UNIVERSITY OF NOTRE DAME

LITURGICAL STUDIES

VOLUME I

Liturgical Studies

LITURGICAL COMMITTEE OF THE UNIVERSITY OF NOTRE DAME

Liturgical Piety
REV. LOUIS BOUYER (OF THE ORATORY)

*

IN PREPARATION

The Psalter as a Christian Prayer Book
REV. BALTHASAR FISCHER

The Building and Furnishing of Churches
REV. J. O'CONNELL

The Primitive Liturgy
REV. JOSEF A. JUNGMANN, S.J.

The Bible and the Liturgy
REV. JEAN DANIELOU, S.J.

Liturgy and Western Culture
REV. HERMAN SCHMIDT, S.J.

The Prayer Life of the Church
REV. BONIFAAS LUYKX, O.PRAEM.

Aphikomen: The Key to the Last Supper
EUGENIO ZOLLI

The Missionary Value of the Liturgy
REV. JOHANNES HOFINGER, S.J.

The Sacred Scripture and the Spiritual Life
VERY REV. MSGR. FRANCIS H. DAVIS

Church Architecture for Our Time
HERMANN BAUR

LITURGICAL PIETY

LITURGICAL PIETY

BY

REV. LOUIS BOUYER

OF THE ORATORY

UNIVERSITY OF NOTRE DAME PRESS

NOTRE DAME, INDIANA

IMPRIMI POTEST: Parisiis, Die 1ª Junii 1954, Maurice Duprey,

Supérieur Général de l'Oratoire

NIHIL OBSTAT: G. Brillet, Pr. de l'Oratoire

IMPRIMI POTEST: Theodore J. Mehling, c.s.c., Provincial

NIHIL OBSTAT: Eugene P. Burke, c.s.c., Censor Deputatus

IMPRIMATUR: ✠ John F. Noll, D.D., Archbishop-Bishop of Fort Wayne

Sept. 9, 1954

First Printing March, 1955; Second Printing
December, 1955; Third Printing October, 1957

LIBRARY OF CONGRESS CATALOG CARD NO. 54-11103

Foreword

In his Encyclical *Mystici Corporis* Pope Pius XII has affirmed that, "mysteries revealed by God cannot be harmful to men, nor should they remain as treasures hidden in a field, useless. They have been given from on high precisely to help the spiritual progress of those who study them in a spirit of piety. For, as the Vatican Council teaches, 'reason illumined by faith, if it seeks earnestly, piously and wisely, does attain, under God, to a certain and most helpful knowledge of mysteries. . . .' "

It is in the light and in the spirit of these statements that the Notre Dame Liturgy Program of the Summer Session has striven to play its part in what the Pope, in the Encyclical *Mediator Dei,* has described as the "remarkably widespread revival of scholarly interest in the sacred liturgy" which "took place towards the end of the last century and has continued through the early years of this one."

Since 1947, the Program has invited some of Europe's most noted scholars to lecture on various parts or aspects of the sacred liturgy. And it is these lectures which, edited and arranged for publication in book form, constitute the Notre Dame Liturgical Studies.

The present work, *Liturgical Piety,* which introduces the series, is one of great importance to everyone who is at all interested in living more fully the prayer life of the Church, especially in promoting active and fruitful participation in the Holy Sacrifice of the Mass. For our gloriously reigning Holy Father says that "the Mass is the source and, as it were, the center of Christian piety." In this work, the learned Oratorian, Fr. Louis Bouyer, undertakes the very difficult but very necessary task of showing us what that prayer life, especially as centered in the Mass itself, essentially is. Of necessity, therefore, he strives to disengage the essential nature of the liturgy from not only the forms it took when misunderstood or neglected, but also from those forms it might be given in various unconsciously mistaken attempts at restoration. The positive value of this book, however, is that of showing how liturgy, as the prayer life of the Church, is primarily concerned with the mysteries of our Redemption, in both their doctrinal and sacramental character. It is through the liturgy that the authentic Christian life is produced and maintained. Hence, this great book makes it very clear that the most profound Christian piety is that of a whole-hearted and joyful sharing in the Cross of Christ in and through the Mystery of the Mass and the Sacraments.

Obviously, a book of this kind can hardly help being controversial. But to make it so has not been the author's primary intent. Rather, he has tried to exercise simply that freedom which is legitimate for a scholar and to proceed in the spirit which the Pope describes when he says, in *Mediator Dei:* "Thus there has developed in this field among many European nations, and in lands beyond the seas as well, a rivalry as welcome as it has been productive of results. Indeed, the salutary fruits of this rivalry among the scholars have been plain for all to see, both in the sphere of the sacred sciences . . . and in the spiritual life of considerable numbers of individual Christians."

MICHAEL A. MATHIS, c.s.c.

Editor, *Liturgical Studies*

University of Notre Dame

Oct. 6, 1954

Contents

LITURGICAL PIETY

CHAPTER ONE

False Conceptions of the Liturgy—
Products of the Baroque Period

THE purpose of this book is to describe and make clear the nature of liturgical piety, in all its fullness and with all its implications. But before we begin to do so, we must understand what the liturgy itself is.

We shall begin, then, with a definition and an explanation of that definition. The liturgy, to our way of thinking, is *that system of prayers and rites traditionally canonized by the Church as her own prayer and worship*.

True, such a definition treats the problem we have to solve as if it were already solved. Many, and perhaps even most of our contemporaries, themselves also members of the Church, would hesitate to accept at first sight a definition of the liturgy that so takes for granted a natural connection between the liturgy and piety or 'spirituality' in general. How many liturgical handbooks begin with quite a different definition. Many of them still tell their readers that the liturgy is merely "the *official* form for the *external* worship of the Church." And if this were so, obviously it would be highly questionable whether we could find in the liturgy any training in prayer, or whether, indeed, we could consider the liturgy itself to be a prayer in any proper sense of the word.

We cannot comfort ourselves, however, with the idea that the handbooks we have just mentioned are merely offshoots of what has been called "the stupid nineteenth century." For they have behind them, if not a real tradition or anything worthy of the name, at least a long series of maxims and more or less systematized opinions, reach-

1

ing much further back than the nineteenth century. And it is most important for us now to examine these opinions, for unless we do so we cannot reach the true root of this false conception of liturgy, nor can we hope to eradicate it.

How, then, during the course of Christian history, did such a notion come into existence? How did it happen that the liturgy came to be considered merely as a compulsory ceremonial, the rule for the external manifestation of the Church's worship? We must look for the sources of this notion first of all in the Renaissance, and in the humanistic period.

Did not even St. Francis de Sales, when about to receive episcopal consecration, make a sort of pious resolution always to say his beads when his duties required him to attend a public Mass? How can such a resolution be explained unless we realize that the holy Doctor was truly persuaded that to take more than a merely external part in such a public celebration was unnecessary for the cultivation of a deep and spiritual piety? And if this was the spontaneous opinion of a great saint and doctor of the Church of that era, what must the ordinary people of the same period have thought of the public Offices of the Church?

No less significant, but perhaps more ominous, is a recorded dialogue between Cranmer and Gardiner, held when both men were still orthodox Catholic priests. Cranmer said, "How sad it is that the people in the nave of the church do not understand anything about what is being celebrated in the sanctuary!" And Gardiner answered, "Don't worry about that, it has never occurred to them that they might want to understand it!" How distressing it is for us now to consider that it was the future heretic who had the more truly Catholic reaction! These examples suffice to illustrate the idea of the liturgy which was taken for granted in those centuries. But if we want the further evidence, not of unrehearsed reactions, but of the well-considered opinion of a theologian, we can look into one of the most famous books about the liturgy written in the seventeenth century: that of the French Oratorian Thomassin *Traité de l'office divin et de sa liaison avec l'oraison mentale*. This work is particularly concerned with clarifying the relation between the liturgy and personal prayer, but it is obvious from the author's whole treatment of the subject that the common opinion of the audience for whom he was writing was that there was no connection whatever between liturgy and personal prayer; rather, indeed, the likelihood was that they were opposed to one another. As for the author's own opinion, it favors conciliation of a sort, even though his methods of connecting the liturgy and personal piety are, to say the least, not quite what we might expect. Two chief ideas emerge from his lengthy dissertation, full as it is of interesting material:—the first is that it is quite possible for everyone to pray during the official services of the Church, for the reason that there are many places in these services when silence is observed; and the second is that the great majority of the faithful, including particularly the nuns who recite the Hours daily, are not really distracted from prayer by the liturgy since they do not understand Latin and, therefore, do not bother about the meaning of the words.

Startling as these examples may appear, the mentality exemplified by Thomassin endures even today. Here, for example, is the answer recently given to a question by another French liturgist, one of our own times, the author of a widely studied handbook of ceremonies. He had just finished instructing some candidates for the priesthood in the ceremonies of the Mass, when one of his young and, we hope, candid students asked: "But, Father, when we are saying Mass, at what moments can we pray?" "What? Pray?" answered the sage, "But, my boy, this is not the time for that."

To go through this gallery of horrifying examples is no waste of time, for it is of the utmost importance for us to realize that such opinions about the liturgy were for a long time so commonplace that nobody was aware of the fact that they were actually horrifying. For there was a time,—not so far from our own, and not yet entirely past, —when it was taken for granted by many Catholics that the liturgy was sometimes to be *performed,* but that to understand it was, at best, optional, never necessary or highly desirable, and, occasionally, considered even objectionable. That the liturgy was not anything in which the common people were to participate, of course went without saying. Not only, until quite recently, was a Solemn High Mass understood to be a Mass with no communicants, but in many dioceses of Europe and elsewhere, the distribution of Communion before or after Mass was enforced as the normal practice, and Communion during Mass was more or less forbidden. It is quite in keeping with all this to describe the liturgy as "the official form for the external worship of the Church"—and nothing more.

But we shall never fully understand this false conception of the liturgy unless we appreciate the whole mental outlook of which it was a part. How could people possibly come to accept as a matter of course such ways of thinking and acting? How could people reconcile such views of the liturgy and such practices with any real profession of Catholicism? How could they actually fancy, as they did, that such ideas and practices were a distinctive feature of Catholicism? For we must emphasize the sad fact that people really held this last opinion. Even now, especially in countries mainly Protestant, you will find Catholics who are genuinely persuaded that to take any real, active part in public worship, and especially to try to understand what is going on and not merely look at it, would be to verge on Protestantism.

Now it is from the sixteenth and seventeenth century idea of court life that Catholics of this kind derived their false notions of public worship. An earthly king must be honored daily by the pageant of court ceremonial, and so also the heavenly King. The courtly atmosphere around Him was to be provided by the liturgy. The liturgy, as many handbooks of the period actually say, was considered to be "the etiquette of the great King." The most obvious features of it were those embodying the external pomp, decorum and grandeur befitting so majestic a Prince. The lack of any intelligible meaning in so many rites and even in the sacred words themselves, was, therefore, praised as enhancing the impression of awe to be given to the dazzled multitude. So also, it would have seemed almost indecent to offer to the common people any opportunity to participate directly in so sublime a performance. They were, rather, only to admire it, dimly, from afar, as a scene of unapproachable magnificence.

Incidentally, the prevalence of such a conception of the liturgy may well explain why so many Anglo-Saxon Protestant tourists, visiting Rome in the last centuries, have been so anxious to attend Papal functions. One would think that what the old Anglican litany called "the tyranny of the Bishop of Rome and all his abominable enormities" would be abhorrent to sound Protestant feelings. But all Englishmen and, even more, some Americans naturally delight in antiquarian pageants, and it was our own Catholic experts who were ultimately responsible for these good people's belief that antiquarian pageantry · was precisely what they should look for in the liturgy. Of course, in such a conception, the plume on a guard's helmet is at least as important to the sacred rite as the sacramental materials.

And here is the place to remind ourselves that this general assumption that the Liturgy is a kind of superlative court ceremonial was quite uncritically accepted by the first pioneers of the liturgical movement in the nineteenth century, both by Dom Guéranger and Dom Gréa. The existence of this assumption explains why the Benedictine restoration, as undertaken by Dom Guéranger, was from the first an attempt to restore medieval monasticism with all its display of Gothic buildings, elaborate vestments, Gregorian chant, and all the pomp characteristic of the later days of Cluny,—a pomp so foreign to primitive Benedictinism. But we must also remind ourselves that it is because of precisely the same assumption about the nature of the liturgy that so many people even today, who are not in the least concerned with Christian belief or conduct, have been for so long faithful to the Church for the solemnization of birth, death and marriage,—considering the Church at least as the most skillful and capable of Masters of Ceremonies for such occasions.

From what has been said already, we can see that the distorted interpretation of the nature of the liturgy now under discussion is a typical product of the Baroque period. But we can see also that the Romantic period, in spite of its horrified rejection of everything redolent of the Baroque, and in spite of the fact that it was itself a reaction against the effects of the Baroque, never actually rejected some of the fundamental prejudices of its predecessor. The reason why it is so difficult for us even today to free ourselves entirely from the influence of the Baroque period, the reason why we are hampered by a kind of uneasiness in our efforts to do so lies probably in the fact that we are not sufficiently aware of the necessity of criticising religious Romanticism as well as religious Baroque. The seeds of the cockle as well as of the wheat are to be found in our own make-up, and therefore it is so hard for us to burn the cockle and harvest the good grain.

Nothing of lasting value, then, can be achieved without a preliminary criticism of both the Baroque and the Romantic mentality, since the false notion of the nature of the liturgy has been formed by both periods.

To begin with the Baroque mentality: it was the product of three main factors. The first of these is what we might call the literary and aesthetic world of Renaissance neo-paganism. The fashion of using the resuscitated mythology of the Greco-Roman era as a literary and artistic medium is typical of this period. And with it goes the fashion, so well satirized by Erasmus, of using an imitation Ciceronian Latin. This was the period when Leonardo da Vinci could paint a Bacchus and a St. John that are almost indistinguishable from each other. And, what is of special interest to us, the result was the destruction, so far as daily practice was concerned, of that Biblical medium, of that world of types and parables which had always been the natural background of Patristic and medieval tradition. The Biblical imagery in which the very Christianity of the Church as expressed in the liturgy, had always been set forth and incarnated, was now displaced by a world of completely pagan figures, entirely foreign to the mentality out of which the rites and words of the liturgy had originally developed. This new intellectual world of the Renaissance pretended to be truly age-old, but it was actually almost nothing but an artificial veneer of a culture, of which the best example is this use of Greco-Roman mythology in the literature and art of the seventeenth century.

But to this first and most important factor a second must be added, —the violent hunger for life, life both of the senses and of the mind, felt by the men of that period, a hunger rather masked than truly expressed by the neo-paganism that they borrowed from antiquity.

In reaction against the spirit of the Middle Ages, that hunger rejected the asceticism, the sobriety and the plainness of the traditional liturgy. It craved the super-human instead of the supernatural, as witness the paintings of Michelangelo; and it took pleasure in the enormous rather than in the great, as witness the statues of St. John Lateran with their hysterical gesticulations, and the tomb of Alexander VII in St. Peter's.

In addition to these two factors in the Baroque mentality, there is a third—the Baroque period was Catholic through an instinctive loyalty to the Church, although it was not genuinely Christian. The artist or man of letters of this period, fearing the hostile forces then arrayed against both Christianity and the secular organization of society, dreading also and far more strongly his own subconscious energies now threatening to explode, took refuge in a loyalty to the Church, the more exaggerated the more it feared its own potential inner weakness. Thus, having no deep or positive inspiration of its own but rather undergoing a process of gradual inhibition, deprived also by neo-paganism of its connatural Biblical medium of expression, the Christianity of the Baroque period was drawn into a soulless kind of conservatism. In the domain of the liturgy, it devoted itself to a

stubborn maintenance of what was then under attack from Protestantism and from liberal humanism. But the way in which it held to and
exalted that legacy was to allow it to become fossilized, while em-
bellishing it with elements almost completely external and foreign to
its true nature.

We must remember here that the great cultural creation of the
period, and its most popular one, was the Opera. And in the Opera
an exaltation of sensual passion is combined with a mythological kind
of imagery almost completely decorative, flowering in courtly music
and ballet. So the faithful of the same period sought to find a religious equivalent of the Opera in the liturgy. Churches came to resemble theatres in plan and decoration. The liturgical pomps displayed in such churches tended to smother the traditional text of the
liturgy under an increasingly profane kind of polyphony, the text
itself having little more importance either for the performers or the
onlookers than did da Ponté's poems for devotees of Mozart. And, in
the end, the liturgy was embalmed in productions which treated it as
reverently and as indifferently as the King's corpse at a royal funeral;
it became as it were the pretext for an "occasion" similar to a soiree at
Court complete with a divertissement by Lully. The chief focus of
liturgical life, therefore, was no more the Mass, which included too
many elements out of harmony with the mentality of the times. Instead, Solemn Exposition of the Blessed Sacrament, a ceremony created and developed just in time to satisfy the new tastes of the age,
managed to assimilate perfectly the courtly ceremonial then fashionable. In the Presence of the Divine King, a kind of heavenly grand
opera could be performed, with all the display of lights, jewels (most-
ly false), exquisite polyphonic singing and pageantry which commonly
accompany a royal reception. And all this was pervaded with that
type of sentimental piety, those pantings after divine love, capable
of competing successfully with the ecstatic expressions of human love
fashionable in the poetry of the time which were so much to the taste
of the aristocratic guests in Arthenice's blue chamber.

We cannot easily recapture today the extraordinary atmosphere
in which this new type of worship originally grew up. Grand it certainly was, though its legacy to us is often little more than the
trappings of a carnival,—machine-made lace, faded ribbons, gilt
plaster, paper flowers and sentimental hymnody. And it was hardly
less foreign to the old tradition of Christian worship than was the

contemporary Calvinist cult, with its Genevese gowns, its ugly benches, its enormous pulpits. Something of this latter spirit is still surviving here and there in southern Latin countries, enough to explain the otherwise incomprehensible fact that a French bishop only some twenty years ago, when he asked Consultors in Rome whether he might sing the psalms during Pontifical Vespers, was answered that to do so would be supremely shocking. For, naturally, his reverend correspondents were judging the question from what they heard and saw in the churches of Rome under their own eyes, and so they fancied that the good bishop intended to sing a solo with a full orchestra to back him, just like a common prima donna!

From what has been said, some readers might infer that I am completely out of sympathy with the spirit of the Baroque period, and that I am prejudiced by an idea that what we do now in liturgical matters is more edifying and more satisfactory. On the contrary, my opinion is that that rigid and unintelligent traditionalism, which is so prominent a feature of the true Baroque mentality, was the providential means whereby the Church managed to keep her liturgical treasures safe throughout a long period when scarcely anyone was capable of understanding their true worth. These treasures were, indeed, preserved in much the same way as St. Peter's chair is enshrined in Bernini's setting, or as the columns of the Lateran Basilica of Constantine's time have been immersed and absorbed into Borromini's pilasters. But the treasures of the liturgy have at least been preserved,—while we may well wonder occasionally what would remain for future generations of the faithful if some modern promoters of a "living" liturgy were allowed complete freedom to remodel the Church's liturgy according to their own ideas.

This thought leads to a further observation,—the striking similarity (which is nevertheless generally overlooked), between the attitudes of mind responsible for the Baroque use of the liturgy, and those responsible for many modern methods. The men of the seventeenth century were sure that the short-cut formulae of their theological and controversial handbooks were enough to hold all the pith and marrow of Christian tradition concerning the Eucharist. Therefore so long as they retained somewhere in the background of a ceremony the substance of the rites and the texts of the traditional liturgy, they believed themselves to be perfectly Catholic, and felt quite entitled to dress up these rites and texts to resemble as closely as possible the profane performances of the culture of that period, paying no attention at all to the ways in which the Eucharistic doctrine had traditionally been expressed in the rites and texts themselves. But do not many people today do exactly the same kind of thing when they try to disguise a rubrically correct low Mass by reading and singing in the vernacular, to make it resemble as closely as possible the style of public meeting now popular, endeavoring also to give to the performance of the sacred rite itself a setting resembling that of the stadium, of the factory, or of the movie-theatre? Is it not of the very essence of the Baroque spirit to transpose into a worldly setting a liturgy envisioned merely as an external formality?

The great lesson, then, that we should learn from this brief survey of the Baroque mentality and its influence on the liturgy, is that a real understanding of the nature of the liturgy as it is in itself, and the will to follow out the implications of that nature is the primary necessity for any living use and practice of it. And, as a consequence, the second lesson is that, to do this, it is necessary not to force upon the liturgy a culture or tendencies foreign to it, but rather to try to put ourselves into its own spiritual world and to attune ourselves to its own modes of thought, feeling and outward expression.

These observations lead us now to a consideration of the Romantic period. For, although the reaction of Romanticism was strongly against the productions and the mentality of the seventeenth century, we find to our surprise that it retained faithfully, if unconsciously, most of the dangerous prejudices held by its predecessors against whom it had rebelled.

CHAPTER TWO

From the Romantic Reaction to the Patristic Ideal of Liturgy

I T WAS only against the most superficial features of the Baroque period that Romanticism reacted, that is, against the Neo-Classicism of its decoration, and, in particular, against its use and abuse of mythology. In opposition to all this, the Middle Ages, and, above all, of course, the externals of the society of that period were exalted as the permanent achievement of a Christian culture, and therefore—what is of interest to us here—as the ideal setting for the liturgy. Certainly the Romantics were not concerned merely with the picturesque, though the emphasis on that side of medieval life was sometimes heavily stressed; the medieval epoch was rather taken to have been characterized generally by that sensitiveness to Christian feelings and Christian motives so conspicuously lacking in the Baroque, and, since it possessed this sensitiveness, the medieval period was taken to provide a clue to the true significance of the liturgy itself. Hence the frenzy for Gothic everywhere—Gothic buildings, Gothic vestments, Gothic singing, Gothic poetry and romance, and so on.

Without entering into a detailed criticism of the Romantic reaction to Baroque, we can easily see that it had a somewhat childlike, not to say childish quality. Catholics of the period made out that Catholicism was once again confident of its own strength, proud of its cultural wealth and sure of its final victory. But even if this were so, Catholicism certainly did not look then its best intellectually. No great place can be assigned in the history of Christian thought to the apologetics of Chateaubriand or Lamennais, still less to their theology!

This weakness of the intellectual side of the Catholicism of the Romantic period was due, of course, to the fact that all the normal means of developing a Christian culture had been destroyed along with the suppression of the great Catholic universities of Europe during the Revolution. This, then, was the great weakness of the Catholic revival in the nineteenth century,—a congenital lack of scientific grounding and even of healthy critical reasoning. This same lack appeared at the very beginning of what we may call the modern liturgical revival, in the form of strange deficiencies in logic, and startling justifications of liturgical practices, sometimes amounting to humbug.

The first point to be emphasized here is the uncritical way in which men of the Romantic period adopted, without realizing they were doing so, a great many of the most serious errors of the Baroque. Errors which, in the Baroque period, had taken the form of mere implicit assumptions now even showed a tendency to assert themselves as a kind of bogus philosophy. Thus, the loyalty of Baroque Catholicism to a tradition no longer understood or vitally apprehended now developed into a so-called philosophy of Catholicism, which took tradition (and tradition alone), as its root principle—that is, tradition cut off from and opposed to any kind of critical knowledge. And this is, in the end, the surest and speediest way to render tradition itself lifeless and dead.

In the domain of the liturgy, the adoption of such theories as those of Bonald and de Maistre managed completely to confuse real fidelity to the Church and her ways of prayer with archaism and archeologism and, in many cases, a most fantastic archeologism at that. The adoption of these theories also put the finishing touches on the two-centuries old process of fossilization and stultification of the rites and formulae of the liturgy itself. The finished product of these developments is the type of worship carried out in the monasteries restored by Dom Guéranger. No one, of course, will deny the fact that this type of worship was far more satisfying than that of the Baroque period. The restoration of Gregorian Chant, scrupulous observance of the rubrics of all the ceremonies, and, above all, a sober and dignified kind of celebration neatly pruned of all those theatrical additions by which Baroque practice had been altering and ruining the lines of the liturgy,—all these reforms made this monastic worship one of the most impressive types to be found in modern times. But neither can we deny that this worship was an antiquarian reconstruction, and one of very doubtful authenticity on many cardinal points. On the one hand, it had lost that contact with the mentality of its own times which the Baroque worship had certainly possessed, and, on the other hand, the antiquity which it re-created was no more what it made out to be than the sham Gothic architecture of Viollet-le-Duc or Pugin was truly Gothic. But the greatest weakness of all was that it could not have become the real worship of any actual congregation of its own period. It could become only the worship of that artificial monastic congregation which Dom Guéranger had brought into existence simply in order to carry it out—a congregation which was a kind of shadowy image of Cluny, existing in a world in which nothing still survived nor could come to life again of the institutions and mentality of which the original Cluny had once been the natural center and focus.

We are confronting here the great problem which the whole Benedictine Order is trying to solve today, caught as the Order is between the tenets of its immediate past and the pressure of present circumstances. We cannot and need not go into this problem here, except to show that it is intimately connected with one of the fundamental problems of the liturgical movement. For no reconstructions of the past—however excellent the period one chooses to try to bring to life —can be achieved without a large admixture of the products of one's own fancy; and such reconstructions are likely to raise more problems than they can solve.

There are further criticisms to add to these primary considerations. The Romantic period endorsed and systematized the philosophy of traditionalism already latent in the ideas of the Baroque period. It also preserved as the very heart of liturgical life the sentimental notion of the Divine Presence of Christ that was developed in that period. In fact, to be precise, it is only during the Romantic revival that this notion emerged from implicit assumption to explicit expression and so gained common acceptance. In his *Les institutions liturgiques,* Dom Guéranger always takes it for granted that the focus of the Christian liturgy is not the sacrificial Action but rather the physical Presence of Our Lord in the Holy Eucharist. One obvious reflection of this view is to be seen in the abnormal proportions of the volume on the Feast of Corpus Christi compiled by Dom Guéranger's successors for *L'Année liturgique.* In *Les institutions liturgiques,* the Eastern Rites were thoroughly gone over and criticized from this standpoint, the idea being emphasized that these Liturgies should no longer be allowed to remain within the Catholic Church unless definite changes were made in their rites, to show that the Mass was now to be considered primarily as the bringing into existence of the Eucharistic Presence of Christ and the adoration of It. All this was, in fact, nothing more than theorizing on the changes brought about during the Baroque period,—the changes by which Exposition of the Blessed Sacrament was introduced into the very core of Christian worship and the Mass itself made more and more subservient to the worship of the Presence in the Eucharist, thus pushing into the background first the communal act of the worshippers, and finally the sacerdotal action itself.

As a result of these new ideas, what is most impressive in the Solesmian worship is not the community Mass, at which nobody receives Holy Communion and the lay brothers are not even present, but rather Benediction, when the whole community is assembled and the height both of personal devotion and public ceremonial is actually attained.

A third flaw in the religious romanticism of the period which we can see at work in the field of the liturgy under the influence of Solesmes, is the incredible weakness of its scholarship. This, of course, is another direct result of the tragic disappearance from among Catholics of a sound traditional learning in the wake of the great Revolution. But we must trace carefully the influence of this weakness on the whole liturgical restoration in order to understand and appreciate the subjective and ultimately sentimental manner in which it interpreted that liturgy which it was trying to reinstate. The most significant production of that sham scholarship is *Les institutions liturgiques* of Dom Guéranger, while in *L'Année liturgique* its logical consequences are carried to almost unbelievable extremes. For one thing, Dom Guéranger, in the neo-ultramontanism which he borrowed directly from Lamennais, tried to exalt the Roman liturgy as being the only purely and perfectly Catholic of all the Christian liturgies. In doing so, he was quite unaware of the fact that the Missal of Pius V did not necessarily represent the Roman liturgy itself in its purest and most perfect traditional form. And—what was equally unfortunate—he was also unable to distinguish in practice between the Neo-Gallican liturgies of the seventeenth or eighteenth centuries and older local usages, in spite of the fact that these latter had been canonized by Pius V himself.

A good example of the achievements of such a defective science of the liturgy is found in the fact that Guéranger denounced the Preface *de Sanctis* as a product of Jansenism because of its words: *eorum coronando merita coronas dona tua* (in crowning their merits Thou dost crown Thine Own gifts), not realizing that the Preface as a whole had been compiled from medieval materials or that the incriminating words themselves are a well-known phrase of St. Augustine's. And *L'Année liturgique* verged even further on the ridiculous by expatiating on the almost divinely inspired manner in which the texts of the Collects, Epistles and Gospels are put together in the Sunday Masses of the Roman Rite. For nobody then realized that this "traditional" order, as it is given in the Missal we use today, at least for the Sundays after Pentecost, is the result of a quite recent breaking-up, through faulty transcription, of an older series, and that this disarrangement had actually destroyed most of the connection which had once existed between the various parts of these Propers. It is not difficult to imagine how many mistakes in the detailed commentary on these texts would spring out of such a fundamental ignorance of historical facts!

It may seem unnecessarily cruel to criticize so mercilessly what was, certainly, the first beginning of a re-discovery of the liturgy. But however much we naturally sympathize with those men to whom we ourselves owe so much, we must also see them as they were. We must not blind ourselves to the fact that the materials out of which they built their reconstruction of the liturgy were of varying degrees of soundness. Without such an open-eyed and dispassionate investigation, we can never go further than did those men themselves along the road that they opened up. And we should risk the danger of being unable to prevent the collapse of the building we have received from their hands, a building made of such a hodge-podge of materials.

Moreover, without bold and well-founded criticism such as this— bold because it is well-founded—some of the most faithful heirs of what is of lasting value in Solesmes' bequest could never have succeeded, as they did, in pushing on to discover the true essence of the liturgy. We shall see later, for example, how great are the lessons we must learn from the Belgian liturgical movement which is connected with the name of Dom Lambert Beauduin. He was a true heir indeed to the most valuable portion of Guéranger's legacy, for he quietly put aside, without even a mention, what was clearly obsolete, and he augmented his inheritance by the discovery of a most important principle—perhaps the most important, as we shall see later. And this principle is, that we must not try to provide an artificial congregation to take part in an antiquarian liturgy, but rather to prepare the actual congregations of the Church today to take part in the truly traditional liturgy rightly understood.

But our aim in these introductory chapters is primarily to explain and criticize the false conceptions of the liturgy still surviving today, in order to go straight on to the sound one. We shall, therefore, leave aside the Belgian movement for the time being, and take up at once a school in the German movement which has greater speculative importance, even though its best results came rather later than did those of the Belgian movement. We refer, of course, to the School of Maria-Laach, as it was called, which came into being as an offshoot of the Solesmian revival, with the aim of rectifying this from within, but has, in fact, been so creative as to transcend its own origins. In it alone, especially in the works of Abbot Herwegen and of the famous monk Dom Casel, do we find any clear perception of the deficiencies of the Romantic movement. These men realized that it was those very deficiencies which prevented it from actually doing away with the results of the Baroque influence that it was so eager to destroy. They saw that these very deficiencies rendered the Romantics incapable of recognizing the extent to which they were treasuring these results and even exalting them by the dangerous tendencies inherent in their philosophy and theology, to say nothing of the unsoundness of their scholarship.

For Dom Guéranger, to go back to the authentic liturgy meant to go back to medievalism. He and his first followers accepted unquestioningly the assumption held by most of their contemporaries that the Middle Ages were the Christian era *par excellence,* and that their civilization and culture provided the outstanding example of a Catholic ideal incarnated in earthly realities. But Dom Herwegen, more forcefully than any other authority, has shown that the medieval period, though its way of carrying out the traditional liturgy was superior to Baroque practice, had already begun to overlay the liturgy with fanciful interpretations and developments foreign to its nature. Therefore, far from demonstrating an ideal understanding and practice of the Catholic liturgy, the Medieval period in fact paved the way for the abandonment of the liturgy by Protestantism and its final disgrace and neglect in so much of post-Tridentine Catholicism.

Dom Herwegen's ideas on this point greatly shocked most of his early readers. But it must be admitted today that the whole tendency of contemporary research tends to bear out his conclusions, and to prove them even more convincingly than, perhaps, he himself would have expected. In the greatest scholarly work of our times on the history of the Roman Mass, Jungmann's *Missarum Sollemnia,* an overwhelming weight of evidence goes to show that the history of the Roman Mass during the Middle Ages is the history of how it came to be increasingly misunderstood by the clergy as well as by the faithful, and of how it began to disintegrate through the fault of the medieval liturgists themselves. A prominent feature of that process as Father Jungmann's book shows, was the appearance, in the medieval *Expositiones Missae,* of those wrong conceptions we have already discussed: disproportionate emphasis on the Presence in the Holy Eucharist and a very sentimental notion of that Presence, which came to play so disastrous a part in the worship of the Romantic as well as the Baroque period. Both can be viewed as expressions of the tendency to be found in those sentimentally realistic explanations of the Mass in which it was taken for granted that the Mass was meant to reproduce the Passion by a kind of mimetic reproduction, each action of the Mass representing some action of the Passion itself:—for example, the priest's moving from the Epistle side of the altar to the Gospel side being a representation of Jesus' journey from Pilate to Herod; or the Lavabo representing Pilate washing his hands. Aside from their intrinsic absurdity, such explanations served to dissolve the traditional conception of a sacramental presence into an anecdotal and picturesque idea of the liturgical actions. As if the liturgy were aiming at reproducing materially and theatrically the acts by which we were saved, as if it intended to suggest not only the physical, but also a carnal presence of Our Lord to be grasped more by imagination than by faith!

This was the first criticism made by Dom Herwegen and the Maria-Laach school of the way in which men of the medieval period understood the liturgy, and so of all subsequent attempts to find in the Middle Ages the principles for a true renaissance of the liturgy; and this criticism has more and more been borne out by modern research. But to this first, Dom Herwegen and Maria-Laach add another and even more penetrating criticism, which does not seem capable of receiving such unqualified agreement either from historians or from theologians.

The fundamental error of the Middle Ages, when they are compared with Christian antiquity, would be, according to the former Abbot of Maria-Laach, in their turning from an objective kind of piety to a subjective one. Here, he thinks, is also to be found the root of all subsequent errors, since the true and authentic spirit of the liturgy is forthright objectivity, while that of medieval and post-medieval piety tends more and more to an all-absorbing subjectivism. This tendency goes along with a shift of emphasis from the union of the whole Church with God to an emphasis on the union of the individual soul with Him. Here is the reason for the title of a small but very meaty book by Dom Herwegen, *Kirche und Seele* (Church and Soul), in which he proposes an opposition between a piety of the Church and a piety of the soul paralleling the opposition between traditional objectivity and modern subjectivism.

With this second conclusion also, it seems to me, Dom Herwegen certainly put his finger on a very real problem. But did he himself do justice to his own intuition by formulating the problem in this way? His opponents at once seized upon this aspect of his system of thought in order to accuse the Maria-Laach movement of lacking any real interest in true personal devotion, and of tending, therefore, to foster a kind of piety which would be the opposite of true piety since it would begin with indifference to personal religion as such. Later on, we shall have occasion to discuss in full the issues of this controversy. Suffice it now to say that Dom Herwegen himself was possibly too greatly influenced by the modern way of looking at things, even while he was criticizing that very way. Is it not typical of modern individualism to separate and oppose subject and object? Would it not be typical of the true tradition to render unnecessary a choice between the two, rather than to favor objectivity alone, an objectivity understood as the opposite of subjectivism? Would not, then, an authentic way of returning to tradition be found in the rediscovery of the inherent and mutual relation of the "subjective" and "objective" in piety, and, in consequence, of the person and the Church, rather than in fruitlessly opposing either subjective to objective, or person to Church?

But let us go no further into this problem for the moment. Our present task is to discover the object on which the whole emphasis of Christian piety must be placed if, according to the School of Maria-Laach, we are to be faithful to the authentic spirit of the liturgy. To define clearly and to deepen our appreciation of that object was the special work of one man, whose name will probably endure even beyond his Abbot's as representing the thought of Maria-Laach. I refer, of course, to Dom Odo Casel and to his theory concerning the *Kultmysterium,* the Mystery of Christian Worship.

This Mystery is the core of the entire Catholic liturgy. An understanding of it is, therefore, the necessary prerequisite for any real understanding and practice of that Liturgy. We cannot here fully define that Mystery,—Dom Casel devoted nearly all his works to it, and many subsequent chapters of this book will be occupied by a discussion of it. But it is important to remember from the first that the development of the concept of the Christian Mystery first proposed by Dom Casel, has been adopted and developed in some of the most authoritative works of modern scholarship. Their authors have labored to abstract the nature and meaning of the mystery from the data of the liturgy itself and from the works of the great exponents of the mystery, the Fathers of the Church, who, obviously, understood the liturgy itself most perfectly since they themselves were chiefly responsible for the main essentials of the liturgy even as it exists today.

To summarize now the content of the mystery:—it is the re-enactment in, by and for the Church of the Act of Our Lord which accomplished our salvation, that is, His Passion and Death in the fullness of their final effects,—the Resurrection, the communication of saving grace to mankind and the final consummation of all things. And, as we have said already, the central property of the liturgy and, therefore, the central fact to be understood about it, is the unique mode in which Christ's redeeming act is permanently renewed and partaken of by the Church. An understanding of this mode, which is entirely different from that of theatrical or imaginative representation or from any physically realistic repetition, is the very clue to the understanding of the whole liturgy which began to be lost during the Middle Ages. And it is this clue which the Baroque period had lost so completely that it kept in view only a shell of the liturgy—a shell which was so much the more externally adorned and built over as the reality inside tended to be forgotten.

So we are now brought back to that very definition of the liturgy which we set as our goal at the beginning of our research, and we are brought also to a justification of that definition which is at once illuminating and immensely suggestive. The liturgy, as we said, is to be regarded primarily not as the official regulation of the external worship of the Church, but rather as that system of prayers and rites traditionally canonized by the Church as her own prayer and worship. The emphasis given the "Mystery" by Dom Casel necessarily presupposes the vital and interior idea of the nature of the liturgy implied in this definition. And this emphasis shows us immediately what is the heart and soul of that visible body, the liturgy, and so prevents us from making any further mistakes by confusing the living organism of this body with any external and artificially constructed vesture— recognizing the fact that the heart and soul of the liturgy prevents us from continuing to treat it like the severed members of a dead body. In brief, Dom Casel's re-emphasis of the Mystery gives us an immediate access to a true understanding of the real life of the body of the liturgy, and so shuts the door on any tendency to exalt it merely as a corpse lying in state.

But, for all that, we cannot ignore the chief objections which have been raised against the Maria-Laach idea of the *Kultmysterium,* or the severe criticisms that it has received. Some of these objections and criticisms are best answered by a purely scientific and objective treatment of the subject rather than by any discussion, and these will be taken up later. But others require some answer here, as a necessary prerequisite to such a treatment; moreover, we cannot get to the work of explaining liturgy by the *Kultmysterium* before we get some of the objections against it out of the way.

We have already noted one objection to the School of Maria-Laach,—that its opposing of an objective to a subjective kind of piety would tend to do away with the very essence of any piety worthy of the name. What has already been said on this point shows that this objection consists in a misunderstanding arising from the poorly balanced expression of a truth, though the truth itself is beyond discussion. It cannot seriously be denied that a certain modern type of piety which is almost entirely psychological tends more and more to feed only upon itself. But the true remedy is not to leave piety completely unnourished, but rather to make sure that it is fed upon the objective content of Christian faith and of the sacraments, in other words, upon the Christian Mystery. This, surely, will be easily admitted. Such an answer is sufficient for our present purposes, since it shows that this particular objection is not, in fact, well founded. We shall see later on how a truly liturgical and objectively centered piety does not attempt

to dispense with any truly traditional forms of asceticism,—far from it!
—but only a mention of this point is necessary for our present purposes.

Far more difficult to answer is the objection that the theories orig-
inating in Maria-Laach are, under a new disguise, nothing more than
that same misguided antiquarianism and archeologism which, from the
very beginning, vitiated even the best achievements of the Romantic
revival. Do not Dom Casel and his followers merely take the Patristic
period as Dom Guéranger and his school took the Middle Ages, fanci-
fully exalting it as a kind of canonical age which is to be reproduced
and set up in the midst of contemporary life by means of the reconstructions of a false archeology? A whole part of Dom Herwegen's
work in particular, might be regarded as a hopeless effort to bring
back to life the men and the Christendom of the first ten centuries, as
if only these men and the Church of that era could rightly understand and practice the Catholic liturgy, and therefore we must try to
substitute them for the men and the Church of today. Were this true,
it would hardly matter which historical period was used as the norm
for such a hopeless endeavor! For if the stubborn rejection of the
Church and the world as they are today were held to be the necessary
preliminary to any authentic liturgical renaissance, this fact in itself
would certainly constitute the most perfect condemnation of that
renaissance.

And it is true that we cannot completely deny this accusation of
archeologism—especially if we take a look at the artistic productions
which have of late been encouraged by Maria-Laach. No less—and
perhaps to an even greater extent than any sham Gothic of the last
century—these works are among the most astounding blunders produced by any Christian aesthetics. And the pity of it is that they are
not blunders by reason of a defective technique, but blunders committed solemnly and on principle. Nothing could be more of an
abortion, dead at the very moment of its birth, than this soulless and
uninspired false byzantinism.

But we must note here that such an art, even though it came
into existence along with the school of theology of Maria-Laach, is
actually not so much an effect of that school as a continuation of the
artistic school of Beuron, whose own masterpieces were destroyed by
the American bombing of Monte Cassino. And, more generally
speaking, everything about Maria-Laach which shows the influence of
this spirit of bogus archeological restoration is due, not to Dom Casel,

but to the nineteenth century origins of the modern Maria-Laach.

It is certainly one thing to single out for recognition a period in the history of the Church when theology, Christian art and the daily life of the Church all gave clear and full testimony to the essential nature of Christianity; and it is quite another thing to try to remodel the external aspects of the Church of today according to the external aspects of that same period. We must, then, take every measure to avoid this fatal mistake. But we must also agree with Dom Casel when he says that we must look to the Patristic embodiment of the Church's tradition if we are to find the clue to what is of enduring value in the liturgy according to that tradition. In the domain of the liturgy, the truth of this statement should be practically self-evident, since the Patristic was certainly the most creative of all periods in this field. What better way is there of understanding any institution than to study it at the period when it is still filled with its primitive vitality? But, on much wider grounds, it must be admitted that the Church has always held that the Patristic period has a special place in her history unlike that of any other age. The Fathers are truly "Fathers" to us and to the Church herself today, and this is because their witness to the truth can never be superseded or even rivalled in its primeval freshness and also in its organic wholeness and its living unity.

But in order to understand their witness rightly, in order not to confuse our perception of its permanent value with any attempt to mimic and copy childishly what they had and what they did that was peculiar to their time alone, it is probably safer not to consider the Fathers in isolation. What we should do rather is to take an all-inclusive view of the development of the People of God, from the first beginnings of this development to its final achievement in those lasting institutions and living ideas which constitute the Fathers' legacy to us as to all ages.

Following, then, this preliminary survey of the rediscovery in recent times of what the liturgy is and means, we shall attempt to see how the traditional liturgy of the Church was developed—in its main parts as in its organic whole—in the very formation of the People of God itself. And this will serve in turn as an introduction to the Church's teaching about the liturgy as it is stated in the Encyclical *Mediator Dei*. In order to obtain this wide and deep vision of the whole question, we shall have to take our materials not only from the technical field of liturgical research in the narrower sense of the word, but from other fields as well. We shall first use the data of Biblical research in order to attain to a theological understanding of the formation of the People of God, but as we proceed, we shall need to include many truths from the theological study of the dogmas of revelation and redemption. In this way alone can we hope to reinstate the liturgy in its rightful place in the history of the Christian dispensation and in any theologically well-grounded vision of what Christianity permanently is and of what it always will be.

CHAPTER THREE

From the Jewish Qahal to the
Christian Ecclesia

ONE OF THE most interesting factors in the development of ecclesiology during the last twenty years has been the gradual realization that the beginning of any true understanding of the Church, as presented in Revelation, consists in an adequate study of the idea of the People of God. God's intervention in the history of mankind since the Fall, God's Word making itself more and more perfectly heard and understood by men, all this Divine action seems from the beginning to be focussed on one clearly defined objective:—the formation, out of common and fallen humanity, of a people which should eventually be God's Own People.

In this light, the Church itself stands out as the great aim of the Incarnation and the Redemption. For the Church is the final actualization of that people which God had been preparing all through the course of history from the first just man to the "Holy and Just" One Himself, that people which God had been creating, as it were, out of the history with whose course He had been merging His Own intervention. To speak more precisely, the results of recent research show with great unanimity that the Church (ἐκκλησία) of the New Testament is (as can be seen through the medium of the Septuagint) to be understood as the final perfection of what the Hebrew Bible from the first had called Qehal Yahweh, (קהל יהוה) "the Assembly of Yahweh."

All through the course of its development, which took place side by side with the development of Revelation itself, this Qehal shows a most striking continuity of essential elements, which we must now try clearly to understand. For in so doing, we shall discover liturgy, our own Catholic liturgy, in its permanent essentials.

Now, the purely secular "assembly duly summoned" (ἐκκλησία) at Athens was the official convocation of the people (from the root καλέω, I call to a convocation). This "calling" was formally carried out by the heralds (κήρυκες) in the name of the regular civic authority, and having been thus gathered together according to law, the assembly of the people acquired as it were a moral personality in order to hear official information concerning its welfare and to take concerted action in response to this information. Similarly, in that Holy City which the people of Israel were always understood to have constituted, the Qahal was called to a convocation, and, having assembled, it heard the words of the King and had to give, as it were, an official answer to them. In the New Testament, the Apostles will be prepared to introduce themselves as κήρυκες, the heralds of Israel's King, whose task it is to call together by the Word of Jesus the new elect of God throughout the whole world, and to enable them, thus brought together, to hear what that same Word has to teach them. One of the most fundamental names for the preaching of the Apostles, therefore, will be the word proclamation (κήρυγμα), which was from the first associated with the idea of congregation or church (ἐκκλησία) in Greek.

Three examples of this Qahal in the Old Testament are especially valuable as leading to a more complete understanding of its nature. The first is the assembly described in Exodus XIX. The multitude which had escaped from Egypt, a multitude up to this time lacking any definite form, is now called upon to go to Sinai to hear the words of its sovereign, that is, God. Let us notice here the fact that it is God's Word which brings about the convocation and God's Word which is also the purpose of it.

But to return to the convocation or Qahal on Sinai,—what were the distinctive features of that first meeting of the people? The assembly which the Word had summoned heard the solemn proclamation of that very Word, brought to them as the climax, following a well-defined series of actions of praise, adoration and collective supplication, after a common preparation by fast and purification. Then, with equal solemnity, the Word was accepted and agreed to by the people, and this acceptance constituted precisely the covenant or alliance between God and His People. But the covenant was not considered to be ratified until a sacrificial offering had concluded the meeting. In that sacrifice, by actually doing what God's Word had formally required of them, the people pledged themselves to that Word and, at the same time, the Word was sealed by God Himself. Thenceforth the covenant stood, founded on God's authority alone, but founded with the free response and obedient agreement of the people. And by this whole process, the people itself was created, formed as a people, and no longer a mere crowd, and more definitely, was made God's People by, through and for the Word of God.

At a second turning-point in the history of Israel, when the covenant inaugurated on Mt. Sinai was again renewed, we find once more the Qehal Yahweh. This turning point is described in the famous scene of 2 Kings 23, when King Josias attempted to make a new beginning, as it were, of the history of the people, by dedicating it once more to Yahweh.

Here again we find precisely the same essential elements as in the meeting on Mt. Sinai. First, the people were called together to a convocation by God's Word as rediscovered by the High Priest in the Sanctuary. Then they heard a solemn reading of Deuteronomy, as in the convocation on Mt. Sinai they had heard the Ten Commandments. After this reading, the people were led to agree, by exultant praise and prayer, to the Word thus newly expressed. And, finally, the renewal of the covenant of alliance and of the people's own agreement to this covenant was expressed and embodied in a solemn celebration of the fundamental sacrifice, that is, the Paschal celebration.

Without insisting on the striking parallelism in the details of this second great Qahal and those of the first on Mt. Sinai, let us now consider the third. We find it described in Nehemias (2 Esdras 8, 17, and 13,1) in the period following the exile of the people and the destruction of the holy city. Through the dispensation of divine providence, the captives had been released and allowed to go back to their former home. The Holy City was still a heap of ruins, but one thing was still standing in the midst of that utter devastation,—God's Word, as it had been finally condensed and embodied in the Bible of the Scribes. The scribe Esdras, then, once more called the Qahal to a convocation, and had this newly-made Bible read to the People.

But here a striking, new element appears. When the solemn reading of the Word was finished, there was no sacrificial celebration such as had concluded both the previous covenant meetings. Instead, representatives of all the various classes of the people took a formal vow to carry out the proper sacrifices when the rebuilding of the city and the Sanctuary had been accomplished, and, at the same time, Esdras himself offered a solemn eucharistic prayer, in which were mingled thanksgiving for the past and supplication for the future, invoking God Himself to realize His Own design, that is, His Own Word, in, through and for His People.

Here we can see, as has been often pointed out, the beginning of the new type of worship which is still that of the Jews today, that is, the worship of the synagogue. It is now commonly admitted by historians that the synagogue type of worship, limited to Scripture reading and prayers with no sacrifice, was not precisely a product of the Exile. But there can be no dispute over the fact that this new kind of worship first gained its importance for God's People as a result of the impossibility of carrying out a sacrificial worship after the destruction of the temple, and then, later on, from the realization noted by Aggeus (2, 3)—at first so disheartening—that the temple as it was rebuilt, far from being the realization of the hopes expressed by Ezechiel, was not even the equal of the older one. The increasing importance of synagogue worship actually, then, accompanied the eschatological expectation sown by Ezechiel himself and by the second part of Isaias, that expectation which is now fostered in us by the Apocalypse. The primitive covenant with all its ritual began to be understood to be only a preliminary dispensation. The true and lasting worship, the eternal sacrifice were still to be looked for, together with the new and everlasting covenant promised by Jeremias and Ezechiel. In the meantime, when God's great deeds of the past for the salvation of His People were commemorated, they were no longer to be praised as the final achievement of what His Word wished to bring about in the history of mankind. These deeds were rather to be recalled as the pledge and foreshadowing of those far greater deeds for whose accomplishment in the future by that same healing and creating Word the people were still to hope for and pray. This is the reason for the general tenor of that new type of prayer which can already be termed a eucharistic (thanksgiving) prayer, first pronounced as we have seen by Esdras. Here is the reason also for the increasing decline in importance of the temple worship, even when it had finally been restored; Israel could no longer realize in any existing sacrifice its hope for the new and lasting covenant. True, this eschatological expectation did express itself in ritual, but it was not the ritual of the old community, the Israel 'of the flesh,' which could not accept this expectation. It was, rather, the ritual of those small pious communities in which the 'remnant' of Israel was preparing itself for the last phase of the kingdom and the judgment to come.

By the time of Our Lord, then, we find that on the eve of each Sabbath and of each festival of the Jewish year, families and pious communities (*habouroth*), were meeting together for a community meal, opening with the breaking of bread, and after the meal itself, coming to its most important feature,—the solemn eucharist, or thanksgiving prayer over the "cup of blessing," in which all God's gifts of the past are commemorated only as a token and pledge of the final gifts to come. We shall study further on in greater detail the late developments of this ceremonial meal but what has just been said is enough for our present purposes.

We can now go on to a study of the primitive Christian community, the nucleus of the Christian Church, as it is described in Acts 2, 42: "And they were persevering in the doctrine of the Apostles and in the communication of the breaking of bread and in prayers." Here, as we can now see, are in brief all the elements of the new Qahal, and these are the same as the elements of the old, but now brought to an enduring perfection.

The "doctrine of the Apostles" is that proclamation (κήρυγμα) by which now the Word, incarnate in Jesus, calls into convocation the People of God in its definitive form, and enlightens it by the definitive revelation of itself. The word "apostle" gives a clue to the nature of the new dispensation. God's Word will no more be heard, as the Epistle to the Hebrews says, in the way in which "at sundry times and in divers manners God spoke in times past to the fathers by the prophets" (Hebrews 1, 1), but God Himself is now speaking to His whole People, since in Jesus, His great ἀπόστολος (the one sent) or *Schaliach* (in Hebrew), He realizes literally the Jewish saying that the "Schaliach or apostle of a man is like another Himself."

God speaks Himself in Christ whom He has sent; and Christ speaks and therefore God also continues to speak in those whom Christ has sent as He Himself was sent. Through having been "sent," therefore, the Church which is the Qahal of the true People of God, always possesses the Word itself in its entirety, both spoken and speaking in her midst. In other words, the Church, being sent, is, first of all, the place in which that Word of God, which is Christ, is finally proclaimed, or, rather, proclaims itself through the apostolate. And this being sent, this apostolate, assuring as it does the permanent presence of God Himself in His People, constitutes the distinctive characteristic of the People of God under the New Covenant.

But—to refer once more to the quotation already cited from the Acts—the apostolic community does not merely listen to God's Word proclaimed in Christ. It invokes that Word in prayers which it inherits directly from the synagogue, and it pledges itself to the Word in the great Eucharistic Prayer of the breaking of bread. This prayer certainly retains, as we shall see later on, all those features of the Jewish thanksgiving at the meals of the *habouroth* which had already become traditional. But it now acquires a new and enlightening meaning and form in that same Christ who now seals the New Covenant in His Blood, that Covenant which He has Himself proclaimed, since He is the definitive Word of God to His People in its definitive form.

In this light, we can now understand why St. Ignatius (Bishop Martyr of Antioch) will acknowledge as a legitimate Eucharist of the true Church, only that which is carried out with the consent of the bishop, to whom Christ's mission (apostolate) has been communicated. For only in this way, as we can see, can the great achievement of the New Covenant be realized—God Himself speaking in His Word made flesh, and putting His seal of graces and blessings on that Word by the shedding of Christ's Blood here formally represented and praised.

Now at last we can understand also the close interrelation between the two poles of the new Qahal, as between those of the old Qahal (or Ecclesia, the Greek and Latin term for Church). St. Paul tells us that as often as we eat this bread and drink this cup, we show forth, that is, proclaim (καταγγέλετε) as in the Gospel, the Lord's death until He comes. In other words, the carrying out of the sacrificial rite of the New Covenant is in itself the most eloquent preaching of God's Word, by means of that Blood more eloquent than Abel's (Hebrews 12:24). But we can turn this statement about and it will be equally true. Through, and only through the proclamation, the "kerygma" of the Gospel by the Apostles, and in the power of that apostolate which makes their words Christ's Word and Christ Himself the very Word of God,—only thus is the new and everlasting covenant not only proclaimed, but also brought about: a new creation which redeems the old is accomplished on the Cross; the same Word which once brought the first creation from nothingness into being now brings it from human death to divine life.

Having finished this brief survey of the Qahal (or assembly duly summoned) considered in its organic development, we can now see, as it were in a nutshell, all the constituent elements of the Christian liturgy. And we can see these elements in their permanent relation to the Church herself as she comes into existence at the very focal point of the redemptive action of the Incarnate Word.

The liturgy in its unity and in its perfection is to be seen as *the meeting of God's People called together in convocation by God's Word through the apostolic ministry, in order that the People, consciously united together, may hear God's Word itself in Christ, may adhere to that Word by means of the prayer and praise amid which the Word is proclaimed, and so seal by the Eucharistic sacrifice the Covenant which is accomplished by that same Word.*

Once we have reached this over-all view of the liturgy, we can indicate some of its most important features and understand them rightly. The first is the close interrelation in the Christian liturgy between speaking and doing. Since that liturgy is predominantly the coming down of God's Word to us, it is fundamentally a liturgy of the Word. It is obvious that this is true of the first part of the Mass, which is actually nothing but the hearing of God's Word expressed to us in the circumstances and atmosphere that befit it. But the Mass is equally a liturgy of the Word in the second part, which we rightly call the sacramental and sacrificial. For the Christian sacrifice, as we shall see later on, is essentially a sacramental sacrifice, and every sacrament is a *verbum visibile,* a word made visible, and every sacrament also essentially implies *verba sacramentalia,* the sacred words which give to the sacred action itself not only its meaning but also its own inner reality.

But the immediate complement of this truth—that the Mass is a liturgy of the Word—is the fact that the Word who speaks in the liturgy is that same Word through which the world was made and now must be re-made, God's Word, His creative Word. As it comes forth to us here and now through the apostolic ministry, it still remains

God's Own, not only because it is His message, but because its Author is actually and operatively present in it, and it therefore possesses the same creative power which it had in the beginning of creation. Just as truly, then, as we can say that the whole liturgy is God's Word, we can and should also say that it is God's action. Since the Christian liturgy is, as we said before, primarily the place where is proclaimed God's Word of the New Covenant, the liturgy is also the place of the new Creation.

The realization of these truths will surely prevent us now from continuing to think of the liturgy as being of limited value, or of somewhat secondary importance in the Church's life. On the contrary, as both history and theology demonstrate, the liturgy in its essence and in its constituent elements is bound up with the chief truths and the central realities of Christianity.

In the light of what has just been said, we can clearly understand the most important fact that revelation itself is not to be considered as an abstraction, the mere communication from God's mind to man's of the articles of dogma in a set series. From the very facts of history, we learn that God's Word addressed itself to His People when it was officially called in convocation in the Qahal, that is, the liturgical assembly. From the existence of this liturgical context for the proclamation of God's Word, the context which is native and proper to revelation itself, we learn also that revelation is not only concerned with ideas or notions, but rather is, speaking most precisely, a call. God's People is called upon by God's Word to do and to become what the Word proclaims, and to do so by the power of the Word itself. God's Word thus calls for a response, both individual and collective. The celebration of the liturgy, therefore, should engage the whole people in its Catholic unity and also every one of its individual members in its whole climactic action of prayer and praise, and, even more, in the final sacrifice which seals the covenant between God and man.

This truth, and only this, can provide us with the right key to the true meaning of the famous sentence of the *De Gratia Dei "Indiculus"*: *"Legem credendi statuat lex supplicandi"* (let the rule of prayer establish the rule of faith). As the proclamation of God's Word was formerly incorporated in the liturgical celebration of the Qahal, so that Word can never be rightly understood apart from the living and enduring tradition of that same celebration. The reading of the Scripture that takes place in the framework of the Mass is not merely one among many types of reading the divine Word: it is the chief and fundamental type, to which all the others refer as to their norm. And, to penetrate still more deeply into this truth, it is in the living liturgical celebration alone, with all that this celebration, as we know already, implies for the living Church, that God's Word can be accepted as it desires to be accepted.

Now we can understand how natural it is to connect the Bible with tradition, how truly harmonious are these two sources of our faith. Tradition properly speaking is the life of the divine Truth in the Church. In the liturgy, that life is taken hold of at its source and in the fullness of its strength. In the liturgy that life is to be found in the context of cult and sacrifice which is native to it. In this context was made the fundamental proclamation of the divine Word; in and for this context the Bible itself was developed. For these reasons, the liturgy is to be considered as the central treasury containing all doctrinal tradition, and is, as Pius XI once said in a golden sentence, the "principal organ of the ordinary magisterium of the Church."

In considering these basic truths, we can also see how closely connected with each other are the apprehension of Christian Truth, the life of the liturgy, and the Christian life in all its fullness, individual and social. First let us note that it is no mere historical accident that the Christian initiation was never carried out as if it were the introduction of an individual into a structure of ideas and practices. From the very beginning it was an initiation into the life of the Church, carried out in the form of an initiation into the celebration of the liturgy. As we shall see later, catechesis, baptism and confirmation as traditionally carried out and explained, should be understood to form one continuous process of introduction to the Mass. Now we can verify what we implied in the previous chapter, that our modern notions of the existence of any opposition between liturgy and the Christian's inner life, between revealed truth and personal spirituality, between the life of the Church and the life of the individual Christian were completely unknown to Christian antiquity. In his Mystagogical Catechesis, St. Cyril of Jerusalem introduces the Christian life to his neophytes as a personal life of faith and prayer, a life which could not be conceived of apart from its incorporation in Christ's Body. And this incorporation consisted precisely in the uniting of the neophytes to the assembly of worshippers.

By this reference, moreover, we are brought to a final and most vital consideration. In the assembly of the Church, the *Qahal,* whose proper activity is the liturgy itself, rightly understood,—in this assembly everyone has something to do, has his own part to play in an action which is essentially communal, an action which allows for no spectators, but only for participants all actively engaged in the whole work.   But this communal activity must not be thought of in any superficially democratic kind of way.   It does not at all imply that everybody should have to do everything, or anybody any kind of thing.   Nor does it imply, as the Protestant belief has it, that it is only for the sake of decency and order that special people are appointed to take special parts of the liturgy in the name of the whole community.   For the idea is completely false—even though many Catholics often assume it to be true—that whatever the priest does at Mass, he does only in the name of the people and as its lawful representative.

On the contrary, although the liturgy is essentially a communal act, it is hierarchically ordered.   And this is not merely to prevent confusion and disorder; it is, rather, the direct consequence of the fact that the Church, the *ecclesia* does not meet on its own initiative, or because its members have spontaneously gathered together, but rather because it has been convoked by God's Word, speaking to it in the manner befitting that Word.

Or, to put the same truth in a different way, the hierarchical character of the liturgical assembly of the Church is the primary effect of the apostolicity which is the very basis and foundation of that assembly in the New Covenant.   It is on God's Word, and on IT alone, that the Church as such has the power to meet and to do what it must do in that meeting.   And, let us repeat, the great fact of the New Covenant in Christ is that God Himself speaks to us in Christ whom He has sent, and Christ speaks in those whom He, in His turn, has sent and through whom He is present, and thus God is present with us to carry out continually His great work among us.   Here is the reason for that statement of St. Ignatius already mentioned: "Only that Eucharist is to be accounted as valid which is performed by the Bishop or by a man whom he has enjoined to perform it."

This statement may be further illuminated for us by some wonderful statements of St. Clement in Chapter XL, and what follows, in his Letter to the Corinthians.   Let us note that this is certainly the first known text in which the word "liturgy" occurs, and here it still possesses its former connotations from secular speech, of a public service performed by one individual for the welfare of the whole community. Let us also keep in mind the fact that St. Clement is writing to the Corinthians for precisely the same reason which had already prompted St. Paul's Epistles to them, that is, their insubordination and the disorders arising in their liturgical assemblies from their ineradicable and stubborn tendency to try to rival one another in spiritual performances. St. Clement begins his letter by a general survey of the behavior of the People of God all through biblical history, as we have already done in this chapter. And then he draws this conclusion, which we can use as our own:

"Since, therefore, this is evident to all of us, and we have explored the depths of the divine knowledge, we are obliged to carry out in fullest detail what the Master has commanded us to do at stated times. He has ordered the sacrifices to be offered and the liturgies accomplished, and this not in a random and irregular fashion, but at definite times and seasons. He has, moreover, Himself, by His sovereign will determined where and by whom He wants them to be carried out. Thus all things are done religiously, acceptable to His good pleasure, dependent on His will. Those, therefore, that make their offerings at the prescribed times are acceptable and blessed; for, since they comply with the ordinances of the Master, they do not sin. Special functions are assigned to the high priest; a special office is imposed upon the priests; and special ministrations fall to the Levites. The layman is bound by the rules laid down for the laity.

"Each of us, brethren, must in his own place endeavor to please God with a good conscience, reverently taking care not to deviate from the established rule of service . . .

"The Apostles preached to us the Gospel received from Jesus Christ, and Jesus Christ was God's Ambassador. Christ, in other words, comes with a message from God, and the Apostles with a message from Christ. Both these orderly arrangements, therefore, originate from the will of God. And so, after receiving their instructions and being fully assured through the resurrection of our Lord Jesus Christ, as well as confirmed in faith by the Word of God, they went forth, equipped with the fullness of the Holy Spirit, to preach the good news that the Kingdom of God was close at hand. From land to land, accordingly, and from city to city they preached, and from among their earliest converts appointed men whom they had

tested by the Spirit to act as bishops and deacons for the future believers" (Chapters 40-42).

Combining St. Clement's phrases with our own, we may put all
this into a single sentence: The Church's one liturgy, ordered by God's
Word in Christ and made operative through that Word, is to be
composed of the harmonious conjoining of the distinctive "liturgies"
of bishop, priest, deacon and layman all working together, in accord-
ance with the apostolic hierarchy,—with no one acting separately by
himself and no one usurping the part of another, but everyone playing
his own part in the divinely ordered harmony of the whole action.

As a result of these considerations, we are now ready to understand both the importance and the meaning of Pius XII's Encyclical
letter on the Sacred Liturgy, *Mediator Dei,* written by the Holy Father
as a guide for the efforts now being made all over the world to regain
a full understanding and use of the Church's traditional prayer and
worship.

The introduction to this document points out the fact that the Encyclical is needed because, on the one hand, too many people are still
ignorant of the Catholic liturgy and are not interested in it, while, on
the other, many people who are eager to have the liturgy developed
and used to the full are not aware of its exact nature and meaning.
The Pope begins, therefore, by exploding completely that false theory
which would make of the liturgy merely the official regulation of external worship. He opposes to it a full and magnificent exposition of
the true idea of Christian worship, that it is Christ's Own worship of
His Father which was begun on earth and now continues forever in
heaven, as carried on and expanded in and through the Church. And
at the end of this exposition, the Pope gives this capital statement
with which we can conclude all that we have been attempting to say
with regard to a definition of the liturgy:

"The holy liturgy, therefore, is the public worship which is offered
to the Father by our Redeemer as Head of the Church; it is also the
worship offered by the society of the faithful to its Head, and
through Him to the Eternal Father; in a word, it is the whole worship
of the Mystical Body of Jesus Christ, that is, of the Head and of
its members."

The Holy Father then confutes, in the light of this definition, the theory which would reduce the liturgy to a merely formal and external worship. He next proceeds to attack that dissociation of the objective and the subjective in worship, which we have already mentioned and condemned. He shows clearly the fundamental necessity of the objective element in the liturgy, but he also shows that it has no end in itself apart from the formal, and therefore subjective, response of the faithful, including the full and methodical use of both intelligence and free will. We shall return later to a fuller consideration of these truths. Let us now proceed to the next section of the Encyclical and take note of the Pope's insistence on the hierarchical nature of the liturgy, which is that of the Church herself. The liturgy, he says, is hierarchical because it is carried out in dependence on the hierarchical ministry of the Church, and because it is so closely connected with the proclamation of saving Truth which was committed to the same apostolic ministry. Here are precisely the same considerations to which we have been led by our historical and theological survey.

The Pope mentions next the human factors which concur in the actual development of the liturgy. Among these, he speaks of the development of the formulation of dogma, the modifications of ecclesiastical discipline prompted by external circumstances, the more or less recent growth of various extra-liturgical practices and works of devotion in which may be found a great deal that is of lasting value, and, lastly, the development of those fine arts which concur in the outward expression of the liturgy. Here the Pope warns those men who try to bring their own creations into the liturgy without regard to legitimate authority, and those who disregard the traditional character of the general content and shape of the liturgy. And he also warns those who, dominated by an idealized vision of some historical period, would attempt an artificial restoration of that period and so tend to that kind of archeologism which we have previously denounced. We have already touched upon various points of this part of the Encyclical, and we shall mention them again later.

The two following sections of *Mediator Dei* apply the principles previously laid down to the two major constituents of the liturgy, the Eucharist and the Divine Office. We shall examine later the greater part of the points here made by the Holy Father. Suffice it now to note how beautifully balanced is the treatment of the subject given in the first part of these sections. The Sacrifice and the participation of the faithful in the sacrifice are once more put in place as the basis of the whole action of the liturgy, and at the same time, the Pope warns us against any antiquarian reaction which would simply try to rid the liturgy of all modern developments. Here and elsewhere in the Encyclical, the Sovereign Pontiff teaches what is, and what will be for us here, the golden rule in all such matters: not to suppress what has come about naturally in the course of history, but to rectify and purify it by adapting it not to the merely superficial, but rather to the basic ordering required by a truly traditional and theological understanding of the Holy Eucharist.

On the second point of this section of the Encyclical, we will notice the spiritual emphasis placed on the permanent use of the Psalter in the Divine Office, an emphasis which will provide us with our main theme when we come to the part of our own study of this subject.

The conclusion of the Encyclical consists of a series of remarks and warnings, applying to various countries and various circumstances. This section indeed has not the general bearing of the preceding ones, and seems to have been intended as a reminder to the Bishops of some of the difficulties they will have to meet, each in his own way, rather than as a formulation of anything like definite decisions with a universal application.

In view of what we have said already about the present historical situation in which our own efforts must be made to restore the full understanding and use of the liturgy, and of what has also been said about the sound basis of tradition on which this effort must be founded, may we hope that these few brief remarks about the Encyclical on the Sacred Liturgy will be all that is needed to convince our readers of the opportuneness of this great document for our times, and of the admirable wealth of traditional doctrine which it has once for all now solemnly proclaimed to the whole Church.

But it may be as well to remind ourselves of the fact that an Encyclical is not a sudden and unprepared revelation, neither is it a magic formula which will act, as it were, *ex opere operato* without our own concurrence. As we can see from the study already undertaken in the previous pages, it is on a lengthy and laborious work, carried on throughout the whole Church but most especially by the toils of certain distinguished members of the Benedictine Order, that this Encyclical has put its stamp of approval. We may well say that this document is in itself an index to the truths of lasting value which have been proposed by the contemporary liturgical movement, and that it is also a climactic product of that movement itself. Far from trying to propose new and startling ideas of his own, the Pope has rather succeeded in giving to the whole Church the benefits of the greatest achievements of modern scholarly research in liturgy combined with the best living and traditional theological thought, and also with a summary of wide pastoral experience. Combining all these kinds of knowledge, in his function of visible Head of the Church and with the grace of that office, the Holy Father has given us in this Encyclical a synthesis to guide and inspire all subsequent work in this field. How to carry out this work in the spirit of *Mediator Dei* is the task to be outlined in the course of the second and larger part of our study. The Encyclical was written precisely to call us to take part in that work. This call will be rendered fruitless through our own fault, if we do not labor as unremittingly and as skillfully as we can to clarify and to apply the charter that has been given to us.

CHAPTER FOUR

The Problems of Liturgical Movements: the Lesson From the Seventeenth Century

IN THE COURSE of the preceding chapters we have tried to arrive at a complete definition of the nature of the liturgy. We have gone about this task, not by means of abstract considerations, but rather by beginning with the false and inaccurate definitions actually common today; trying to understand in the light of history how these definitions once came to be made, and why and how through a slow and complicated process of development, they have come to be criticized and to be proved unsatisfactory. At the same time, we have followed the tentative work of scholars and theologians getting back to the true idea of the nature of liturgy; we have seen something of their surmises, of their early defects, of their growing perception of the essentials of the liturgy and their final attainment of a well-balanced view of the whole.

In this way, we have tried to consider all the elements of the problem—historical, scriptural and patristic—and to take advantage of all the research and experiments that have already been made, without committing ourselves to any particular school. And we have done this, in order to propose a definition of the liturgy that will be wide enough to include all the essentials, and, at the same time, precise enough to dispel many of the conflicting errors still extant.

Having proposed such a definition in the light of these preliminary studies, we then found in the Encyclical *Mediator Dei* a confirmation by authority of the ideas we had already ventured to propose on a purely scientific basis. Thus we have applied the golden rule which is that of all true Catholic theology,—not to substitute a merely external acceptance of what authority teaches for personal research, but to try to explain and justify the teaching of authority through personal research, while, at the same time, verifying the results of research by the test of authority.

Up to this point, although we have had occasion to mention several liturgical schools of thought, we have as yet given nothing like a history of the liturgical movement as such. We have only made a kind of sketch of such a history in order to arrive at the correct definition of the liturgy and to make ourselves sufficiently aware of the difficulties which beset all such liturgical research.

We must now ask ourselves, therefore, what does the historical fact of the existence of the liturgical movement mean for the Church herself. And we must then try to formulate the requirements which a liturgical movement must fulfill in order to attain its rightful purpose.

We can best begin this new section of our work by the following definition:—*the liturgical movement is the natural response arising in the Church to the perception that many people have lost that knowledge and understanding of the liturgy which should belong to Christians, both clergy and laity, and in consequence, have lost the right use of the liturgy also.* So the Encyclical *Mediator Dei* explains that it has been written to help both the rediscovery and the renewal of the liturgy. The necessity for both these aspects—the mental rediscovery and the renewal in practice,—presupposes the existence of a fact which we have already made clear; they presuppose, that is, that the true nature of the liturgy itself and what it should mean in the daily life of Church and of Christians have been neglected for a long time and allowed to fall into apparently hopeless oblivion. And the Encyclical's declared purpose of aiding both the rediscovery and the practical renewal of the liturgy presupposes also that a healthy and widespread reaction to this neglect and oblivion has already sprung up in the Church.

Once such a definition of the liturgical movement has been given, we can easily grasp the problem inherent in the very nature of it. Since such a movement arises necessarily during a period when both the understanding and the practice of the liturgy are at a low ebb— otherwise there would be no need for such a movement—it will be tempted to look wistfully toward a period when things were different. For this reason, the nineteenth century pioneers in the present movement first emphasized the state of the liturgy as it was in the Middle

Ages, and their efforts were, therefore, in some part mistaken. More recently, as we have seen, emphasis has been laid rather on the Patristic period, and this has produced more satisfactory results. But here is the source of the danger which we have already pointed out, the danger against which the Encyclical most particularly cautions us,— the danger, that is, of any artificial attempt to revive some period of the past in all its details,—whether that period be well or badly chosen, and its practice of the liturgy be well or poorly understood.

We can easily see, then, that the liturgical movement must necessarily go back to the well-springs of tradition; but it is always in danger of the fatal mistake of letting itself become hypnotized by such a return, and therefore of considering itself as merely a reaction to what is being done at present, or as a restoration of what was done in the past.

There is an equally grave danger of succumbing to the opposite temptation just when one is conscious of this first danger of antiquarianism and is guarding against it. This second temptation is that of false modernity, of a so-called adaptation to modern needs which actually causes the loss of true tradition as the result of an idolatry of ephemeral fashion, and as the result of the unregulated fancies of individuals. Against this second danger, the Encyclical warns us no less urgently than against the preceding one. And we should take note of the fact that today, as at other historical periods, we are often faced by both dangers at once, sometimes at war with each other, but sometimes also allied in a peculiar, but perfectly understandable fashion. For it is certainly desirable to go back to a higher and purer source in order to discover the permanent essentials of the liturgy and then to adapt these essentials to modern needs. But too often we find that people who are, in fact, only interested in carrying out their own preconceived ideas, unmindful of any other considerations, are appealing to a more or less hypothetical antiquity simply in order to evade the regulations of contemporary authority.

In other words, the task which we now face is that of making a clear and working distinction between a true rediscovery of the liturgy which will be a new upsurge of its eternal vitality, and a false rediscovery which would be a mere wandering off into a more or less fantastic past. And, at the same time, we must distinguish between a true renewal of the liturgy which will enable what has been lost and forgotten in the dust of the obsolete to spring up again into actual life, and a false renewal which would actually be merely a superficial love of change for the sake of change, or one which would pay due attention, it may be, only to the claims of a passing fashion. These two false kinds of renewal need to be distinguished from the true, if only for the sake of the true.

After what has been said already concerning the slow but continuous disintegration of sound liturgical thinking which took place during the Middle Ages, we need not be surprised at the fact that the beginnings of a true liturgical movement, as we have just defined it, are to be found during the sixteenth century. In the Christian humanism of the first quarter of that century, we see a craving for a more widespread and more profound access to the Bible and to the Fathers; we find also the desire for a more pure and authentic type of piety, based on a better knowledge and understanding of the liturgy together with a more perfect practice of it. For a most beautiful expression of these desires, we have, for example, a text of Erasmus from his Colloquia, instructing a young man in the way to attend Mass.

But, sad to say, it was among the adherents of this nascent liturgical movement that the Protestant Reformation found its promoters. As a consequence, not only did Christian humanism as a whole often seem somewhat suspect because of the falling-away of some of its most famous exemplars, but the program of liturgical reform which Christian humanism had been promoting has remained permanently scarred and crippled. Here we can see, in the first beginnings of a liturgical movement, a most forceful example of how "back to the primitive Church" can be perverted to mean "down with the Church of today." And we can see also how, under the guise of resurrecting the practices of antiquity, people can come to promote the most unprecedented kind of novelties.

The first mistake, that of trying to go back to the primitive Church in the wrong kind of way, resulted perhaps from the very mentality of the humanism of that time, formed as it was under the domination of an ideal of antiquity imbuing many people with the typical humanist thirst for an idealized past. A kind of mechanical reproduction of the past, therefore (in the case of the liturgy meaning a reproduction of the primitive Church and its worship so far as these could be imagined by the very imperfect scholarship of the time), was confused with what might have become a healthy return to apostolic and patristic sources.

But it may be said in fact that, in this field as in many others, the Reformation was shipwrecked not because it was too daring, although this has often been said, but because it was much too uncritical of its own assumptions, the assumptions generally common at the end of the fifteenth century. The so-called Reformers imagined, for example, that a return to the primitive liturgy meant taking the low Mass as the norm, suppressing everything in the Canon except the actual words of the Institution of the Eucharist; enlarging upon penitential features of the low Mass, such as the Confiteor; and, in general, not only centering everything on the memory of the Passion, but reducing everything to it.

But all these points, far from being primitive practices, were actually the most recent and the most questionable accretions or modifications of the Mass introduced during medieval times. As every scholar knows, not the low Mass, but the High Mass is the primitive form. Again, the exclusive emphasis on the words of Institution alone as against the whole Canon is a distorted exaggeration resulting from a lack of balanced liturgical thought and appearing only at the end of the thirteenth century. Or again, the lengthy acts of confession in Protestant services were adopted, not from the true primitive liturgy, but from practices once a part of the private administration of Holy Communion outside of the Mass, and which were only introduced into the Mass itself in late medieval times. And, finally, the idea of the Mass as an absorbing contemplation of Our Lord in His passion only, to the total exclusion of any thought of His Resurrection and of His final glory in His Whole Mystical Body, together with the reduction of the liturgical mystery to a mere memorial of the Passion,—all this is nothing but the final development of the medieval over-emphasis on the suffering Humanity of Christ, combined with the effects of the gradual disappearance of the true idea of the liturgy as sacramental, this idea having already been buried under a merely sentimental and allegorical remembrance of the past, in the *Expositiones Missae*.

In all this, we can see an example of the fact that the men who wanted to dig up and reintroduce a long dead past, while systematically ignoring all later developments as mere corruptions,—these same men were in fact only clinging to and over-developing practices which were actually recent liturgical accretions of more or less doubtful value, whilst losing everything truly primitive which had been handed down to them by tradition.

This strange but undeniable fact is worth keeping in mind as a permanent warning against all rash and ill-considered attempts to get back to a so-called "purer" or "higher" type of worship. There was at least something in the suggestions of the early Protestant reformers that could usefully have been retained. But their suggestions about the liturgy not only were rendered false as concerned externals, but were warped in their inner essence by a fantastic view of antiquity. And this view was the direct consequence of an attempt to reproduce antiquity in a mechanical fashion coming from the people who paid insufficient attention to the prejudices underlying their own aspirations, or to the constituent elements of their much too hastily attempted reconstruction of antiquity. For it was these uncriticized prejudices which unconsciously determined all their reconstruction although they supposed that it was the vision of the reconstruction that caused them to desire what they put into practice.

For these reasons, the beginnings of a true liturgical revival are not to be sought in the so-called Reformation, but rather to be looked for in the reaction to it,—a reaction which should have been at once critical of the Reformation itself and of the state of things which the Reformation opposed. Unfortunately, at first this was not so: the great weakness of the Counter-Reformation lay in its inability to achieve quickly a balance between criticism of the Reformation and criticism of its causes—and Baroque Catholicism was the result. And in spite of its praiseworthy preservation of a tradition which it did not rightly understand, Baroque Catholicism did little more than hasten, in the field of liturgy, that process of stultification that had already become evident during the Middle Ages.

After what has been said above about the changes made in the liturgy by the Lutherans, we can see how much Baroque Catholicism actually had in common with the errors of Lutheranism, although it fought so desperately against it. Both movements, far from escaping from the failings of the preceding period, often merely exaggerated these failings; and they were the same failings in both cases, though exaggerated in ways superficially different. Clear evidence of the truth of this statement may be found in a remarkable fact:—the style of church decoration that is commonly called "Jesuit," very closely resembles the style used in most of the Lutheran churches of the North which were built or re-decorated during the seventeenth century. No building could be more like the famous Roman Church of the Gesu than the chancel of Jung Sankt Peter in Strassburg or the Storkyrka in Stockholm. (This resemblance, it is true, has not often been pointed out; but only owing to the provincial fashion in which the history of the fine arts is still being studied). The same could be said of literature: for example, the religious poems of the English metaphysical school could certainly be taken as most valuable and typical specimens of what the Baroque mind could achieve in such a field,—and they are not the work of devout Catholics, but of devout Anglican parsons!

Yet, in spite of the Reformation and of the most prominent tendency of the Counter-Reformation, the sound elements in early Christian humanism still endured somehow in the Church, and, together with them, there was a continued perception of the way by which both the Charybdis of Luther and the Scylla of Baroque Catholicism might have been avoided. But this trend of thinking was very slow to recover from the double blow which it had received from the Protestants, associated as it was now in the minds of good Catholics with Protestant errors, and sharing as it actually did in at least some of these errors.

We have already alluded to some of the Anglican writers of the Baroque period,—let us notice, then, that in the Church of England were found also some of the men who first perceived that the way to a true liturgical renewal lay neither in Protestantism nor in the Baroque mentality. And here also were some of the first men to see more or less clearly where the true way should lie. We need not be afraid to acknowledge this fact, for the worst of heretics may sometimes have some very useful truths to tell us, truths which need only to be put back in a Catholic setting to take on their full value. Nor were these men we have just mentioned, the Caroline Divines, the worst of heretics,—far from it!

We are quite aware of the risk we are taking in saying such things, the risk of appearing to some readers to suffer from that too common delusion which causes French and Belgian Catholics to view Anglicanism through a golden cloud. Against such a notion, we can appeal to the authority of Pope Clement VIII, who exclaimed after reading some of the most important passages in the *Ecclesiastical Polity* of Richard Hooker: "There is no learning that this man has not searched into: nothing too hard for his understanding: this man indeed deserves the name of an author: his books will be reverenced as they grow in age, for there is in them such seeds of eternity that if the rest be like this, (that he had read) they shall endure until the last fire shall consume all learning."[1]

There is nothing, after all, very startling in the fact that some Anglicans could see the way out of the chaos of the Reformation and out of a merely negative and superficial Counter-Reformation even sooner than most Catholics. Such a fact is easily explained by historical causes. For Richard Hooker and his disciples, the Caroline Divines, were reacting from within Protestantism itself against its own excesses. They naturally possessed, therefore, both a clearer and a deeper perception of its root fallacy than most Catholics could have, since Catholics could only see the final effects of this fallacy from outside Protestantism, but could not have learned from the same personal experience what were the fundamental failures from which these final effects had flowed. On the other side, these same Anglican Divines were not prevented in the least by their position from maintaining what had been good in the original surge of Protestantism and what had been good in the general movement of Christian humanism from which it had proceeded. To defend their allegiance to their own church against the Puritans, these men were actually led on to emphasize the best tendencies in the primitive Reformation,— and to emphasize them the more as the Caroline Divines wanted to discard the evils of the Reformation as it appeared in its full development.

Such a desire, of course, often succeeded in making up a *Via Media* that was merely an illogical and ineffective compromise between yes and no. But in some superior minds and loftier souls, it produced at least a few beautiful sparks, potential beginnings of something far better than a compromise. Not only Hooker, but Andrewes, Laud, and later Cosin and many others of that school saw clearly wherein lay the great failures of Protestantism:—that its pretense of going back to the Church of antiquity was unsound, and that it was in itself as much of a novelty with no precedent as was that state of affairs against which it was rebelling. And these same men saw clearly that in order to answer the Protestant rebellion it was hopeless to treasure, along with practices that were truly tradional, the merely medieval corruptions out of which the errors of Protestantism had previously developed. In these ways, and to this

[1] Quoted in his *Life* by I. Walton.

extent, the Caroline Divines rediscovered something of what Christian humanism might have become in the midst of Catholicism itself, had men like Cardinal Quignonez in Spain or Cardinal Pole in England and Italy been in the forefront rather than Luther and Calvin.

How, then, can we best sum up these primary intuitions of what the liturgy should be which the Caroline Divines exhibit both in their written works and in practices that were actually carried out for a time in the Church of England?   These men felt, first, that the liturgy should be the common and effective worship of the Christian people. They were opposed, therefore, to any re-building of those screens between the sanctuary and the nave which some modern Anglo-Catholics were later to make so fashionable.   The services were not to be performed by some specialists instead of the people, but actually by the people.   And this desire did not imply anything anarchic or out of order, for these men had suffered from the Puritans' recklessness in such matters and abhorred it.   On the contrary, they understood that the Christian people as such was to constitute a Church only with due reverence paid to the hierarchy as instituted by Christ and His apostles, and to the institutions which had been received from authentic Christian antiquity.

According to the Caroline Divines, this Christian tradition was not to be received as a dead letter to be carried out only materially, in the exact shape in which they had received it from its most recent and more or less untrustworthy transmitters. The true tradition was rather to be disengaged from all spurious and unhealthy additions, and thus renewed in its primitive freshness, in order to be re-expressed in a frame which should make it accessible to the people of that day. Hence the insistence on the use of the vernacular, and on a systematic educational effort to make the people understand not only the letter but the spirit of the liturgy. Hence also the attempt to have the whole Bible read during the course of the ecclesiastical year, but read in its traditional context of praise and prayer, in constant reference to the mysteries of Christ's life and Passion seen as permanently actual and living, in and for the Church.

However, what was the actual success of the Caroline Divines, and what was best in their thought and in their lives? The limitations of that success are no less instructive for us today than are their first principles themselves.

We must say, first of all, that in everything done by these men there was too great an element of intellectual aloofness, of a refined but unpopular aristocracy of the mind, to make their efforts successful except among the very few. We cannot admire too much the personal piety which is exhibited in the *Preces Privatae* of Lancelot Andrewes, or the familial way of worship and of Christian living shown by the community of Little Gidding with Nicholas Ferrar. But we must realize that these beautiful achievements were appreciated by very few people, and had no power of widespread influence, for they had too many of the qualities of the scholar and of the highbrow English gentleman to appeal to more than a very small élite.

Secondly, and in close connection with this first defect, we must realize that although their reconstruction of antiquity was much more successful than that which was so unjustifiably the boast of Protestantism, still it was an artificial reconstruction and not a true revival. They acknowledged occasionally that good qualities were to be found in many aspects of the Middle Ages or even in the Roman Catholicism of their times against which they struggled ceaselessly; yet these men were, in their deepest hearts, antiquarians. To recapture the past—a very beautiful past, it is true—and to make it stand immobile was their ideal. And such an ideal separated them from the living Church no less than from the living world.

But the most striking failure of their work arose directly from their being out of communion with the Church. What was admirable about their work, and what had such a measure of success that it has endured even until our days in the larger Anglican churches, and, especially, in the cathedrals, is a Divine Office which is not a devotion of specialists but a truly public Office of the whole Christian people. This Office has some defects:—an exaggerated brevity in the Psalmody, a too easy acceptance of the contemporary fashion for elaborate polyphony which tended to make the Office once more something heard rather than sung by the people themselves; and, finally, too lengthy prayers of intercession (along the lines of those *preces feriales* and litanies of all kinds which were a legacy from the Medieval period). But, in spite of these defects, we must admit frankly that the Offices of Morning Prayer and of Evensong, as they are performed even today in St. Paul's, Westminster Abbey, York Minster, or Canterbury Cathedral, are not only one of the most impressive, but also one of the purest forms of Christian common prayer to be found anywhere in the world. This success makes even more striking the almost complete failure of the work of the Caroline Divines with the very core of the Christian liturgy, that is, the Eucharistic celebration.

With regard to the Eucharistic celebration, the Caroline Divines were imprisoned in the frame of worship already elaborated in the Prayer Book, a frame which abandoned in practice almost everything that was most primitive in the Mass. Everywhere in this field, therefore, we can see their obvious embarrassment. Only by returning to the undivided Church could they have regained the ground on which to build up the true Christian worship in its fullness. And since they were not prepared to make such a return, they could devise nothing better than a *via media,* a compromise in the worst sense of the word. In spite of their abortive efforts to reinstate a doctrine of the Real Presence and at least some of the features of a sacrificial Eucharist, they were tied to the Prayer Book. Not only did that frame of prayer with which they were determined to be contented at any cost preclude their rediscovering the traditional Eucharist in any practical or effective fashion, but, what is far worse, they could not recapture what is only to be recaptured in the true Church, that is, the full and organic intuition of what the Christian Eucharist is in its wholeness and in its unity.

For this reason it was not until the nineteenth century that the Anglican service again took on something of the appearance of the Catholic Eucharist, and even this was achieved only as a result of those disconcerting imitations of the Catholic practices of the time which are one of the most bewildering features of the so-called Ritualist Movement, that unexpected offshoot of the Oxford Movement. Therefore this mechanical imitation of modern Catholic practice was not to prove much more fortunate than the equally mechanical return to antiquity formerly advocated by the Caroline Divines. For what the Anglo-Catholics of a hundred years ago were able to borrow from the Catholics of the time were precisely those features which now appear to Catholics to be among the weakest points in their recent liturgical practice. For example, a preference for low Mass (as private as possible) rather than a public celebration; the high Mass itself carried out so as to do without Communion or any participation at all by the faithful; and, above all, an enthusiasm for Benediction of the. Blessed Sacrament which tended to make it, rather than the Mass itself, the focus of congregational worship.

All these last criticisms may be most useful to us now if they cause us to realize that any imitation of what is being done today anywhere, no less than of what was done in any period of the past, is completely ineffective as the basis for a sound liturgical movement. An interior and deep understanding of what is being done must be first attained, for any liturgical renewal is doomed to fail which is not basically, in its very beginnings, soundly theological.

These remarks about the Church of England are a useful preliminary to a discussion of what came about a few years later in the Catholic Church itself, for they gave us the clue to the causes of some of the difficulties which rendered sterile some very promising achievements in this case also.

During the first part of the seventeenth century in France, a wonderful renewal of piety and Christian learning took place, a renewal unfortunately that was soon to be obscured by the unhappy controversies of Jansenism and Quietism and to be at last almost, though never completely, stopped by the general disintegration of belief and practice in the eighteenth century. At the same time, in France there were also some very promising beginnings of an initial Catholic liturgical movement. We need now to study that movement with the greatest sympathy; it failed in some respects, not always through its own fault, but it accomplished a great deal that is of lasting value, more lasting, perhaps, than anything later achieved during the nineteenth century. It is regrettable that Dom Olivier Rousseau was not aware of how favorable to the seventeenth century liturgical movement is the comparison between it and that of the nineteenth century. In his interesting book, *Histoire du Mouvement liturgique,* he accepts almost without criticism some of the most untrustworthy and baseless statements of Dom Guéranger unfavorable to the seventeenth century movement. But, happily, other scholars have not so readily endorsed the dicta of the first Abbot of Solesmes—for example, Dom Henri Leclercq in his article: *Liturgies neo-Gallicanes* in the *Dictionnaire d'archéologie chrétienne et de liturgie,* and, more recently, Henri Brémond in two volumes of his *Histoire littéraire du sentiment religieux,* (t. IX and t. X)—and they enable us to go over and revise our opinion of the comparative progress of the liturgical movement during the two centuries.

Most promising conditions for the growth of a strong and healthy liturgical movement existed in France at the beginning of the seventeenth century. A magnificent revival of theological learning was to be found in the Sorbonne and other schools of theology. Jesuits such as Maldonat in the field of Sacred Scripture and Petau in Patristic studies, secular priests such as du Val and Gamache and, later, their great pupil Bérulle, were cultivating a wealth of knowledge of Christian tradition as admirable as that which was so evident among their Anglican contemporaries. And these Frenchmen possessed a deep and wide experimental knowledge and love of the Church in its living and enduring reality, together with the solid foundation for speculative thought that they constructed out of the best elements in medieval tradition and renewed by their biblical and patristic learning. No men could have been better fitted to promote and guide a liturgical renaissance. During the same period, as we shall see later in more detail, a scientific study of the liturgy was being undertaken in Italy by two great scholars who were also saintly men, the two Cardinals Bona and Tommasi. And only a little later, similar works were produced in France by the Benedictines Dom Mabillon and Dom Martène, by the Oratorian Lebrun, and many others.

One of the first effects—most interesting for us today—of this nascent liturgical movement, was a great effort to make the faithful understand the liturgy, both by translations and by explanations that were soundly historical and theological, and not fantastic like those of the Middle Ages. As examples we must mention at least the translation of the Roman Missal by Voisin, published in 1660; the translation of the Office of Holy Week, also by Voisin, published in 1662; the book of Letourneux *La meilleure maniére d'entendre la Messe* (The Best Method of Hearing Mass) (1680), and also, in 1679, shortly befor the Revocation of the Edict of Nantes, the translation of the Missal and of the Ordinary of the Mass by Pellisson, a convert. In 1682, Letourneux also published his *Carème Chrétien* (The Christian Lent), and before his death in 1682, he had finished the six volumes of his famous *Année chrétienne*. All these works, we must remember, contained not only the Latin text of the Liturgy with very beautiful translations, but also detailed explanations that are marvels both of scholarship and of pedagogy.

But, sad to say, all this marvellous work of educating the faithful was ultimately thwarted, first by purely political motives, and next by those unhappy controversies at the end of the century, the worst being the Jansenist, in which, again, political motives appear more and more clearly.

The first blow to this nascent liturgical movement was the condemnation of Voisin's translation of the Missal by a papal brief of Alexander VII, in 1661. This brief has enormous importance historically, because its text is the only argument from authority which, until recently, has been used again and again in attempts to show that translations (especially of the Canon of the Mass) have been condemned by the Church and are at least dimly heretical, as being opposed to the "secrecy of mysteries." But this brief does not, in fact, prove any such contentions, for, as Bremond convincingly shows in the ninth volume of his History (p. 117 and ff.), this "brief" is the most perfect example of what the canonists call a "surreptitious decision." It was obtained by the Prime Minister Mazarin by means of the forged accusations that Voisin had composed his Missal in order to say Mass in the vernacular. And Mazarin made this accusation for the purpose, actually, of compromising and discrediting the vicar generals of Cardinal de Retz, Archbishop of Paris, who had given their approval to the publication. By means of this barefaced forgery, Mazarin hoped to ruin his great enemy in the eyes of the Holy See. This brief of Alexander VII was so obviously inspired by a completely fictitious presentation of the state of affairs, that at first it had no practical effect. But it was to be used later in more serious controversies and then to prove a fatal weapon.

The fire of Jansenism began to blaze up and rage some years later. And very soon, as in many similar instances, everyone was listed on one side or the other. Jansenius, Saint-Cyran and Arnauld were Patristic scholars, great admirers of Christian antiquity, concerned with both the liturgical and the biblical movements of the time. And so everyone who had undergone the same spiritual and mental formation, or who had the same sympathies, either did in fact side with the Jansenists (as did many Benedictines and Oratorians who had no liking for the famous five propositions ascribed to Jansenius), or was considered to be on the Jansenist side or likely to be on it. Thus many of the most important and, as we can see now, most innocent productions of the liturgical movement of the time came to be condemned,—for example, the *Année Chrétienne* of Letourneux, although it is now certain that Letourneux was never implicated in Jansenism. He was, as a matter of fact, selected by the archbishop of Paris, Harlay, who was himself most opposed to Port-Royal, to confess the nuns there, precisely to avoid their remaining under Jansenist influence!

Not all the liturgical work which had been already accomplished was actually suppressed, but it all suffered heavily. A fantastic two-volume book, Vallemont's *Du secret des mystères,* published in 1710, shows us to what an extent, in the general mental confusion of the times, the reaction could go. Vallemont combines constant references to the Protestants (implying that their unique and principal heresy consisted in the desire to have the Christian people read their Bible and understand their prayers), with the most offensive and abusive references to the Brief of Alexander VIIth and to some propositions of Quesnel favorable to the liturgical movement, which had been put into the Bull *Unigenitus.* Thus Vallemont manages to identify allegiance to Rome and to the Church with a complete rejection of any effort to translate, to explain, or to promote widely any general understanding by the people of what is being done in the liturgy. Sad to say, this book represented one tendency of the times which was able so to monopolize the name of orthodoxy that even such a lover of the liturgy in the nineteenth century as Guéranger was fascinated by it and proved quite unable to criticize its most fantastic lies.

Here we can see the final victory of what we have termed the Baroque mentality over all the potentialities, at first so promising, of the liturgical movement which sprang up in the seventeenth century. And here also we can see, naively acknowledged, the purely pagan character of Baroque religion when it is examined in its essence. Vallemont certainly regards the liturgy as something sacred; but, to his mind, sacred means untouchable, something to be preserved intact at any price, and something which cannot be kept intact without the complete renunciation of all attempts to make the practice of it intelligent and living. No notion more fundamentally unchristian can be imagined: here, in fact, the kind of false "holiness" of the pagan mystery-religions is given the place and the name of the true holiness of Christ. •

But there was another aspect of the seventeenth century liturgical movement, in addition to the intensive literary activity of translation and explanation which we have just described. Paralleling this activity, most interesting attempts were made to revivify the actual practice of the liturgical rites and participation in them by the faithful, and to do so by means of a more perfect historical and theoretical understanding of the rites.

But these attempts were rendered suspect from the first, even more than was the work of translation and explanation, by the fact that some of their most prominent supporters were more or less attached to Jansenism. And the same unfortunate effects were produced as had formerly come about in the wake of Protestantism;—tendencies and ideas that were good in themselves were spoiled by an admixture of false tendencies and opinions, or, when they were not actually spoiled in themselves, they were discredited by being given the label of a heretical party. And so for generations afterwards men were disheartened, and prevented from advancing any further along the way which, in fact, was the right one.

The most famous among those liturgical pioneers of the seventeenth century was later denounced by Dom Guéranger as having been a living combination of heresies of all kinds, although, as a matter of fact, he can only be reproached for having signed the Appeal against the Bull *Unigenitus,* as did many of the most respectable churchmen of the time. This pioneer's name was Jubé, and he was the parish priest of Asnières, at that period a small place near Paris on the west bank of the Seine. Jubé insisted first of all on the public and collective character of the Mass. As a consequence, he never used the high altar in his church except on Sundays and feast-days when the congregation gathered together. He also restored the old Roman usage (which had endured longer in France than in Rome itself) of placing the linen cloth on the altar only just before Mass, and of having no other cross or lights on the altar than the processional cross and tapers, which were set in place at the beginning of Mass. Jubé began Mass by saying the Psalm *Judica* and the *Confiteor* along with the people; then he sat down on the epistle side of the altar, and listened to the Epistle and the Gospel as they were sung by the assistant ministers, after having sung the Collect himself. He sang the *Kyrie, Gloria* and *Credo* along with the people, instead of saying them in a low voice by himself. He also restored the offertory procession, (which had never entirely disappeared from French churches), and had offerings of all kinds made in this procession which he later blessed at the *Per quam haec omnia* at the end of the Canon, according to the original practice. He never began the Canon before the Sanctus had been sung in full, and he said the prayers of the Canon loudly enough to be heard by the whole congregation in his small church. In other words, he wanted once more to make the readings, the singing, the prayers, the Offertory real, rather than merely conventional acts; and he wanted to have the sacrifice offered with the full, though always hierarchically ordered, participation of the Christian people. Dom Guéranger later regarded all these practices of Jubé as so many reasons for horror and dismay. But we of today can see in most of them intelligent and healthy improvements, had they been introduced with the consent of proper authority.

But the same mistake of archeologism made in the tentative reconstruction of the Caroline Divines appears once more in many of these French attempts to restore the liturgy. There was, for example, the typically Jansenist notion of reintroducing the public penance of the ancient church. In fact, one of the most characteristic features of French Jansenism, especially as exemplified by Saint-Cyran and his followers, was the vague idea that the only truly satisfactory practice of Christianity had been that of the first five centuries, and that to reform and reinvigorate the contemporary Church, the necessary and sufficient means that must be taken was to return to this primitive practice. Also subject to this delusion, which perpetually haunts so many would-be reformers, was the type of Jansenism that later developed in Tuscany, exemplified especially in the famous Synod of Pistoia held by Bishop Scipione Ricci, the Synod which was finally condemned by the Bull *Auctorem Fidei* of Pius VI. This delusion of primitivism was here combined, as is so often the case, with a fancy for ideas far from primitive (for example, notions about the hierarchy of the Church which seem to treat pastors of parish churches as being divinely appointed in the same sense as are Bishops). Thus in Jansenism, excellent suggestions about liturgical practice such as those applied by Jubé were combined with doubtful or completely erroneous prescriptions or prohibitions. And for this reason, practices such as that so highly praised in *Mediator Dei* of using altar breads offered and consecrated at the Mass for the communion of the faithful at the same Mass, rather than hosts previously consecrated and reserved,—were discredited as seeming of the same order as the desire for a rationalistic simplification of the liturgy, an exclusive use of the vernacular, and an indiscriminate rejection of all kinds of modern devotional practices (the Rosary, devotion to the Sacred Heart, etc.)

But such unfortunate deductions from principles that were, in general, essentially sound, were not the only results of the practical aspect of the seventeenth century liturgical movement. Much more important in themselves and much more lasting in their influence were the revisions of the local French liturgies made at the beginning of the eighteenth century and not abandoned until the end of the nineteenth. These so-called neo-Gallican liturgies were completely caricatured and ridiculed by the *Institutions liturgiques* of Dom Guéranger. But the time has now come to revise this condemnation, made far too hastily, for, as is too little known, the liturgical Reform officially undertaken by Pope Saint Pius X borrowed a great deal from these reformed Gallican liturgies and incorporated it permanently into the Roman liturgy itself.

The capital accusation made against these liturgies by Dom Guéranger was that they were direct products of Jansenism, and bore the marks of this heresy everywhere. But, as Brémond points out very pertinently, the prelates who undertook the revisions embodied in these liturgies, including the most popular among them, were actually among the most deadly foes of Jansenism, for example, both Harlay and Vintimille, who were perhaps more responsible for the Parisian liturgy than any other bishops of the period.

Such being the case, when we consider the manner in which the revision was accomplished, and the points in these liturgies which were so indignantly censured by Guéranger as being not only Jansenist, but Protestant, anti-Roman, anti-traditional and so on,—what do we find? A tendency to return as much as possible to the use of the Scriptures themselves in preference to ecclesiastical compositions of a later date and dubious origins; a desire to purge the Breviary readings of the lives of the saints of all obvious inaccuracies and gross historical errors; an avowed preference for the temporal rather than the sanctoral 'cycle'; and the weekly use of the entire Psalter. All of these are deadly heresies, if we are to believe Dom Guéranger! But, as is now well known, all these points are actually contained in the program for the reform of the Roman Breviary itself which was drawn up by Pope Benedict XIV, the most learned and saintly Pontiff of the eighteenth century. And the majority of these same reforms were advocated by Pius VI, (the same Pope who condemned the Council of Pistoia) in a letter to the archbishop of Cambrai.[1] And, finally, all these points either have been already applied in Pius X's reform of the Breviary or seem to be about to be applied in the new reform now being planned in Rome.

[1] See Dom Henri Leclercq. *Op. cit.*

We shall have an opportunity later on to examine the Gallican liturgies in more detail. What has been said so far is sufficient to show the clarity of thought, depth of learning, ardor of piety and zeal for souls contributed to the liturgical renewal by that vast movement begun by the Catholic Renaissance in the France of the seventeenth century. And we must the more deeply deplore the fact that so brilliant and valuable a work was spoiled by a combination of human politics and unhappy and sterile controversies, and spoiled also by an admixture of biased opinions, among which was the perennial mistake of putting archeologism in the place of a living return to the sources of the liturgy, and the no less fatal error of projecting into an imagined antiquity some of the most unfortunate fashions of the time.

CHAPTER FIVE

Contemporary Movements: Solesmes, Belgium, Germany, France Since the Last War

Fʀᴏᴍ what has been said, in the last chapter especially, some readers might conclude that Dom Guéranger has been given the part of the villain all through our story. Nothing could be further from the truth. We are forced to point out his greatest mistakes in order ourselves to avoid their inevitable and disastrous consequences. But doing so must not blind us to the fact that there is no achievement whatever in the contemporary liturgical movement which did not originate in some way with Dom Guéranger. The very least that we can say in his praise is that he brought the liturgy back to life as something to be lived and loved for its own sake. This new life, as he understood it, had a galvanic quality, in both senses of the word; for while it implied a measure of artifice, it had also a thrilling power to arouse the interest and to stir the mind and heart of a good many men of his time. His love of the liturgy, like so many passionate loves, embraced something that often was more chimerical than real, but nevertheless this love was on fire with a burning passion, and so was capable of communicating itself to others. And we must also praise, not so much the intrinsic beauty with which the liturgy was performed at Solesmes and its dependent monasteries—since this beauty attracted the few but repelled the many, and among them some of the best men of the period—as the deep reverence that always pervaded it. This characteristic, along with others that might also be mentioned, sufficed to indicate to some lofty souls and deep minds what treasures of religious thought and sentiment — of

57

piety in the best sense of the word—were hidden in the Roman Liturgy, and what a complete expression of human needs and aspirations could be found in it.

After his time, it was slowly discovered that the "Roman Liturgy" in the form that Dom Guéranger had tried to make supreme and exclusive was not, in fact, the Roman Liturgy at its best. It was rather a late embodiment of that liturgy, an embodiment produced by many conflicting forces, and the very Popes who had canonized the liturgical books of Pius V had never intended the liturgy they prescribed to remain unchanged. Even before this discovery of the true nature of the "Roman" liturgy, people began to feel that the setting which Guéranger had worked so hard to provide for the liturgy was not, perhaps, so much in tune with its enduring mentality as he had innocently imagined. Even in the recent, post-tridentine form in which it is embodied in the books of Pius V, the Roman Liturgy everywhere implicitly protests against the attempt to make of it an impersonal ceremonial in which none of the people take part, designed merely to provide a few spiritual dilettantes with an exquisite but highly sophisticated kind of nourishment.

But all these criticisms were made by Dom Guéranger's own disciples sooner than by anybody else; and the best way to provide a balance for the criticisms we ourselves have made of his work is to realize that his followers were only able to go deeper and further than he himself into the true nature of the liturgy because he had already given them so much of positive value.

In my opinion, the decisive turning point for the Liturgical Movement came in 1909, when, at a Catholic Conference held at Malines in Belgium, Dom Lambert Beauduin, a monk of Mont César, proposed what was to become the basis of the Belgian liturgical renewal.

In the years preceding this conference, Saint Pius X had paved the way for such a revival. By his proposed reformation of the Roman Breviary (which was carried out two years after the conference), by his strenuous efforts to make Holy Communion once again a normal and regular practice in the Christian daily life, by the motives for the fostering of the chant emphasized in the *Motu Proprio* on Sacred Music, the Pope had led the way toward a rediscovery of the liturgy as true prayer. And he had, by the same means, led the way toward a new realization of the fundamental principle that the liturgy is something which we are not meant merely to see or to hear, but in which we are, above all, to take part, as in the traditional and collective glorification of God, bringing before Him the whole individual man in the whole Christian community.

But to gather up all these lines of rediscovery, to apply all these implications of the work of Pius X to actual personal and pastoral practice required the soul of a contemplative and a priest. The task called for a man imbued with the perception and the love of the Church as a living mystery, a man also to whom liturgical life should be life itself, and who would be inspired with an intense desire to make it possible for all his brethren in Christ to enjoy the same experience. This man, this priest, was found in the person of Dom Lambert Beauduin. In him we should revere one of the most simple and unpretentious yet one of the greatest figures of the Church in the twentieth century. His great mind, possessed both of clarity and depth, his open heart, his intense devotion to Our Lord and His Church, his acute perception of the needs of both the faithful and the clergy, made this humble monk able to lead some of the most courageous and providential enterprises of the Church in our times, enterprises whose lasting value cannot yet be ascertained.

We should never forget that Dom Beauduin, before he became a Benedictine at Mont César, had been a secular priest of the diocese of Liège. He had worked there for eight years in an extremely active ministry, especially among working men, as one of those "Chaplains of Workmen" appointed in this diocese to forward the practical application of the great Encyclical of Pope Leo XIII, *Rerum Novarum.* But Dom Beauduin was attracted to the cloister by the need he felt for a more deeply founded piety. And, as a monk, he was called to teach theology to the younger monks. Thus were providentially combined in this priest of wide experience, zeal for the souls of modern men, desire for a true and deep kind of piety, and interest in a better understanding of Christian dogma.

All these qualifications caused Dom Lambert to realize, first of all, that the liturgy itself, properly understood, is the fundamental catechesis of Christian doctrine, and that its presentation is the means most capable of stimulating and feeding the highest and purest spiritual life. And he also realized that the liturgy itself, thus understood, is meant to be the well-spring of spiritual vitality and to provide the framework for Christian living, not only for individuals, not only for some Christians, but for the whole Christian people in the

Church. As he says in his little book: *La Piété de l'Eglise* (first published in 1914) he often thought that great marvels could be accomplished by the clergy in reinvigorating Christian life in their parishes if only they worked to have their people find in their parish church the house of God and the gate of heaven; in their parish priest, the man who offers, blesses, leads, teaches and baptizes; in the parish Mass, the great weekly meeting of the Christian people in which, by the action of the visible priesthood, men united in bonds of brotherhood are to be transformed into the whole Christ! What pains priests take, he often thought,—this priest who had been active for so many years in so many kinds of social work—what labors they undergo to organize so many works that are certainly useful, but of secondary importance! But what would be the effects if priests took the same pains to promote the rediscovery of essentials through a rediscovery of the liturgy, if they labored to have the liturgy understood and practised by the whole Christian people as its collective and personal life of prayer and worship in Christ and the Church? One sentence in the *Motu Proprio* of Pius X could sum up this program and express its ideal aim, and to this sentence Dom Lambert referred again and again: "Our deepest wish is that the true Christian spirit should once again flourish in every way and establish itself among the faithful; and to that end it is necessary first of all to provide for the sanctity and dignity of the temple where the faithful meet together precisely in order to find that spirit at its primary and indispensable source, that is . . . the active participation in the most holy and sacred mysteries and in the solemn and common prayer of the Church." No man of the time was so well prepared as Dom Lambert to listen to the words of the Blessed Pope, and no one else was so ready as he to proclaim these words so forcefully.

In the Catholic Conference previously mentioned at Malines in 1909, where the Belgian Liturgical Movement actually began, Dom Lambert's aims and his practical program met with the complete approval of Cardinal Mercier, one of the most eminent prelates of modern times, and of Godefroy Kurth, a famous layman and historian. These desiderata were, therefore, formulated under Dom Lambert's direction:

1) That the Roman missal should be translated, and its use promoted widely among the faithful as their chief devotional book, to popularize at least the complete text of Sunday Mass and Vespers.

2) That an effort should be made to have all piety grow more "liturgical," especially by means of the recitation of Compline as evening prayer, by attendance at the parochial Mass and Vespers, and by teaching the people to find in their participation in the prayers of the Mass the best preparation for receiving Holy Communion and the best way of making their thanksgiving afterward. All this should be accompanied by the attempt to restore earlier liturgical traditions in Christian homes.

3) That Gregorian chant should be fostered, according to the Pope's desires.

4) That the choir members in each parish should be encouraged to make annual retreats in some center of liturgical life such as a Benedictine abbey.

In the years following the Conference at Malines, Dom Lambert and his brethren at Mont César were the leading and principal workers in carrying out this program. But, as Dom Olivier Rousseau emphasizes, Dom Lambert himself soon came to widen the scope of the last point and thus to transform it. For he came to find his foremost liturgical apostolate in winning not so much lay people who were choir members, but first of all the priests themselves, especially the parish priests. Here is shown most clearly the perceptive genius of this great Benedictine. He himself, led by the teaching of the Pope and by his own Christian and priestly experience, had come to rediscover the liturgy as the prayer and worship of the Christian people. In the same way, he now realized that since the liturgy is the pastoral work *par excellence*, the pastors must be the first to be convinced of its value; they must be encouraged not only to promote the liturgy for the sake of their parishioners, but, first of all, to find in it for themselves the true source of their spiritual life and apostolate.

But we must add that however important was this vision of Dom Lambert's, it would probably have produced no fruit if he had not also possessed in abundance the practical insight into men's minds and the sympathetic fraternal affection required to help his brethren in the priesthood to make for themselves and for their people the discovery of the liturgy that he had already made for himself.

We do not need to go thoroughly here into the history of the review *Questions liturgiques et paroissiales* and of the *"Semaines liturgiques,"* the two main organs through which the liturgical movement was soon to become the focus of the life of the Church in Belgium. But we must point out some of the characteristics of the work which Dom Beauduin accomplished through these means and many others.

The most striking characteristic is what we might call its realism, taking the word in its best sense and referring it to two complementary aspects of the work of restoring the liturgy. In the first place, Dom Lambert and his followers have always kept in mind the actual people whom they were addressing, both priests and lay people, and the actual parishes of these priests and people, each with its own problems. So Dom Lambert and his followers spared no pains to make everything that they proposed quite clear to priests and people, in a patient and prudent, but decidedly progressive fashion. They also tried in every way to arouse the interest of their audience, and to establish and develop the natural connection between whatever was already in the minds of their readers and what the liturgy had to offer them. And by this we mean not only the way in which the liturgy could answer needs of which priests and people were already aware, but the way in which it could correct, purify and enrich their whole view of religion and of the Christian life.

The Belgian liturgical movement has also showed this character of true realism in a second way: by always going to work with the actual liturgy of the Church of today. Dom Lambert was far too learned to imagine that the Roman Missal as it now stands is in a state of perfection that has never been surpassed or that never could be surpassed. But he deliberately refrained from any attempt to confuse liturgical renewal with liturgical reformation, either by going back to more ancient rites and usages or by undertaking new and unprecedented experiments. With a wisdom which we cannot esteem too highly, he always held to a principle which could be expressed in this way: the liturgy belongs to the Church; let us, then, take it just as the Church of today has treasured it for us and as she offers it to us; let us try to know it, to understand it, to carry it out *as it is,* as perfectly as we can. Let this work suffice for us now; when we have done our best to accomplish it, then will be the time to see whether there is also something further to be attempted.

This wisdom proceeded, of course, from Dom Lambert's own most personal experience. The life of a Benedictine had shown this young and active priest, in search of a source of a more intense and effective spirituality than that he already possessed, that we have a forgotten treasure in the actual liturgy of today, the liturgy of the modern Roman Missal and Breviary. Nobody would ever dream how much a man could rediscover in it and could strive to carry out in his own life and priestly ministry. For anyone, then, to allow himself to wander about in dreamy fields of anticipation of future reforms or restoration of practices of the past before he had attempted fully to make use of what exists in the present,—this would be to give in to the most foolish kind of temptation.

Here, then, is the clue to the great importance of the Belgian movement,—that it never got lost in archeologism or antiquarianism, and it was never tempted to wander off into innovations of doubtful value. This movement consisted in the pure and strong rediscovery of living tradition as it is: not a thing of the past, but the actual reality of the Church of today to be lived by the people of today, a reality so continually overflowing with riches as yet unknown as to render foolish any wish to look for something different until this reality as it is has been once more fully explored and put to use. We have now in the liturgy of the Church, treasures that we do not make use of because we do not know of their existence. Let us come to know them. What could be more matter-of-fact, more simple, and more healthful than this modest program?

This was the first foundation of all Dom Lambert's work; and it is wonderful to see how his wide and deep knowledge of history, and his piety that was so soundly doctrinal, springing as it did from the highest sources of tradition, contributed so much to a real understanding of the rites and prayers of the Church and to their appreciation. We would admire him even more greatly, if we were to follow all his activities for the purpose of restoring a vital practice by priests and people, and observe the balance of true learning, a most personal piety, pastoral experience and love of souls shown throughout all his work.

This true realism of the Belgian liturgical movement was ruled and inspired by a wide and deep devotion to the Church, the actual hierarchical and collective Church of today, acknowledged and loved as the living body of Christ. This *ecclesiastical* characteristic of all Dom Lambert's work, and, in particular, the completely revitalized understanding of the sense of that word "ecclesiastical" which his work brings about, is, perhaps, the true reason for its astonishing success. But also, in close connection with this rediscovery of the Church in and through the rediscovery of the liturgy, we must realize the importance of Dom Lambert's understanding of the nature of the priesthood and of its unique role in the Church and in the liturgical renewal. For this understanding is the key to the practical method used by Dom Beauduin in going about the work of renewal, as it is also the key to that pastoral character which is an essential quality of the liturgical movement. We must always remember that Dom Beauduin himself did not go to the monastery in order to escape from the priestly responsibilities he had already assumed, but rather to be more capable of being faithful to them. So he was able to explain vividly to his fellow priests how the two purposes a priest should have in studying the liturgy are actually one: how will the liturgy enable me to live as God wants me to live; how will it enable me to have my people live that same life, the life of Christ in them? So also Dom Lambert was able to understand so well and to make others understand the two-fold aspect of the liturgy, that since it is, as we have said, the possession of the Church, it is both the possession of the whole Christian people in its vital unity and the most important reality at the basis of every Christian's most personal life.

The perfection of this synthesis, so completely and spontaneously achieved by Dom Lambert, may perhaps be described best by saying that it shows us how to appreciate that word, Catholic; and no better praise can be given that great priest and religious than to say that in all his work he shows himself to be *homo Catholicus* par excellence.

In connection with the Belgian liturgical movement, we must mention the new missals that were produced with complete translations and sound explanations. Such missals were proposed first of all at Malines, and became the main instrument of the movement. And the movement itself was largely responsible for their astonishingly quick and widespread diffusion. In this field, we need only mention the names of Dom Fernand Cabrol, Abbot of Farnborough, and Dom Gaspar Lefebvre, the famous monk of Bruges.

Another great characteristic of the Belgian liturgical movement was that it was not the work of a party or of specialists, nor was it a kind of separate activity in the Church. From the first everyone understood it to be a general renewal of Christian teaching and life, both individual and collective, a renewal of the Church itself through the renewal of its parochial life. And so the whole movement had the same outstandingly Catholic quality as Dom Lambert, its chief inspirer.

After the first World War, while the Liturgical Movement in Belgium was once more beginning to develop and to attain its full success, two new advances were taking place in Germany. But we must admit that the first beginnings of the German movement (as described so well in the long introduction by Count Robert d'Harcourt to the French edition of Guardini's *Spirit of the Liturgy*), did not possess that complete and healthy balance which was so distinctive a quality of the Belgian movement. The movement in Germany, as it was connected with the monasteries of Beuron and especially with that of Maria Laach, was at first rather the concern of the few, of an intellectual élite, than of the whole Christian people. In this it held closely to the primitive Solesmian tradition. But it soon began to depart from that tradition inasmuch as the deep historical and theological culture of men like Abbot Herwegen and Dom Casel differed from the amateurish kind of scholarship of Dom Guéranger. What has been said in a previous chapter about these men is enough to show how greatly they contributed to a complete renewal of our fundamental conceptions of liturgical questions. Especially in the field of theology, the work of Dom Casel was to strengthen and deepen that comprehension, so vital to Dom Beauduin, of the liturgy as not a detail, however important, but the center and, in a way, the whole of the life of the Church and of all Christianity.

But we can only realize the full importance of the German contribution, when we perceive that the work of the somewhat aristocratic and high-brow school of Maria-Laach was complemented by the more popular work of the school of Klosterneuburg, in Austria, under the leadership of Pius Parsch. This afterwards became the widespread work of many parish priests and religious in Germany and Austria, including such pastors as Pinsk in Berlin and such Jesuits as Jungmann of Innsbruck. Thus a movement sprang up in Germany which closely resembled that of Belgium in its practical inspiration and undertakings, while being able to make full use of the vast stores of scholarship and speculative thought, as well as of the intense and magnificent piety of Maria-Laach.

A most important new development of the modern liturgical movement which was due primarily to the Augustinian canons of Klosterneuburg, and especially among them, Pius Parsch, consisted in the explicit promotion of a biblical movement in conjunction with the liturgical movement itself. The review *Bibel und Liturgie,* which

was distinguished by the same remarkable psychological and peda-
gogical tactfulness as animated Dom Beauduin's work, initiated the
task of showing how a living understanding of the Roman Liturgy
could be effectively deepened and enriched by a wider knowledge
of the Bible.

The advance caused by this development cannot be too greatly
emphasized. First, it enabled men to grasp the full significance of the
liturgy itself by uniting it once more with its chief source, this source
also now being valued in its fullness. At the same time, the liturgical
movement came in this way at last to promote that direct and abund-
ant use of God's Word in all forms of Christian spirituality which for
so long had been rendered suspect in the eyes of Catholics rather than
effectively promoted by the sixteenth century reformers. This particular effect of the Biblical movement was accomplished by giving
the Bible that living commentary without which it cannot be properly
understood. For it is in the liturgy that the Church best prepares us
to understand God's Word, both by means of the light thrown on the
texts of Holy Scripture by one another as they are placed together in
the liturgy, and also by the way in which the liturgy itself handles the
inspired themes which make up the unity of Revelation itself.

This widening of the scope of the liturgical movement is a fact of
the very greatest significance in the history of its development, for the
importance of this biblical renewal inside the liturgical movement goes
far beyond the sphere of practical methods, and involves theological
implications of the greatest value. From what has been said in a previous chapter, we can see how close is the interrelation between Revelation and the liturgy, or, more exactly, between the Divine Word
and the congregational worship of the Church. To realize this interrelation and to grasp its full significance will prove to be one of the
decisive factors in our attaining a true and renewed understanding of
the nature of the Church itself. And such an understanding is certainly the supreme aim of the whole liturgical movement. Thus we
are led to believe that it was the work of divine providence to bring
together in a harmonious balance the work of the two great liturgical
centers in Germany, Maria Laach and Klosterneuburg, for it is only
in and through each other that the Mystery of Christian worship and
the living Word of God can both be rightly understood in the living
Church.

And we may hope that this synthesis will, in a few years, become the outstanding characteristic of a third phase of the movement, a phase which is now beginning in France,—if this phase develops as it should.

It is only since the second world war that France has become at last the theatre of new developments in the liturgical renewal. Long before, of course, the Abbey of Solesmes, and, in spite of all its defects, Dom Guéranger's work, *l'Année Liturgique,* had already exercised a wide influence in France. The great school of Catholic literature which includes Péguy and Claudel had educated many minds and given them a new perception of Catholic teaching and practice. None of this, however, had really won the clergy or affected to any great extent the rank and file of ordinary Catholics.

But, in the years immediately after the war, a new beginning was made, inspired by some French Dominicans and a few secular priests. From the outset, these men were eager to profit by all the experience of their Belgian and German confreres. On the other hand, the fact that they began their work in the milieux already prepared by Catholic Action, especially by the various Catholic Youth Movements, established it firmly in contemporary life. We must note the fact that the French movement gained its first adherents from among those men who were, at the same time, beginning suddenly to realize the necessity for a true home missionary effort in the great de-christianized centres of industry. As a result of all these factors, the French movement, like the Belgian, was from the start directly pastoral in its orientation. But it is important to remark that the French movement did not so explicitly identify its pastoral purpose with a parochial one as had the Belgian movement. We may even ask ourselves whether some men in this French movement were not perhaps too quick to admit that the parish could not be made once more the actual center of Christian worship. And along with this tendency went another to give precedence to missionary work among modern pagans rather than to the work of helping faithful Christians in the Church to rediscover their own treasures.

These various factors could lead, and sometimes have led to some neglect of the traditional aspect of the liturgy, and to an interest perhaps not perfectly balanced in making up or re-making the liturgy. The creation and overwhelming success of what have been called "para-liturgies" are proofs of what we have just been saying. Composed first to be a means of education, a transitional device preparing the way for an understanding of the liturgy itself, these "para-liturgies" have often become ends in themselves. Some people, that is, have been tempted to find in these para-liturgies, not a means toward taking part in the real liturgy, but rather a "liturgy of the future" which will more or less replace or refashion the official liturgy itself.

It cannot be denied that there are grave dangers threatening such a mode of thought. In their generous desire to meet today's unbelievers on their own ground, are not some Christians unconsciously inclined rather to canonize modern ideologies than to communicate the Christian faith?

But it is precisely here that we can see clearly the vast import of the connection so recently reestablished between biblical and liturgical renewal,—and also the great importance of the Patristic revival which provides the living link between the Bible and the liturgy, and which is so conspicuous a work of the Church in France today. For the most effective counter-balance to those dubious missionary efforts which tend to bring the spirit of the modern pagan world into the Church rather than effectively to christianize that world, will certainly be the new discovery of the Word of God, set down in the Bible but only to be truly understood in Catholic communion with the Fathers and in the midst of the liturgical assembly of the Church of today and of all ages.

The problem that now besets us is, of course, that of reconciling permanence with adaptation in the tradition of the Church and especially in its liturgical tradition. There is no longer any question of considering the liturgy as something set once for all in the forms now established, something that can never be altered in any way. But the only alternative to a deadly anarchy must be sought in a revival of tradition itself which will have the combined strength and suppleness of a truly living organism. And nothing will prove more effective for such a purpose than a return to the sources of tradition, a return entirely free of all archeologism.

One most reassuring phenomenon now visible in the midst of a confusion which might otherwise seem disquieting is a new development, daily more clearly discernible, in the various "para-liturgies" themselves. Sometimes in the recent past they have exhibited a tendency to lay aside the traditional liturgy and to try hastily to embody modern ideals more or less foreign to the spirit of the Church and of the revelation that has been entrusted to her. But now we see an exactly contrary tendency. "Para-liturgies" are tending more and more to take the form of meetings for reading the Bible and for prayer, and this reading and prayer is determined by the great themes of the Christian mystery as laid out in the authentic tradition of the liturgy itself. So we are beginning to find once more a spontaneous and vital atmosphere similar to that in which the liturgy was developed in the great creative period of its history. Nothing could be more conducive to a true rediscovery and revitalization of the liturgy, a renewal which would give back to the liturgy all that richness and fullness of life which it once possessed and which, through the Middle Ages, was increasingly lost.

The recent restoration of the Easter Vigil and its immense success in France,—greater, perhaps, than in any other country,—is a striking proof of what can be accomplished through a return to authentic tradition. But, in order to promote this return, nothing is now more urgent than a careful consideration of what the liturgy is in its permanent essence and in the laws of its vital development. The task we must now undertake before proceeding any further, therefore, is that of laying out the way by which to approach such a consideration, using the light of the Encyclical *Mediator Dei* and taking advantage of all the recent work of research and of the accumulated experience of the past which we have just been reviewing.

CHAPTER SIX

The Catholic Tradition Concerning
the Shape of the Eucharist

In APPROACHING the reform of the liturgy, we must, first of all, keep in mind the danger of either a false traditionalism, on the one hand, or of a rash modernism, on the other. The spirit of false traditionalism would reduce the liturgy to a sort of framework to be accepted purely on authority, a completely stylized, purely external routine—in other words, something virtually dead. Rash modernism, at the other extreme, would, by reaction, awaken in the people the desire for a "new" liturgy—a so-called "living" liturgy—and then satisfy that desire with "paraliturgies" which spring full-fledged from their sponsors' minds, regard having been paid, not to tradition, but only, under the pretext of meeting the needs of the present, to expediency or even to momentary fashion.

Both these results, let us not forget, have much the same source. To attain them together, therefore, it is only necessary that we continue to leave the liturgy of the Church untouched, even if this means its gradual disappearance as a living thing, while in its place the newly made "paraliturgies" may prosper freely if they but stop short of using for themselves the official title of the liturgy.

Priests will continue to say the Breviary in their spare time; they will say Mass and administer Baptism at record speed, without changing a single word to be sure, but also without taking the trouble to make the people understand what is going on, much less to take part in it. On some special occasions, a solemn or pontifical Mass will be correctly performed as a distinctive pageant of Catholic loyalty. And

70

at the same time, the people will continue to be fed with pious devices of all kinds, with individual exercises of devotion, more or less spiritual practices, revelations to nuns, and so on. Or, in some modern quarters, mass religious meetings will take place on the pattern of contemporary pagan worship of the nation, of man's work, of earthly ideals, only "christianized" by their mode of expression. . . . And everybody will be happy, living and letting others live. . . .

But if the Church were ever to acquiesce in such a state of things, she would abandon her most sacred duty and practically give up everything for which she was designed by her divine Founder.

Here, then, we come to the necessity for a rediscovery in the field of the liturgy itself, which is its principal locus, of what tradition truly is, and what are its authentic relations both to authority and to individual initiative and personal needs. For tradition is not a dead thing to be accepted blindly only under the external pressure of authority. Nor, in order to bring it to life again, should tradition by any subterfuge be taken away from the regulation of authority and developed by anybody in his own irresponsible way.

The true idea of tradition held by the Council of Trent in entrusting the Holy See with a much needed reform of liturgical books, was equally opposed to both mistakes. The Council of Trent was far from allowing any individual the freedom to make up a liturgy or paraliturgy of his own which would usurp the place of the Church's one whole liturgy. But it was far from any desire to impose any prefabricated and immovable liturgy on the Church. The authority of the Council and its appeal to the authority of the Holy See itself was to be understood as the safeguard at once of the genuine authenticity and of the continual adaptability of tradition. And this has always been the case with authority and always will be in the Catholic Church.

Therefore—as was still clearly understood by all the canonists who wrote on the liturgy during the seventeenth and eighteenth centuries, from a private author like Lebrun to a great Pontiff, who was at the same time a canonist of genius, like Benedict XIV—the authority attached to the liturgy is not dependent completely and solely on that of the actual Popes or Bishops who have canonized such and such books with their rubrics, or who have guaranteed such and such answers of any commission, from the Sacred Congregation of Rites down to the commission appointed for the reformation of the Parisian liturgy by Hardouin de Perefixe. No, the authority attached to the liturgy was for these men fundamentally that of tradition itself. And it was only as the guarantor of tradition under both its aspects of permanence and of living adaptability that the authority of Popes and Bishops gave their sanction to the liturgy.

More exactly—as can be seen in the statements of the Council of Trent and in the detailed formulations of the various Pontifical Bulls canonizing the Missal and Breviary of Pius V, and, finally, in the Encyclical *Mediator Dei,*—in the field of liturgy as in every other, the living authority of the Holy See itself and of all the Bishops, at Trent and elsewhere, intervenes precisely in order to *canonize what it considers to be the most perfect vehicle available in our age for the maintenance of the tradition which through Christian antiquity has come down from the Apostles themselves.*

This definition seems to give a clue of paramount importance to the understanding of the liturgy as a living thing, along the lines of the forceful formulations of *Mediator Dei.*

Just because the liturgy is in no way merely a detail of discipline to be changed at will either by authority with no precedent to guide it, or by individuals deferring to their own irresponsible hobbies, just because the liturgy is the living heart of the Catholic tradition, that is, because it embodies the ultimate revelation of the eternal Word of God to His People, while it includes the act of redemption and new creation realized by that selfsame Word,—the liturgy shows the distinctive features of the Catholic tradition in its most solemn form.

The Catholic tradition is not a thing of the past, fixed once for all in detailed written form, never to change or progress. Neither is it a changeable thing to be remodelled at will either by individuals or by an authority which, if it did such a thing, would be as unfettered and irresponsible as an individual. This tradition is, rather, a living pattern given once for all in its essentials by Christ and His apostles. And this pattern has to be lived out through all the ages, not by individuals separately, but by a living community, grounded on Christ and His Apostles through being always in communion and one with the successors of the Apostles and the vicars of Christ.

In this living communion, the Popes and the Bishops are not to do everything while the rest are to accept their governance in a purely passive way. Nor are individuals allowed to do as they like.

Still less is the authority meant to be all-powerful in some field isolated from real life, while the individuals are left alone to do everything or nothing in all other fields of activity.

Rather, we may apply here most effectively Newman's fruitful statement about the two component parts of tradition in the Church and their mutual and necessary interplay. As he says, there is only one tradition, which is that of the whole body, head and members; but this tradition takes two complementary forms which are never to be confounded, which can never be reduced to one, and which are never to be separated from each other.

What may be called the episcopal tradition is the whole body of decisions which have arisen from the extraordinary magisterium of the Church. Only this form of tradition may be considered to be properly and strictly authoritative. But it must never be seen as separated from, let alone as opposed to, what Newman calls prophetic tradition, that is, as Newman uses the word according to St. Paul's phrase, *"the mind of the Spirit,* the thoughts, the principles which are like the breathing of the Church, the way in which habitually and, as it were, unconsciously, she looks at things, rather than any set of dogmas, static and systematic."[1] This prophetic tradition is maintained throughout the whole body of the Church, not only passively but also actively, always of course in conjunction with those who are at its head. It expresses itself in countless ways; and the records of these ways are kept for us by history, or, more exactly, by all the documents and monuments on which the study of history must be built. But the great point is that this tradition cannot be recognized in these records except by those who are living in the Church, who are breathing with her breath, who are living in her life and praying her prayer. And the episcopal tradition itself is, as it were, plunged in that prophetic tradition, always leading it, but also founded on it, in order to guarantee it at every step, to be able to distinguish its main stream from divergent backwaters; making solemn and definite pronouncements which are never meant to take the place of the continuous life and light of the "prophetic" tradition, which is far too rich ever to be fully defined, but rather to preserve it both from stultification and from alteration.

Now we can see how the individual in the Church is meant to respond to the stimulation given by authority, especially in the field

[1] Via Media, t. 1, p. 249-251.

of the liturgy. He is not meant to answer by a strictly correct but purely passive and external adherence to the material injunctions of authority. He is, rather, to make an ever-renewed effort to know, to understand in a living way, to keep faithfully, by adapting it to new needs, "the faith once given to the saints," not as a naked and abstract idea but as a living body. Knowledge of the past, then, and personal understanding of the actual present are not to be renounced for the sake of a dead acceptance of authority; rather they are to be used to promote a filial obedience to authority, to illuminate and vivify what is received from authority. In so doing, far from ever coming into conflict with authority, we shall be preparing the way for it. We shall at once help to develop the seed which the preacher is to sow and make ready for it not a hard rock, but fertile ground. We shall provide authority with a living material which it can correct and perfect by its paternal injunctions, not with a dead carcass which it could only galvanize into action artificially and from the outside.

Having reached this point, we are now faced with the task of trying to encourage this attitude which we have progressively been defining. We propose to do so by three consecutive steps. First, we shall attempt to disengage from history some of the essential features of what has happily been called the permanent shape of the liturgy. Then, we shall try to develop the deep theological significance of this shape. And, finally, we shall propose some means whereby this ever constant wealth of Christian tradition may be applied to the present situation and its needs. But from everything that has been said so far, we must realize that the important point for us is not so much any particular detail of our own tentative work, but rather the promotion of that true spirit of living and faithful orthodoxy in regard to the liturgy which we have been at such great pains to define.

*　　*　　*

We shall now try to find out from tradition, then, what we called the permanent shape of the liturgy. But we must be careful not to confuse this research with a search for any abstract or purely logical scheme, still less for an abstract formula or concept from which to deduce the whole of Christian worship. Precisely because the liturgy is so living a thing, no development along a straight line, no exact concept of reason can be the clue to it. Of course, from what has already been said on the "Qehal Yahweh" and on the brotherly meal of those who are expecting the consolation of Israel, it has already been made sufficiently clear that the core of the Christian liturgy is to be found in the Eucharistic *synaxis,* in the Mass. But the Mass as found in liturgical tradition is not to be reduced to any single idea, not even to any single trend of thought. It is an action which possesses in itself, certainly, the perfect unity of a great living thing; but this unity is one of elements which are very complex because they are very rich; it should not be allowed to disappear in a confused mixture of these elements; we should rather learn to see these elements in their unity, each and all taking value and depth of meaning from their mutual interaction.

From this point of view, we may welcome, at least as a great incentive to our research, the summary of the question proposed by a Swedish scholar, Yngve Brilioth, in his book *Eucharistic Faith and Practice*.[2] He insists precisely on the fact that, without doing violence to the texts, it is impossible for us to reduce any of the great historical forms of the Eucharistic liturgy to one single element, or to one single set of elements in logical combination. He even goes so far as to say, what seems to us to be simple common sense, that any period in the history of the Church in which a tendency arises to make such a simplification and logical ordering of the Eucharist is shown by this very fact to be a period of decay, preparing only for further corruption.

In the traditional shape of the Christian liturgy, as Brilioth believes, there are to be found at least four irreducible elements. And to these must be added what is not properly another element, but a deeper and almost indefinable reality which permeates all four elements but leaves to each its own individuality. These four elements are: communion, sacrifice, eucharist properly speaking (that is, thanksgiving) and memorial. The further reality, which cannot be separated from these four elements which it is to animate, is the Mystery. We shall soon try to state just what is to be understood by each of these words. But let us first consider their necessary connection with one another. When these four elements are combined in proper proportions and are wide open to the illumination given them by the Mystery—without losing their own individuality—then we have the full Catholic tradition in all its wealth and purity. But when a given age overemphasizes one

[2] London, 1930. Through the next few pages I am following Brilioth's treatment of the subject very closely (see his book from page 18 to page 69).

of these elements so that the others are partly lost sight of, or so that they are subordinated to it, then the fullness of tradition is lost, the spirit of the authentic liturgy is endangered as well as that of authentic Christianity, and one may look for the appearance of all kinds of errors, in doctrine as well as in practice. Let us, then, take each of these five terms and try to understand them.

Communion, as the word is used here, is not to be understood in its modern usage, that is, as the reception of the Sacrament by an individual believer. Rather it is to be understood, as κοινωνία was always used by the Fathers, to mean "communion with" other people in a common partaking of the same gifts. This use of the word combines the two different meanings of the Latin phrase "communio sanctorum," and explains each by the other: that is, "communio sanctorum" (taking *sanctorum* in the masculine) as meaning the communion among the saints, which is brought about through "communio sanctorum" (taking *sanctorum* in the neuter), that is, communion *in* the holy things. Thus, the element of "Communion" means that the Eucharist is a meal, a community meal, in which all the participants are brought together to have a common share in common goods, these common goods being first of all the bread and wine of a real human meal, whatever their deeper significance. And to describe this element, we have the Apostle's sentence: "Because the bread is one, we though many, are one body, all of us who partake of the one bread."[3]

Sacrifice, then, is to be understood as the actual sacrifice which the Church has always intended to offer when it is assembled to celebrate the Eucharist. It is striking to find that Brilioth, a Protestant author, emphasizes the fact that in the most primitive and basic usage of all the ancient liturgies, the terminology of sacrifice is directly applied to what the Church does when she meets for the Eucharist.

The use of these sacrificial terms did not arise, as might be supposed, from an idea of the Cross as being in some way represented in the Mass. Far from it,—historical evidence leads us rather to the supposition that the terminology of sacrifice came to be applied to the Cross by the Church because the Cross was felt to be at the heart of the sacrifice which is offered by the Church in the Eucharistic celebration. We may note, as a fact in support of this interpretation, that in the New Testament, it is practically only in the Epistle to the Hebrews that we find a sacrificial explanation of the Cross, and this

[3] I Cor. 10:17.

explanation is given by reference to the liturgy of the Old Covenant taken as an allegory of the New. We may also note that the earliest Christian ecclesiastical writers habitually use all the notions of sacrifice in direct reference to the Christian liturgy. It seems to be true that the continuity from the "Qehal Yahweh" to the Christian *synaxis* which we ourselves brought out earlier in this book, was so well understood from the very beginnings of Christianity that the whole sacrificial terminology of the Old Testament was applied without any intermediate stage to the liturgy of the New Testament. This fact can be seen most strikingly in the Apostolic Fathers, no less in the writings of St. Clement or St. Ignatius than in the Epistle of Barnabas, famous for its radical idea that the ritual of the Old Testament had never had any other meaning than to be an allegory of the New.

But just here, of course, the question arises: what, then, according to that primitive view, is properly sacrificial in the Christian *synaxis* (the Christian assembly)? We must answer that, from the ways in which the first Christian authors, beginning with St. Paul, express themselves, everything in the Christian *synaxis* is sacrificial. The distinctive feature of the New Testament, as these men understood it in the light of the 31st chapter of Jeremias, is precisely that its sacrifice is now no more confined to any special rite, but is the whole of the Christian life inasmuch as it is a life in the *agape,* the divine Love. This is, of course, to say that the meal which expresses and, as it were, incorporates that *agape,* is itself and in all its details sacrificial in the highest sense. Thus, not only are the eating and drinking in this meal sacrificial, but so, too, is the sanctifying prayer which is said over the food; and when we understand it in this way, this prayer becomes the perfect form of that sacrifice of pure lips which the teaching of the Prophets had already so strikingly outlined. But, since the Christians have partaken in the meal of *agape,* the whole Christian life of each individual is now imbued with that sacrificial virtue. So we must realize that St. Paul is not using a figure of speech when he speaks in sacrificial terms of the offerings made by the Corinthians for the poor of Jerusalem, or when he speaks of the oblation that he himself is making of his own life and his labors for the benefit of souls, as he concludes with: "I rejoice now in the sufferings I bear for your sake; and what is lacking of the sufferings of Christ I fill up in my flesh for his body, which is the Church" (Col. 1:24). One of the most perfect expressions of this synthesizing view of the Eucharist and the Christian life is that given by St. Augustine in the *City of God:* "Tota redempta civitas est unum sacrificium quo seipsam offert Deo Patri"; "The whole city of the redeemed is one sacrifice through which it offers itself to God the Father." And this is the "unceasing oblation" properly speaking which was foreseen by the Prophet Malachias[4] whose words are so often quoted by the Fathers, since they understood this oblation to be realized in the Christian dispensation.

Thirdly, then, the Eucharist is the *thanksgiving* which finds its central expression in the great prayer always said by the president of the *synaxis.* It is a thanksgiving to God for all His gifts, including in one view the whole of creation and redemption but always taking as a starting point the bread and wine, typical of all created things, and the consuming of which is the actual occasion both of the meal itself and of the celebration attached to it. But this element of thanksgiving, the jubilant acknowledgment that everything is a grace, and that the grace of God is marvelous, is also as it were a general atmosphere which pervades the whole Eucharistic service. This thanksgiving finds another expression that, in its own way, is also essential, in the "sacrifice of praise" which is the purpose of almost all the psalmody that from the first inhered in the celebration of the Eucharist. In conjunction with the Christian sacrifice, this element of thanksgiving is, in a still deeper sense, a new attitude of man, as he stands before God in the Church, an attitude which springs from the exultant faith which receives and drinks in the divine *agape* as it flows from its source in the Holy Spirit. The keynote of the thanksgiving here is, therefore, the *Alleluja,*—what we might call a contemplative prayer which penetrates the whole of life, but penetrates it with the contemplation, not of a sublime and lofty abstraction, but of the divine condescension of the living God.

For the fourth element in the Eucharist is what we have called the *Memorial.* This is, of course, first of all the Memorial of the Cross as the great saving act through which the divine *agape* overflowed into this our world, a memorial, effected through the *anamnesis* made over the bread and the chalice, of the broken Body and of the Blood that was shed. But the Eucharist is also the Memorial of everything that led up to the Cross throughout all history, not only from the Birth of Christ, but from the sacrifice of Abel, the offering of Abraham and the sacrifice of Melchisedech, through the whole sacred

[4] I, 11.

history of the People of God. And it is also the Memorial of everything that has resulted from the lifegiving Passion of Christ, that is, His resurrection, His glorification (which includes the outpouring of the Spirit, the building up of the Church and, finally, the consummation of everything in the divine *agape*). In this way, we can understand the apparent strangeness of some ancient liturgies which make the *anamnesis* not only of Christ's sitting at the right hand of the Father, but also of His coming again to judge the living and the dead, just as St. Paul speaks of us as already risen again and seated in heaven with Our Lord.[5]

But this is not enough. The whole Eucharistic celebration is also a memorial. And here we must keep in mind a most important point,[6] which we have touched on already and to which we shall again return, namely, that there is an inseparable connection between the two parts of the Christian *synaxis,* that is, between the Bible readings and the meal. For the readings lead up to the meal. They recall to memory God's action of entering into human history, redeeming it and fulfilling it from within; while the meal itself commemorates the climax of this process in the Cross of Christ. And the meal needs the readings to point out to us the way to see it aright, not as a separate event of today, but understandable only in reference to a decisive action accomplished once and for all in the past. Such a consideration will bring us in due time to see that the whole Mass is a single liturgy of the Word, Who began by speaking to man; Who continued speaking to him more and more intimately; Who finally spoke to him most directly as the Word-made-flesh; and Who now speaks from the very heart of man himself to God the Father through the Spirit.

Having thus paved the way by what has been said so far, we are now prepared to understand the decisive importance of the Mystery as synthesizing and elevating all the preceding aspects. If each of the constitutive elements of the Mass which we have examined is better described than defined, how much more difficult is it to give any definition of what the Mystery is! Following still Brilioth's lines of thought, but using now our own words, we may say that the Mystery embodies the Church's three-fold conviction when she celebrates the Eucharist. She believes that Christ is present in an ineffable way in the celebration; she believes that what she does today, He Himself is

---

[5] Eph. 2:6.
[6] Made especially well by Brilioth, op. cit.

doing and through her; she believes that this action of today, which is His as it is hers, is, finally, the one saving action of God in Christ throughout history. That is to say, that the Mass is the Cross, but the Cross always seen in the whole perspective of which we spoke when we were discussing the Memorial.

We shall need to examine other definitions of the Mystery; but we may well keep the above as a particularly plain definition carrying with it no serious difficulties, a definition which, from the outset, gives a whole view of the idea, even if it does not go as deeply into it as we shall wish to go later on. The Mystery, then, is not a fifth element of the Mass to be added to the four others; it is rather a new depth in each of them, through which all are brought together into a single living unity, entirely supernatural. In his exposition, Brilioth warns us of the grave danger of trying to make of the Mystery, not that ineffable quality common to the four elements of the Christian Eucharist, but a distinct element added to them, and an element which, because of its intrinsic importance, may easily tend to absorb all the others. We may, of course, notice here some influence on the author of Protestant prejudice. But we may well ask ourselves also whether there is not a good deal of truth in his warning. In some forms of modern Catholicism, certainly, the overemphasis on the Real Presence (which, in a way, corresponds to the first aspect of the Mystery as described above) has eclipsed people's appreciation of the Eucharist as communion, sacrifice, thanksgiving and memorial, and has also degraded rather than exalted the Christian apprehension of the Mystery itself. As Brilioth sees it, the true balance would emphasize equally the fact that the holy things, the partaking of which makes us one, are nothing else but Christ Himself; that the substance of all Christian sacrifice is the one sacrifice of the Cross; that the Christian thanksgiving is Christ's own, our thanksgiving making us all acknowledge His God and Father as our God and our Father; and, finally, that everything that is "announced" to us in the liturgy is announced, not only as part of the past, but as the one great reality of the present also, as well as of all the future.

Clearly, this balanced view of the celebration of the Eucharist can enable us to grasp fully the idea of the real presence of Christ in His Church. We are not, in a word, to focus our contemplation on the sacramental bread and wine alone, but on two other realities as well. If there is a necessity, first of all, to consider the presence of Christ as victim in the eucharistic elements, we must not for that reason neglect His presence as high priest in the whole hierarchy. Christ will be present in the elements only because He is present in the man who is to preside over the *synaxis* and to say the thanksgiving in Christ's own name, this presence being brought about through the apostolic succession. And, thirdly, Christ is to be present in the whole body of the Church, for the Church enjoys the Eucharistic presence only to be made one, *in* Christ and *with* Christ, through the Eucharistic celebration, and especially through the consummation in the holy meal. When these three realities of the divine presence are not seen in their right interrelation, they are seen falsely and misconceived—just as, according to Brilioth, the whole celebration is not understood unless it is understood in all its constituent parts and their unity.

Now, as we said above, in the final stages of such a disintegration, there tends to be a retrogression from true religion to magic. Brilioth himself explains this by his insistence on the idea that the Mystery, though from many points of view the most characteristically Christian quality in the Eucharist, making Christ all in all as it does, yet from another point of view may be regarded as that quality of the Eucharist which links it up with natural religion, and, more particularly, within the Greco-Roman world contemporary with primitive Christianity, those religions which were precisely called "mystery religions."

This idea of a similarity between the Eucharist and the pagan "mystery-religions" certainly poses a question of great importance, which is difficult to treat but which we cannot evade, if we are trying to understand fully the Christian tradition of liturgy. In discussions of this similarity, the so-called "mystery religions" are seen to bear an analogy to the Christian religion in so far as they involved a δρώμενον, that is to say, a ritual enactment of the death and return to life of a god, this enactment being carried out in such a way as to make the "mystes," or initiates, partakers of the life of that god, becoming in some way identified with him. Even if we thus put the case in terms as plain as possible, and make no attempt to force analogies into close similarities, we still cannot but be struck by the resemblance of the δρώμενον with the Christian mystery. It is true also that this resemblance belongs only to the Mystery proper. The religions of the Roman empire had no interest in a Memorial of anything; they had no interest in history as such, but rather in a myth, that is, in a symbolic picture of events always recurring in a cycle—in this case, the cycle of the seasons—; for the mystery gods were above all gods of nature, with its perpetual recurrence of death followed by a return to life. Nor did these religions have any element of thanksgiving,—this idea, as we shall see later, being purely Jewish in its origins and Christian in its developments. These religions must undoubtedly have had a certain contemplative aspect, but this was simply the contemplation of the unchanging cosmos, not at all of an intervention of God in the world once for all, to make an irreversible change in it.

Certainly in these religions there was some kind of sacrifice, but merely in the ancient sense in which all natural and pagan religion was sacrificial; they knew nothing of that transformation of the idea of Sacrifice which the prophets had prepared, and which is shown so conspicuously in the primitive Church. These religions may, perhaps, have achieved some limited Communion between fellow initiates, but here it is well to remember the distinction made by Bergson between the closed communions of the old religions, and the communion inaugurated by the Christian *agape* which is radically new because open to everyone.

It is the Mystery, then, which fully seems to afford the only line of continuity between these mystery religions and Christianity. To see how far one can go with this idea, we shall now consider one of the most important books of the last generation on the origin and development of the Christian Eucharist, Lietzmann's *Messe und Herrenmahl*. We might say that Brilioth wrote his book simply to answer Lietzmann's. But he attempted to do so by holding in the main to Lietzmann's idea of the Mystery, and trying to complete it by showing how, in authentic Christianity, the Mystery is inseparable from the four fundamental elements which he himself emphasized so strongly.

Are we, then, to follow Brilioth in his acceptance of this major point in the thesis of Lietzmann and many other modern scholars, that is, that the Christian Mystery as such and the pagan mysteries must be considered to be at least analogous to each other? In order to answer this very important question, we must begin by considering Lietzmann's ideas more fully.

Lietzmann holds that we find in the Catholic Eucharist not so much a tension between irreducible elements, as in Brilioth's conception of it, but rather an inner opposition between two conflicting factors. Only one of these factors is Christian, coming from Our Lord through the primitive Christian community. The other factor is foreign both to Christianity and to Judaism; it was an import from Greco-Romanism, borrowed from the mystery religions by St. Paul. If we may put it in such a way, there are not one but two, Christian eucharists and these two are irreconcilable. One of them comes straight down to us from the the community meals of the disciples before the Passion, meals in which they had Our Lord in their midst. This form is eucharistic properly speaking, because it is full to overflowing with exultant faith in Christ's presence, but it has no connection with the Lord's last supper on Maundy Thursday nor with the Cross. And we must add that, even if it is full of the conviction that the Lord is invisibly present with His own, yet there is nothing to focus that presence on the elements of the meal, which are not necessarily even bread and wine. The Lord is present, yes, but not as the spiritual food of His disciples. He is present as an invisible guest who is still taking part in the community meal, and so bringing to it an inexhaustible source of gladness. It is in just this way that the word of the Apocalypse is fulfilled: "Behold, I stand at the door and knock; if any man listens to my voice and opens the door to me, I will come in to him and will sup with him and he with me."[7]

In Lietzmann's theory, the other eucharist comes completely from St. Paul. This eucharist beholds a radical transformation of the primitive community meal which the Apostle attempted to introduce for the sake of converts from paganism, especially those at Corinth. It imposes a completely new meaning on that meal, one that goes hand in hand with an interpretation of our Lord's death which is also purely Pauline,—both interpretations coming from the same source, the pagan mysteries. The emphasis is no longer on the resurrection but on the death of our Lord: "For as often as you shall eat this bread and drink this cup, you proclaim the death of the Lord, until he comes." St. Paul, in other words, has interpreted the Cross as a life-giving mystery concentrated on the ritual reenactment of a God's death, and so he implies that the Cross is to be understood as the $\delta\rho\dot{\omega}\mu\epsilon\nu o\nu$ in the pagan mysteries. From this fact also would be derived the idea of the localization of the presence of the Lord in the bread and wine, since these are seen as the supernatural means of union between men and the saving death of Christ, through an identification of the believer with his God —this idea itself being as congenial to the pagan mysteries as it was foreign to the thought of Judaism.

[7] Apoc. 3, 20.

Later on we shall see how every line of this theory poses more problems than it pretends to solve, attributing to the pagan mysteries a great many purely Jewish or Christian ideas simply in order to enable these mysteries to be able to give us an explanation of Christianity itself. But now let us only ask what should be our opinion of this distinction between a primitive Jewish and a completely remodelled Pauline Eucharist?

Oscar Cullman, one of the greatest contemporary scholars of the New Testament,[8] stresses very strongly a point which Lietzmann entirely neglects. And it is precisely from the neglect of this particular point that the possibility can arise of making such a sharp distinction and opposition between the two supposed types of eucharist. Lietzmann takes as alternative possibilities for the origin of the eucharist, the meal that the disciples took with Christ on the eve of His death, and the meals they took with Christ before His Passion. But what he does not see is that the Lord's supper on Maundy Thursday, the meals taken with Him in the past and the meals of the primitive Church were all in continuity, *through the meals after the resurrection,* in which He had appeared to His disciples as the Conqueror of death. No ground of opposition, therefore, can be found between them. And we must also add the fact that Lietzmann completely misunderstands the relationship between the Cross and the eucharistic joy as it was understood in primitive Christianity, because he is interpreting this relationship from the viewpoint of modern sentimental forms of piety wholly foreign to the ancient Church. Certainly, there never was any opposition in the minds of primitive Christians between the eucharistic joy which springs from the resurrection, and a fancied sad and gloomy piety concentrating on the Cross. From the very first, Christians saw the Cross as illuminated by the resurrection; the resurrection was not to them the reversal, but, so to speak, the natural product of the Cross. Thus, the whole construction of Lietzmann falls to pieces.

But to say this is not enough. Why did Lietzmann conceive the idea that there must have been two origins for the Christian Eucharist? Because to him, as to all the scholars of the "liberal" school at the end of the last century, it was unthinkable that Jesus on the first Maundy Thursday evening should have created a sacramental reli-

[8] See his essay: La signification de la Sainte Cène dans le Christianisme primitif, Strasbourg, 1936.

gion and told His disciples, "Do this in remembrance of Me." According to these scholars, the idea that Christ gave the command to continue the rite He had made up was absolutely out of the question, not only for Him but for the whole primitive Church, since it did not believe that it would continue for many years, let alone centuries, but rather that it would soon be met by the Parousia.

Whatever our opinions may be on this last point, however, we have still to make it clear that Lietzmann's whole argument derives from a radical misconstruction of the sentence: "Do this in remembrance of Me." The reasoning we have just set forth puts the emphasis on the "do this" as if Jesus was seen as really creating a new rite and imposing it on a community still entirely in the future. But, following Gregory Dix, in his well known study, *The Shape of the Liturgy,* we must frankly say that such a notion is completely mistaken. Recent scholarship shows with perfect clarity that, far from creating a new rite, Jesus was only performing once again a thoroughly traditional rite of Judaism, while infusing into it a new meaning and a new reality. This fact, as we shall see, makes wholly useless the supposition of any fundamental influence of paganism on the Christian Mystery, and forces us to conceive that Mystery and the liturgy of which it is the living heart along purely Jewish lines.

CHAPTER SEVEN

Liturgy and Mystery—Dom Casel's Theory
Explained and Discussed

From what has already been said, it must be clear that we cannot evade the problem of the historical relation between the Christian mystery and the mysteries of natural, or pagan religions. This problem is not only a matter of Apologetics. If it were, what has been said in the preceding chapter would be enough, perhaps, to show that the Christian Mystery cannot be traced back to the pagan mysteries, or to any influence that they could have had on the development of primitive Christianity. In the conclusion of the preceding chapter, we saw how genuinely Christian is the Mystery, how directly it springs from the most distinctive and original elements in the Christian message.

Nevertheless, there are some analogies, which we have already described briefly, between the Christian Mystery and the pagan mysteries, analogies so striking that they certainly cannot be neglected. If they cannot explain the origin, properly speaking, of the Christian Mystery, these analogies surely may, if carefully worked out, cast great light on the grafting of grace upon human nature, and the grafting of God's work in Christ on human endeavor. Here lies the great importance of the references Dom Casel constantly makes, in speaking of the Christian Mystery, to the pagan mysteries which were contemporary with it. The significance of these references is that they demonstrate how wonderfully human is the Christian Mystery, as well as how wonderfully divine. Thinkers like Lietzmann, as well as Bousset and Reitzenstein and their French follower, the ex-abbé

Loisy, made use of their knowledge of the pagan mysteries to belittle and try to reduce to nothingness the importance of primitive Christianity. But Dom Casel did not retreat before their arguments, nor answer them merely by negative counter-criticism. His great and courageous feat was, rather, to accept all the materials brought forward by the 'comparative' school, and to propound a new interpretation of these materials, much deeper and richer than that of his opponents.

Let us then, first sum up once more the main themes of Casel's theory. The "mysteries," it is said, using this word as a common name for the Eastern religions which were being introduced into the Roman Empire at about the same time as Christianity,—the mysteries of the Syrian Adonis, the Asiatic Attis, the Egyptian Isis and Osiris, and the Persian Mithra, to quote only the most important—were all formed on the same pattern. Each of them was a "dromenon," that is, a kind of religious drama, a liturgical representation of the death and resurrection of a god. By being associated, in the actual performance of this representation, with the saving act of the deity, the initiates or "mystes" were to be saved. They were to be thought of as born again to a new and divine life, the life of the god himself triumphing over death.

Now, says Dom Casel, these mysteries were a kind of providential preparation in human nature for what God was going to do for it in Christ. The pagan mysteries did not, properly speaking, influence the beginnings of Christianity, but they provided a frame for Christianity to fill with its divine grace, the pattern which would make that grace appealing to human nature, as showing how grace brought with it precisely what human nature most desires and had been attempting to obtain for itself.

But what, then, is the Christian Mystery? If we mean to ask what it is in its deepest reality, it is nothing less than the *transitus,* the passage from death to life, through the Cross to the resurrection, which was once for all accomplished in Christ. The Mystery, therefore, is an action; and it is an action which took place in the past and can never be repeated, because it is perfect. The Mystery is the Cross of Jesus, the Cross seen primarily as an accomplishment, fulfilling His own human history and the sacred history of God's People and, finally, the whole history of mankind which had been disrupted by the Fall but which, by the Cross, has been reconstituted and brought to an unutterably glorious conclusion by God Himself. The Mystery is, then, the Cross seen also in the fullness of its wonderful fecundity, that is, as including the resurrection of Christ, His ascension into glory, and, through the Christ Who has now Himself become *Pneuma,* life-giving Spirit, the radiance of all the wonderful gifts which He has given to man.

This action is as it were the inner essence of the Mystery. But the Mystery is permanently embodied in the liturgy,—more especially in the Mass, but also in all the sacraments and even in the sacramentals, in the Divine Office, in the feasts of the liturgical year, and in the whole Christian life, since this life is nothing less than the expansion of what is given in the sacramental order. In all this, of course, the Mystery is hidden. Nothing is present of the historical circumstances by which the divine action was set in its place in time and space. But the substance of the action is present, in a mysterious way, entirely real to faith; and it is through this substance that the Christ-*Pneuma* encounters the lives of all men and diffuses in them His own life.

On this point, Dom Odo Casel and his greatest disciple Dom Victor Warnach also, insist that it is not only the divine virtue of the Mystery which is present now—that is, its power (as Professor Söhngen would put it) of continually creating and infusing grace in our hearts. The grace of Christ cannot be separated from His Person; His life *in* us is not a different thing from His life lived *among* us and *for* us. Therefore, Dom Casel and Dom Warnach think that, however puzzling the theory may sound, we must firmly maintain that in and through the liturgy, the all-saving act of Christ, giving life through His death, is truly and really present in its fullness as in its unity.

In this connection, Dom Casel elaborates on the patristic use of the word *eikon,* the image, a term borrowed from Platonism and used in a sense much fuller and more realistic than that to which we may be accustomed. An *eikon* is not an external image, foreign to its model, made from without and therefore without life in itself. An *eikon* is the living image of the model through which the model is present, through which it imposes itself on the material which is to receive it.

We do not need to emphasize the richness and beauty of this whole synthesis of Christianity. By underlining its providential resemblance to the most striking outlines of the natural spirituality of mankind, as these began to show themselves just when the Gospel began to be preached, it helps us to understand more easily how Christianity is the divine answer to all human needs.

This synthesis also brings Christ and His own life, the life that He won for His whole mystical body by the Cross, into contact with the daily life of each one of us. And in so doing, it shows how the whole sacramental order is nothing else than the realization of that Christ-mysticism which is at the heart of St. Paul's teaching.

And, finally, this synthesis gives us a significant view of the liturgical life, a view entirely derived from the sentences of the Fathers, whom Dom Casel is never tired of quoting: *"Quod Redemptoris nostri conspicuum fuit in sacramenta transivit,"* "That which was visible in our Redeemer has now passed into the sacraments," says St. Leo. *"In suo mysterio pro nobis iterum patitur,"* "In His Mystery He suffers again for us," says St. Gregory. The Council of Trent also says that in the Eucharist *"mortis ejus victoria et triumphus repraesentatur,"* "The victory and triumph of His death is represented"; and finally the words of Pius XII himself in *Mediator Dei,* which Dom Casel, sometime before his death, acknowledged as the exact statement of the thought he wished to proclaim: *"Id agit quod jam in cruce fecit,"* "(Our Lord) does that (in the Mass) which He did on the Cross."[1]

We must add also that a most powerfully convincing testimony is given to this sublime theological synthesis by the whole life of prayer and contemplation of the great monk of Laach. Nothing could more perfectly express the inherent strength of that personal witness than the words in which his brethren announced his sudden death, which took place in the Abbey of Herstelle just as he had sung the "Lumen Christi" in the Easter vigil:

"Lumen Christi clara voce confessus, paschale celebraturus praeconium, dilectus nobis pater in Christo, sacri mysterii cultor et mystagogus, Odo Casel, monachus lacensis, holocausto perfecto, nocte sacra cum Domino transiens intravit in visionem beatam paschalibus mysteriis quae initiatis tradidit ipse consummatus: Deo gratias!"

"Just as he had saluted with a loud voice the Light of Christ and was preparing to celebrate the Easter Praise, our well-beloved Father in Christ, the devoted servant of the sacred mystery and initiator into its richness, Odo Casel, monk of Laach, made perfect his holocaust and, passing over with His Lord during the holy night, entered into

---

[1] See especially *Das Christiche Kultmysterium,* and *Glaube, Gnosis und Mysterium* by Casel himself.

the vision of the Blessed, being made perfect by means of the Paschal mysteries which he himself had handed on to the initiates: Thanks be to God!"

But this is not to say that we are merely to receive this doctrine from Dom Casel's hands, without wishing to go into it more deeply than he did, or to criticize the expression he himself gave to it. Nothing could be more absurd in itself, or further from what Dom Casel himself would have desired. Therefore we shall follow the example already given by his dearest disciple Dom Victor Warnach, and set about answering the objections that have been raised against the Mystery Theology as we have just formulated it.[2] And we shall set about this task not by means of sterile discussions of isolated details, but by going into the whole problem afresh, using the new lights which recent advances in the history of religion, biblical and patristic research, as well as theological considerations, have cast on it since its first formulation by Dom Casel.

If there is one particular element in Dom Casel's theory which needs modification, it is the general view of the mystery religions which he had accepted. He himself felt this need and, with remarkable modesty, said that he was quite willing to abandon this view if it was proved necessary. But let us note the fact that his weakness on this point resulted, not from any lack of depth or breadth in his own thought, but rather from his magnanimity of mind, which made him accept too readily possible objections to his own position. So, from the first he accepted and never discarded a theory about the pagan mysteries which had been worked out by the "comparative" school. The theory was used by the men of this school against Christianity until Dom Casel was able to demonstrate convincingly that all the materials out of which the theory had been constructed were, actually, more apt to exalt Christianity than to disparage it. But we must admit that the original theory is no longer tenable. No serious scholar today, whether opposed to or indifferent to Christian belief, would accept it as did Dom Casel. What, then, is a true picture of the relation of the pagan 'mysteries' to the Christian Mystery? We shall try to state it as briefly as possible, elaborating only on the points where some of Dom Casel's expressions need to be re-stated.

The first step is to see clearly what the pagan mysteries really were and what they were not. It is now quite evident that Bousset

[2] See his book *Agape*, Dusseldorf, 1951.

and Reitzenstein in particular described these mysteries in terms not at all proper to them, unaccountably attributing to them purely Christian notions. It was not surprising, therefore, that, in the pagan mysteries so described, one could discover the whole content of Christianity, as it were pre-fabricated in some way. The reality is rather different from this far too simple picture.

All the pagan mystery religions which we have mentioned, like the Eleusinian mysteries of Greece whose terminology was later adapted to the others, had begun among agrarian peoples as simply the primitive worship of the gods concerned with vegetation. Core-Persephone, Adonis, Attis, and Osiris were originally thought of as the living power shown in the trees and the grass, and, especially in the various kinds of grain which these peoples cultivated; the power which seemed to die each autumn and come to life once more each spring. The word 'worship' is perhaps too solemn a word to be used in connection with the rites here. In their primitive form, these mysteries were simply an imitative ritual of the death of vegetable life followed by its rebirth, a ritual making use of sexual symbols, the purpose of which was to assist, by a kind of imitative magic, and stimulate the energies latent in vegetative life.

The second phase of the development of these rites came about, in each case, as the result of a foreign invasion. To the invaders, the original rites began to seem mysterious, for they were not the common inheritance of their own people, but rather the old-fashioned worship of the few survivors in the country they had taken over. And the fact that these survivors would treasure these rites as one of the few possessions they had been able to keep for themselves, would naturally make the newcomers the more anxious to be initiated. Under the pressure, then, of a conservative archaism and an ill-informed curiosity, the rites began to acquire a new significance. Nobody, to tell the truth, knew precisely what had been their old meaning or what was to be the new one. But now the old gods receded into a legendary and idealized past; men did not seek any longer to constrain them by magical practices to give aid on a purely material plane; they rather asked them to give a vaguer blessing, but one of a nobler kind. For they were, precisely, gods of the earth and of the under-earth concerned with the place where the dead are to lie. Perhaps, then, they might give to these dead, not so much immortality (which was regarded as a natural property of the human soul) as a happy immortality, to be enjoyed in the company of these gods who ruled in the realm below.

At a still later stage in the development of the mysteries, initiation was open, not only to the recently arrived citizens of the country, but to people from everywhere who flocked to the primitive shrine. And so the shrine became a cause of the triumphant growth of the city around it, since its myth had given to the origins of the city a legendary and superhuman dignity. Then, as civilization progressed, all kinds of deeper and wider interpretations of the original myth and rite sprang up and were proposed to the dazzled barbarians who came to the sacred spot, as happened with the Eleusinian mysteries. But we may notice here a most important point. Throughout this entire process of development, the primitive form of the rite was stubbornly maintained while the interpretation of that rite underwent all kinds of amplifications and transformations. The priests, that is, the few survivors of the original primitive population, like the "Kerykes" and the "Eumolpides" of Eleusis, were not concerned with these developments although they profited by them. Their job was the performing of the rites themselves. All the fuss about these was the work of literary men, poets or philosophers. And we must notice one more detail, perhaps the most important of all and yet the most easily forgotten: the "mystery" was always the *rite,* the rite as jealously preserved by the few specialists who had kept its secrecy inviolate. The interpretations of the rite were free. The "Mystagogus" did not bother about them, but he was very much concerned lest he be deprived of his age-old privilege in the performance of the rites. Plato in his *Phaedo* could suggest to his public that all kinds of sublime meanings, hints of future blessedness, were to be found in the Eleusinian mysteries. The respectable "Kerykes" or "Eumolpides" were politely indifferent to his words, except perhaps to appreciate the gratuitous advertisement. But when Alcibiades, after a drinking bout, imitated the rites with some joyous friends, this was seen to be a sacrilegious violation of the rites, a profanation of the mysteries; and, in spite of his great usefulness to the state, Alcibiades had to be banished.

In the case of the other mysteries, those of Eastern origin, the final stage of evolution was rather different. It was not so much that the whole world flocked to the shrines of these mysteries, as that they came out of their shrines to make contact with the whole world. But in spite of this difference, the underlying religious process was exactly the same as in the case of the Eleusinian mysteries. In the East, exoticism played the part that archaism played at Eleusis. But in both cases, whatever interpretations of the rites were developed by neophytes and more or less discreetly encouraged by a sagacious clergy, the "mystery" as such was not the myth, the divine history which was the oldest explanation of the rite and the first transformation of its original purpose into a higher one; nor was the "mystery" the theologico-philosophical digressions which at a later date elevated the myth itself into a higher and purer realm of thought: from first to last, the "mystery" as such was the rite and nothing else.

Before we make a closer examination of the rite and the myth, and of the theologico-philosophical explanation attached to both, let us first compare this genesis of the pagan mysteries with that of the Christian Mystery.

Everybody admits that the first use of the word "Mystery" in the Church, as far as we can go back, is St. Paul's. And everybody also admits that it is his use of the word which has been the chief factor in bringing about the subsequent development of the term in Christianity and especially among the Fathers. Now, is there any ground for a true analogy between the Mystery of St. Paul, and the pagan mysteries? We can frankly say that the overwhelming evidence of all contemporary research answers "No." The pagan mystery was first of all a rite, and it was always to the rite itself that the word "mystery," and the idea conveyed by it, were properly applied. All kinds of interpretations were given to the rite, as time went on, but the mystery was always the rite itself and nothing else. Yet nothing could be, in every detail, less like the Pauline Mystery.

The Mystery of which St. Paul speaks is not a rite formerly known to everyone but now become secret; the Mystery of St. Paul is a plan of God for the salvation of the world, which had been hidden in the depths of the divine wisdom, inaccessible to man until it was to be proclaimed to the whole world in the Gospel. And we can also say that this plan, in itself, is not connected, at first sight at least, with any kind of rite. The plan touches the actual history of mankind and not, directly, any ritual religion, least of all that field of natural energies which the primitive religions wished to stimulate.

The fundamental text concerning the Mystery of St. Paul is to be found at the opening of the second chapter in the First Epistle to the

Corinthians. Here St. Paul says: ". . . But we speak the wisdom of God, mysterious (ἐν μυστηρίῳ) hidden, which God foreordained before the world unto our glory, a wisdom which none of the rulers of this world has known, for had they known it, they would never have crucified the Lord of glory. But, as it is written, 'Eye has not seen nor ear heard, nor has it entered into the heart of man, what things God has prepared for those who love him.' But to us God has revealed them through his Spirit. For the Spirit searches all things, even the deep things of God. For who among men knows the things of a man save the spirit of the man which is in him? Even so, the things of God no one knows but the Spirit of God. Now we have not received the spirit of the world, but the Spirit that is from God, that we may know the things that have been given us by God . . ." (I Cor. 2, 7 ff). Here we see clearly what are the proper connections of the Pauline μυστήριον they are together wisdom and revelation, σοφία καὶ ἀποκάλυψις, which are two keynotes of a very Jewish tradition.

Wisdom, in the beginning, was the practical art of leading and governing men, the art which was acquired in the ante-rooms of the king's palace, handed on by the elder functionaries to their young colleagues as a wealth of considered experience. This wisdom was common to the great kingdoms of Egypt and of Assyria. Together with the institution of kingship itself, this wisdom was brought from these kingdoms into Israel. But here it slowly underwent a radical change. At first the Israelite scribe or wise man began to be distinguished from his foreign colleagues by the fact that the fear of Yahweh was to be his first obligation. But soon Jewish wise men began to realize that true wisdom must be a gift from God. Thus Solomon, the sage par excellence, began his reign by asking God for wisdom, as the gift he needed most of all. Then the idea of wisdom was carried along in the general trend of prophetic piety, and men began to think that God alone was wise, properly speaking. The exile and destruction of the Israelite kingship deprived the idea of wisdom of its primitive earthly object; but the whole content of experience and meditation of that primitive wisdom, together with its more recently acquired religious considerations, was then ordered, no longer to the human government of earthly matters, but to God's own deeply mysterious governance of all kingdoms. One result of this may be seen in the Book of Job, in which the inscrutable wisdom of God is shown in contrast to all the rational and experimental wisdom of man.

At this point, the idea of wisdom was ready for a radical change. Man came to despair of arriving at true wisdom by his own efforts, even if these efforts were sustained by God. He could only hope for a free revelation of wisdom through an act of condescension by God. Here we pass from σοφία to ἀποκάλυψις, from wisdom to revelation.

In the book of Daniel, we can find a most striking passage which contains the entire vocabulary of the passage of St. Paul's which we have already quoted. In the second chapter, when he is about to interpret the dream of the king of Babylon, Daniel says: "Blessed be the name of the Lord from eternity and forevermore; for wisdom and fortitude are his. And he changeth times and ages: taketh away kingdoms and establisheth them, giveth wisdom to the wise, and knowledge to them that have understanding. He revealeth deep and hidden things, and knoweth what is in darkness: and light is with him" (2:20). And, further on, (2:29): "Thou, O King, didst begin to think in thy bed, what should come to pass hereafter: and he that revealeth mysteries (the Greek Septuagint has ὁ ἀνακαλύπτων or Theodotion: ἀποκαλύπτων μυστήριον) showed thee what shall come to pass."

Let us repeat what we said above, that we find in this passage from the Book of Daniel the whole vocabulary which St. Paul uses in speaking of the Mystery, with the most characteristic connecting of "mysterion" both with σοφία and with ἀποκάλυψις. But the similarity is not merely a matter of vocabulary. The whole frame of thought of the two passages is the same. In both cases, the problem is that of the conduct of history. And the whole context in both cases presupposes an opposition between the way in which men, or created things in general, pretend to lead and make history, and the disconcerting and all-powerful way in which God does so, bringing their plans to nothing and accomplishing His Own unchanging plan. The Mystery is the clue to this secret way of God's, planned in His own "wisdom," and it is through His "revelation" to man that something of His secret way can be known. For, as St. Paul says in another passage, the wisdom of God looks like foolishness to the wise men of this world, but "the foolishness of God is wiser than men" (I Cor. 1, 18).

To St. Paul, however, the great Mystery now, in which all the partial mysteries are disclosed, in which the conflict of the two wisdoms reaches its climax, is the Cross of Jesus. The "foolishness wiser than men" is precisely as he states it, "the preaching of the Cross" (I Cor. 1, 18).

Let us now notice that, from its first appearance on, the Mystery will always refer, in St. Paul's epistles to these same things.

In the Epistle to the Colossians, St. Paul speaks of the acknowledgment of the Mystery of God the Father, that is of Christ, in Whom are hidden all the treasures of wisdom and knowledge (Col. 2, 2-3). In the same way, in the Epistle to the Ephesians (3, 9-11), he says that to him the grace has been given "to enlighten all men as to what is the dispensation (οἰκονομία) of the Mystery which has been hidden from eternity in God, who created all things; in order that through the Church there be made known to the Principalities and Powers in the heavens the manifold wisdom of God, according to the eternal purpose which he accomplished in Christ Jesus our Lord."

But we notice in both these epistles a great deepening of the content of this Mystery. Always remaining centered on the Cross, it appears here not only as including the victory gained by the Cross through the resurrection, but as also being the key, in a most remarkable way, to the whole history of redeemed mankind and to the understanding of the Scriptures.

The Epistle to the Colossians sums up the whole question by the idea of *reconciliation* (ἀποκαταλλάξαι). That is to say, the Mystery finally is that in Christ Himself through the Cross, all men, both Jews and Gentiles, are reconciled among themselves as both are reconciled with God. Then St. Paul himself defines what he calls "the mystery which has been hidden for ages and generations, but now is clearly shown to his saints" (Coloss. 1, 26) as being that the Father "through Him should reconcile to Himself all things . . . making peace through the blood of His cross" (Coloss. 1, 20).

The Epistle to the Ephesians explains the Mystery rather by the idea of *recapitulation,* of the taking up again and summing up of the whole history of humanity, marred by Adam in its first beginnings, but resumed and brought to perfection in Christ. Here St. Paul describes what he calls "the mystery of God's will" as being "to be dispensed in the fullness of the times: to re-establish (re-capitulate, take up again and gather into one) all things in Christ" (Eph. 1, 9-10). Let us notice here a point already brought out in Daniel: the Mystery of the divine wisdom is properly concerned with "the fullness of the times." This fullness, as we see now, is to be attained through the fullness of Christ Himself. And so we see also the connection between the Mystery, as St. Paul sees it, and the Church, considered as the body of Christ through which, as the Epistle to the Ephesians says, Christ Himself attains "the fullness of him who is completely filling up all things (τὸ πλήρωμα τοῦ πάντα ἐν πᾶσιν πληρουμένου) (Eph. 1, 23). So St. Paul can say so strikingly in the Epistle to the Colossians that the Mystery is finally nothing else than "Christ in you, your hope in glory" (Coloss. 1, 27).

Here we can gather together all the elements of St. Paul's inspired thought on the Mystery. It is the Cross, but the Cross seen as the climax of human history, inasmuch as God's wisdom devised it as the solution of the problems of human history. The Mystery is the Cross also inasmuch as through it, in His Son's blood, God reconciles in the body of Jesus all men, who are brought together to make one body, the Church. Thus the history of fallen mankind which had led only to death, is taken up by God and brought to a happy conclusion, that is, to eternal life in Christ, through His death.

It is now time to consider once more the pagan mysteries and to see whether, in any of the explanations of them, made up by their own devotees, we can discover anything resembling the Christian Mystery. But the mystery of the pagans was not a divine fact nor any ideas about such a fact; it was merely a rite, and even the explanations that were given of that rite are seen to have very little resemblance to the Christian Mystery when we look at them closely.

The most important point in St. Paul's idea of the Mystery, the very essence of the Mystery as such, is that the life and the victory have been won by means of death itself. It is precisely because Christ has undergone death that He is the Savior of mankind.

But in none of the pagan mysteries is there the least perception of such a truth. The death of the god in the mysteries was not part of the saving process, but merely a disaster which the god had not been able to avoid. If he was, at the end, not to conquer death properly speaking, but rather to be born again (only, let us not forget, to die again, and again to come to life), this was in no way due to any value inherent in his death; it was, rather, in spite of that death. The gods of the mystery religions were, as has been very well said, not so much savior gods as gods who themselves were saved. And the same thing is formally stated in one of the very few ritual formulae of the mysteries which have come down to us: "Take courage, mystes; since the god has been saved, there will be for you also salvation from your troubles."

What, then, should we think of the alleged identification of the mystes with the god? It is very doubtful whether it ever really implied anything more than a special protection of and association with the god. Never, in any case, can we find in connection with the mysteries the least approach to anything like the idea of the Church as the body of Christ.

But the greatest difference of all, the one which includes all the others, is that the Christian Mystery is a realization in history of a creative and redemptive plan of God, through which, once for all and definitely, everything is changed in man himself and in the whole "kosmos," and history itself is thus brought to an end. There is nothing in the least like this in the pagan mysteries. They had no implications of anything creative, of anything accomplished once and for all, of any definitive change of creation for the better. They merely intended to associate man with the cyclical law of the visible world, with the unvarying succession of death and birth, new death and new birth. In the beginning, the pagan mysteries were supposed to accomplish this association in order that man himself could have some power over that natural process, to intensify it and so to profit by it. Later, in the more religious phase of the mysteries, man attempted rather to receive vitality for himself from the natural process. But nothing of a supernatural order, in the Christian sense,—the supernatural order of which St. Paul's description of the Christian Mystery is the best embodiment—was ever, even from afar and dimly, outlined or revealed in any way by the pagan mysteries; they had no thought, no eye or ear, for the saving and all powerful intervention of God in human history, which is the whole of the Christian Mystery.

Having come to such a conclusion, we might well wonder what we can retain of Dom Casel's theory of the mysteries. But we shall see in the next chapter that, far from being annihilated by these radical alterations that have been made by modern research in some of the scientific data on which it was based, Dom Casel's theory will finally emerge more clearly, more securely established than before, when it has been given the new formulation which these alterations obviously make necessary.

CHAPTER EIGHT

The Pauline Mystery and Its Proclamation: From the Synagogal Service to the Missa Catechumenorum

IN WHAT WAY, then, can it still be fruitful to compare the Christian Mystery with the pagan mysteries, even though recent research has thus radically changed the modern theories concerning both? In answer to this question, it is now time to remember what we said earlier in this book concerning the importance for our purpose both of modern psychology and of the new developments in the history of religion.

As to the importance of modern psychology in this connection, even the most severe critics of Freud and his doctrine, when they are fully candid and honest, admit that he was right in his two fundamental discoveries, even though he erred in his way of expressing and explaining them. It is certainly true that a constant preoccupation with life and death underlies all human psychology—life being seen primarily as the communication of oneself and the achievement of oneself by means of and through that communication; death being seen as the necessary loss of one's own life without which one cannot save that life, to use once more the Gospel's phrase. The sexual instinct, then, together with its strange ability to transform itself into a death instinct, if not actually the source of the constant human preoccupation with life and death as Freud wished it to be, is, surely, nothing else than the most elementary and instinctive form taken by the fundamental pulse of our being. And it is precisely this fundamental and living unity underlying all the diversities and changes of human psychology which accounts for the striking continuity between the most unexpected dreams of modern men and the myths of primitive humanity, and between these and the ever recurrent themes we find in the poetry of many peoples,—love and death seen as related to one another and as reflected in the rhythms of nature.

And, in the latest developments in the history of religion, religion is no longer considered to be merely one compartment of human nature, however lofty a one, but rather as the total, whole reaction of human nature awakening to life, to the universe in which it finds itself. It is, therefore, quite natural that the deepest expression of the love instinct and the death instinct, precisely in their radical and mysterious conjunction, should furnish a permanent form for religion itself. We find this very form as a most prominent factor in the pagan mystery religions of the Greco-Roman world, religions, as they were, of a human nature fully developed along its own lines. Precisely in the disconcerting crudity of their sexual symbolism, and in the amazing wildness of their murder-rituals, they expressed strikingly the obscure intuition that in religion itself human life would find the absolute realization of its craving for a fullness of life to be found in a fullness of communion, and of its impulse to seek the fullness of life through a way of death.

It is well for us to recall here that throughout the whole religious story of the Old Testament, the attempt was not made to suppress the sexual symbolism inherent in all primitive religions, but rather to refine and transform it. Thus, perhaps, the loftiest revelation of the prophets is found in Osee's use of the image of human marriage to depict the "rahamim," the merciful love of God for His people, in an outline of the Agape of the New Testament. And St. Paul himself acknowledged this revelation when he says of human marriage as seen in a Christian light, "This is a great mystery—I mean in reference to Christ and to the Church."[1]

In the same way, we see that the greatest revelation in the Old Testament of the ways of God to man is that found in Isaias LIII, in his portrait of the Servant of the Lord as one who is suffering, crushed, murdered, but who in His death heals the wound of human sin and so gives new life to the world. And this image of the suffering Servant is the one used first of all by Our Lord Himself and by His apostles to make clear the Mystery of His saving Passion.

On these grounds, we can certainly begin to see an indisputable

[1] Eph. V, 32.

connection between what the grace of God has given us in Christ in a purely supernatural way, and what the mind and heart of man, groping in the darkness, dimly projected in those waking dreams which were instinctively acted out in the older rites of the mystery religions and illustrated by the myths which later tried to explain these rites. And this connection is only one of the most obvious and superficial manifestations of the deep relationship which God has established between divine grace in Christ and human nature in all of us, the relationship which makes the Christian Mystery meet us, come into intimate contact with us, whenever there is question of life and death.

But these considerations do not in the least imperil the transcendance of the Christian Mystery. For since it is, as we have already seen from St. Paul's epistles, the perfect disclosure, through the self-revelation of God's own Word, of the divine wisdom unattainable to man, this Mystery is also the great creative act of God's alone, the act which baffles all man's suppositions and expectations.

It is true, therefore, that in order to grasp the divine Mystery in its integrity we need to see how perfectly it answers, not simply one particular need of man's, but his whole basic need. But we need even more to accept that Mystery, first of all, in its own way. That is to say, we need to understand just how the Mystery is, above all, the supreme grace of God. To express this fact in the way in which the Mystery itself has been revealed, the way of all God's revelation, we shall say that the Mystery has to be contemplated first of all under the aspect of its being God's Word *par excellence,* as it is exactly designated by St. Paul. For the *mysterion* is defined by him as an *apokalypsis* of divine *sophia,*—that is, a *mystery* which is the supreme *revelation* of divine *wisdom.*

Our great purpose, therefore, will now be to develop the full meaning of the Pauline Mystery as the very heart of a fully developed theology of the Word of God. And in carrying out this study, we shall see how the permanent truth of the theological as well as of the historical intuitions of Dom Casel is brought out more clearly and established more firmly by the recent additions to and reordering of much of the Biblical and historical material which he himself had used in making his synthesis.

The Mystery, then, as seen by St. Paul, is a divine design. More exactly, it is the key to God's whole design for mankind, a key which could not be obtained by man except through God's own revelation, because it is the exact point at which the unattainable and unsearchable Wisdom of God confounds man's own wisdom.

We can very well say, then, that the Mystery first of all lies in the abysses of God's essence. It is with the vision of this great idea that St. Paul exclaims in a famous text from the Epistle to the Ephesians: ". . . the mystery which has been hidden from eternity in God, who created all things."[2] In the same way, the Epistle to the Colossians speaks of ". . . the mystery of God the Father of Jesus Christ, in whom are hidden all the treasures of wisdom and knowledge."[3]

But clearly we must not think of the Mystery as if it were only one among many of the secret designs of the divine wisdom lying hidden deep in the recesses of divinity to which no man could attain. First of all, the way in which St. Paul speaks of *the* Mystery forbids this. In the Apocalyptic literature of the Jews, all kinds of mysteries are spoken of as being hidden in God and only known through His own revelation. The Synoptic Gospels also still speak of the "mysteries" of the kingdom of heaven. But the plural disappears with St. Paul, as if, to him, all particular mysteries were summed up and transcended in the one single all-embracing Mystery. Indeed, there is no doubt that for him the Mystery includes the whole plan of God for man, and not only for man, but through him for all creatures, that is, all spiritual beings and the material world as well. Only in this sense can the meaning be understood of the sentence in the Epistle to the Ephesians which comes just after the text on the Mystery which we have just quoted: ". . . in order that through the Church there might be made known to the Principalities and Powers in the heavens the manifold wisdom of God, according to the eternal purpose which he accomplished in Christ Jesus our Lord."[4]

This inclusiveness of the Mystery is also to be seen in that succession of ideas so familiar to us in the Epistles to the Colossians and to the Ephesians, that the Mystery, finally, is one with Christ Himself, and that Christ is the "fullness," the plenitude, *to pleroma*.[5] But these texts take us a step further. This idea of the *pleroma*, the "fullness," as applied to Christ in connection with His revelation of Himself in the Mystery, must be understood in a double sense. Christ is

---

[2] Eph. 3, 10.
[3] Coloss. II, 3.
[4] Eph. 3, 10.
[5] Cf. Ephes. I, 10, 22-23, III, 19, IV, 13, and Coloss. I, 19, II, 9, etc.

the fullness, and in Himself He reveals the fullness of what God intended to make of His creation. This "fullness," therefore, is that of God's work, as achieving ultimately the perfection of God's one and whole design. But it is also the "fullness" of God Himself. And this is certainly the most important point for us to consider.

What does this mean? First of all, that God's work for man and all creation is not something merely external to Him, but something in which He is, if we may say so, personally concerned as much as any workman can be personally concerned with what he does. But this is not all. Not only is God concerned with His work, so to say, but this work, especially in its final achievement, cannot be separated from Himself. What He does is not only a mysterious revelation of His ideas, but of Himself. He is, in some mysterious way (and precisely here is the Mystery, properly speaking) putting Himself into His work. Christ both is and reveals the Mystery in its fullness, because in Him we find both God and man, not as two beings, two separated realities, but as ·one. Thus, man himself cannot be known in his fullness except in the revelation of the fullness of God: both revelations, both fullnesses are one.

Now we can see the need for the great emphasis which Dom Casel gave to the idea of the "image," the *eikon,* as a true participation in the very reality of that of which it is the *eikon.* It is not only because of the Platonic mentality of some of the Fathers that this idea of the *eikon* became so important in ancient Christian thinking. It was important to St. Paul himself, for example when he says: "Therefore, even as we have borne the likeness (*eikon*) of the earthy, let us bear also the likeness of the heavenly."[6] Or when he says that Christ is "the image of God" and that we "are being transformed into his very image from glory to glory, as through the Spirit of the Lord."[7]

But here we must also keep in mind that other great statement of Odo Casel's,—that in some higher sense from which all other senses are derived, the Mystery is God Himself, God as He is in the innermost depths of His being and as He is revealed to us in Christ.

But how are we to understand this statement? In what way is God Himself so perfectly revealed in the Mystery that the Mystery is Himself? For St. Paul, certainly, God is so perfectly revealed in Christ and His Cross that our knowledge of God is quite different after this

[6] I Cor. XV, 49 (*Eikon* is used by St. Paul; *eidos* by the Fathers).
[7] 2 Cor. IV, 4 and III, 18.

revelation than before. And the great difference lies in this, that now we know His love, His *agape,* that love which St. Paul contrasts so strikingly with human love (in I Cor. XIII) and which he says (Rom. V) is poured into our hearts by the Spirit. And it is the Cross which is the great revelation of the divine *agape,* because it is in the Cross that we can clearly see that God's love does not wait for us to merit it, but is a purely generous and creative love, that it does not need to find some good in us to love, but rather makes us good by loving us as only God can love. "For," as St. Paul says, "scarcely in behalf of a just man does one die; yet perhaps one might bring himself to die for a good man. But God commends his charity towards us, because when as yet we were sinners, Christ died for us."[8]

This certainly is the great revelation of the New Testament. And it is properly a revelation of God in His deepest nature, transcending not only all creatures but all ideas which creatures could fashion concerning their Creator. This revelation has rightly been contrasted with the celestial *eros* of Platonism, an idea which embodied the highest religious thoughts ever connected with the pagan mysteries. In Platonism, the celestial *eros* is distinguished from and opposed to the terrestrial *eros* because it does not want anything material or sensual. But the celestial *eros* does desire, just as the terrestrial one does, with the difference that it desires only celestial realities. The gods, therefore, who already possess their fullness and have nothing to want, cannot love in this sense. They can move us when they are loved by us, in the sense that they have moved us to become worthy to love them. But they do not move us by loving us; and to say that the gods should love sinners would have had no meaning at all in Plato's thought. But that God loves sinners is eminently true of the divine *agape* as it is shown to us in the Cross, because the divine *agape* is not desire or want in any sense, but rather gift, the pure and absolute gift of the creative God.

This revelation had, of course, been prepared for by the whole of the Old Testament, first of all by the presentation of God as Creator, but still more by the revelation of *hesed,* that is, of the long-suffering and merciful love of God to Israel in spite of its unworthiness. This is shown most forcibly in the prophet Osee's preaching and in the history of his own dealing with his prostitute wife. But only the Cross of Christ could actually manifest, through the death of a man

[8] Rom. V, 7-9.

Who was God, that superabounding flow of the divine life, and so display in a single act all the recesses of the divine wisdom.

Only when we have reached these supreme revelations of St. Paul can we, as he himself says, "know Christ's love which surpasses knowledge, in order that you may be filled unto all the fullness of God."[9] And here St. John gives us as it were the final clue to St. Paul's teaching of the Mystery when he says that "God is love,"[10] and when he adds: "in this is the love, not that we have loved God, but that He has first loved us, and sent His Son as a propitiation for our sins."[11]

Now, perhaps, we can see and fully understand how it is that the Mystery is only to be grasped through a theology of God's Word, and as the very summit of that theology. For what is a word, if it is not the communication, the personal disclosure of a person to other persons? And what better realization of this definition can there be than the disclosure of God's love to us in Christ? Here, if anywhere, God speaks, and He speaks Himself, reveals Himself in a Word which is the most personal form of communication possible, since it is itself a Person. And here again we see that St. John's theology expresses the idea which underlies the whole movement of St. Paul's thought, when, as St. Paul identifies the Mystery with Christ Himself, St. John identifies Christ with God's Word.

The Mystery, then, is the Word of God in its one and whole fullness, for it is Christ Himself: Christ seen as producing in His coming to us the great event of human history, as being in His person the great intervention of God in that history, as being the recapitulation, that is to say, the new beginning and also the definitive summing-up of that history.

And here we see how this great Word of God is also and inseparably a fact, the greatest and most creative fact of all history, the fact in which the great reality of divine life, that is, divine love, as it were invades our own human life. For the great distinction between God's Word and man's word is that when God says something He also does it: He does it by the very fact that He says it. In Him, saying and doing are one and the same thing. Certainly, no idea is more fundamental than this one throughout all revelation. The coming of Christ to us, then, is to be considered both as the final utterance of what God intended to say and as the final realization of what He intended to do.

[9] Eph. III, 19.
[10] 1 John IV, 16.
[11] 1 John IV, 10.

For both word and deed are the same:—the love of God, which He is in Himself and which He shows to us.

But precisely because Christ's coming to us is the final utterance of what God intended to say and the final realization of what God intended to do, the entire history of mankind and of the world before the event of the saving Cross of Jesus is permeated with the Word of God making ready for its ultimate expression; the whole history of mankind and of the world is powerfully attracted and channelled toward the coming of Christ and His Cross. We cannot, therefore, hear the Word of God in such a way as to understand its meaning unless we read the whole Bible as it leads us by its own deepest impulse to the Gospel. Nor can we see by the eye of faith that the great and newly creative act of God is accomplished in the Cross unless we see this act as bursting forth at the end of that immense effort of God's to intervene in human history, not by suppressing, but rather by accomplishing man's freedom, that effort which makes up the whole dispensation of the Old Testament.

And now that God's Word has been spoken in its fullness, now that God's creation through that Word has been brought to its full accomplishment, what is still to be done during the last ages of human history in which we are living, except to hear the Word and to be replenished by the fullness of its creative power? And this precisely is the meaning of the life of the Church in the dispensation of the New Testament, and the meaning of her liturgy also, of that "public service" which she performs before God through her liturgy for man and for man's world. The liturgy makes us hear God's Word in Christ, and it makes us experience in our own lives the power of that Word of God as it is shown forth in the Cross.

But in order to understand the meaning of the liturgy, we must now try to understand more deeply the statement that Christ Himself is the Word of God, His creative Word, Whose power is nowhere shown so fully as it is shown in the Cross.

We can now understand how, when God sends His Word to us, He is Himself present in Him Whom He sends. For, eternally, in speaking Himself in His Word, He gives Himself, His Word being nothing else than that love which is His divine life and absolute self-giving. Therefore, the Word of God as sent to us not only keeps among us its full creative power, which is the power of God, but also it is God Who, properly speaking, is given to us through It, the fullness of God becoming the fullness of the new creation. But, as we have said already, as Christ has been sent by the Father, so He also sends His apostles so that the Word which He Himself is should reach, not only a few men in a small place for a short time, but all men throughout the whole world to the end of time. And this is to say that, as God was present in Him Whom He sent, so the Word is and will ever be present in those who have been sent in their turn. Let us repeat once more the Jewish saying which must be considered to be the clue both to the mission of Christ and to the apostolate of the Church: "The schaliach, the apostolos of a man is like another himself."

And why does the Word act in this way? Why is it the will of Christ to be present everywhere and for ever? In order that the eternal gift of God in the procession of His Word, the eternal gift of His love, that is of His deepest being, should replenish and fulfil all time by becoming the fullness of all being, newly created in Christ. Therefore, as God's gift of Himself proclaimed by Christ the Word became by means of His Cross the actual reality of that new creation in this world of ours, so the Word of the Cross has to be proclaimed through the Church by those whom Christ has sent, in order to speak through them to all generations, so that God may effectively be all in all.

In the light of these truths, we can now grasp the two aspects of the Church from which flow the two aspects of tradition which, following the thought of Newman, we distinguished above. The first aspect of the Church is the instrumental: by means of the apostolic hierarchy, the Church must extend itself everywhere in order that the Mystery of Christ be proclaimed in its permanent actuality until the end of time. The second aspect might be called the vital aspect, and it is the end of the first: the Church which until the end of human history is still in the making must receive the Word in the Mystery in order that the Word should replenish all mankind and the Church herself be revealed as being "the fullness of Him who is wholly fulfilled in all."[12] And this process implies that the apostles as well as all the members should "fill up in their flesh what is lacking of the sufferings of Christ for His body, which is the Church."[13] But it is always by means of the proclamation, the kerugma (heralding) of the Word that the Mystery of the Cross is to be accomplished, that God's own love is to be shed abroad in men's hearts through the Spirit.

12 Eph. I, 23.
13 Coloss. I, 24.

Now perhaps we can see, at long last, what is the fundamental ministry, the fundamental "service," the fundamental *leitourgia* of the Church: it is the permanent proclamation, the *kerugma* of the Mystery, through the ever living and acting Word which is always present in its apostles as God is present in It. Under her first, or instrumental aspect, the Church continues that proclamation of the Word for the new creation. And under the second aspect, the vital, she is created through her reception of the Word by faith. And, as the effect of this reception, the Mystery is diffused through all mankind, the Mystery which was accomplished in the new Adam of definitive humanity, Who is the Head of the Church, Whose body is to grow "until we all attain to the unity of the faith and of the deep knowledge of the Son of God to perfect manhood, to the mature measure of the fullness of Christ."[14]

The first thing that the Church is to do when it assembles together, therefore, is to hear the full Word of God as given in Christ and as brought to us by the apostolic ministry. That Word, of course, is always and for ever that which is given to us through the whole history of redeemed mankind, from the just and holy Abel to the One who is holy and just par excellence, Christ. Therefore, inasmuch as we are what we are as the result of the one and complete history of mankind of which we are the heirs, so we must hear the Word throughout all the phases of its proclamation to mankind in order that we may be able to understand the final and full Word of God in the Gospel, the Word which desired to be proclaimed in our own time here and now so as to bring to it Its own fullness and so bring us to the fullness of the divine eternity.

Of course the Mystery is not only "word,"—in so far as for men "word" can be opposed to "deed" or to "being." But since the Mystery is a personal love that desires to communicate itself to living persons, it must be accepted by us first of all under this aspect of word; and the other implications of the Mystery can be revealed to us only in dependence on this primary aspect. Herein lies the profound difference between the celebration of the Christian Mystery and the celebration of the pagan mysteries. The mysteries of the Graeco-Roman world may have contained a *hieros logos,* a sacred word, but it played a very minor part. It was a more or less optional addition to a rite whose primary implications were merely those of magic. But in the

14 Eph. IV, 13.

celebration of the Christian Mystery everything depends on God's Word and on our hearing it with faith. No magic can find place in the rites which are performed in the Christian Mystery, for from beginning to end everything is ruled by the most free and most generous disclosure of God's heart to His children in His only Son.

We can now appreciate the importance of that development of the *Qahal* in Israel which, as we have said, put an increasing emphasis, in the synagogal worship, on the reading of the Word, of the full Word of God which was already drawing near to its complete disclosure by the ending of the Old Covenant and the dawning of the New. The eucharistic prayer of Esdras, as we have said already, came as the natural conclusion to that reading of the full Hebrew Bible. For this prayer was one of acknowledging, praising and accepting by faith in its unity and completeness the great design of God which was then ready to be accomplished, and of asking in hope for that final accomplishment. In this prayer we can see how the thanksgiving, the eucharist which arose from the lips of a believer after reading the Old Testament, tended of its very nature toward the final fulfillment of the Old Testament in the Incarnation, in the Mystery of the Cross, in the realization of the great prayer of the Old Dispensation which is summed up by the sentence of Isaias: "Oh that thou wouldst rend the heavens and wouldst come down!"[15]

But in order fully to understand the meaning of what is now the first part of the Mass, we must notice that the second part, the sacrificial and sacramental one properly speaking, is in direct continuity with the first. From all that we have just said, it must be quite clear that "deed" and "being" in the Mystery are not opposed to "word," but are, rather, the ultimate consequence of that Word which is God's. It is because God has spoken in Christ and because Christ now speaks in the Church through the apostolic ministry that the Mystery is always active in and through the Church. Its activity depends on its proclamation, on the apostolic preaching of a Word which is not that of man, but is that of God even when it is proclaimed by men's lips, for on the lips of His Own it remains the Word of Him Who has sent them.

We must not, therefore, include an implication of anything magical in our understanding of what we call the "sacramental words" and their supernatural power to *conficere sacramentum,* as the Fathers

[15] Isaias LXIV, 1.

said. When the sacramental words, in the assembly of God's People, here and now, are pronounced as the conclusion to the whole disclosure of God's Word which culminates in the Gospel, it is like the coming of that same Word in Christ to Israel in the fullness of times, of that Word which had been spoken "at sundry times and in divers manners in times past to the fathers by the prophets."[16] The sacramental words, therefore, are not something other than the living Word of God proclaimed to the faith of the Church by the apostolic ministry of the Church; but they are the one and whole fullness of the Word revealing itself as Deed, as Being,—in Christ "the same yesterday, today and forever," in His Cross which is permanently planted in the earth of our world like the "tree of life . . . for the healing of the nations."[17]

Let us now try to see more clearly how these truths are embodied in the Missa Catechumenorum, the first part of the liturgical assembly of the Church. Scholars in this field are finding more and more striking evidence of the direct way in which the Mass of the Catechumens developed from the worship of the Synagogue. This fact has been particularly emphasized by the comparative study, carried out by Anton Baumstark, of the Jewish and Christian lectionaries.[18] Let us first of all notice a fact which illustrates very clearly what we have said already concerning the innate relationship between the Bible and the Qehal Yahweh, the liturgical assembly of the People of God. For one thing, the books of the Old Testament are disposed in a liturgical order in the Hebrew Bible, for they are arranged in the order in which they are read through the course of the Jewish liturgical year, which is ruled by the succession of the great festivals. But the relationship between the Bible and the liturgical assembly is much more profound than this. For it certainly is responsible, in great part at least, for the ordering of the materials within the Books of the Bible themselves. And this fact may very well account for the structure of the Books of the Bible, a structure which often seemed illogical to nineteenth century critics because they fancied that the books must necessarily be read just as they themselves read them, like any modern book, not realizing that the books had been compiled to fit into a general scheme of integrated lessons for a whole year.

[16] Heb. I, 1.
[17] Apoc. XXII, 2.
[18] A fascinating survey of the whole question is to be found in his book, *Liturgies comparées,* Chevetogne, 1939.

And the same thing seems to be true also of the New Testament, at least of the Synoptic gospels. Critics now think that the Gospel of St. Matthew, for instance, has been very definitely arranged to provide the synagogal worship of Christian communities with a series of readings about Our Lord, a series which would fit in with the already existing system of Jewish readings of Old Testament so as to show how everything in His life and teaching was a fulfillment of "Moses and the prophets." But we need not go into any further detail here; the book of Baumstark may be consulted by anyone who is especially interested in this question.

What we need to emphasize here is the fact that when the people of God met to hear the Bible read, even in Old Testament times, it did not seem to them to be a mere succession of more or less edifying episodes in a story without a plot, a collection of more or less instructive teachings without any unity, any inner deep consistency. Quite the contrary:—all the history of Israel was seen as dominated first of all by the historical fact of the Exodus, the intervention of God to redeem His People from slavery, to bring them from darkness to light, from death to life by means of the death-mystery of the sacrificial lamb and of the passage through the depths of the Red Sea, when the first-born of Egypt were slain by the "passing" Angel, and the pursuers of God's People were drowned in the waters of the sea.

In the light of this first intervention, as the last of the prophets saw it, the new tribulations of the Babylonian exile appeared as the preparation for a new Exodus, for a rebirth of the people of God, a rebirth of its faithful remnant, brought about through the sufferings of the Servant of the Lord, enabling God's People once more to serve Him in the light and life of His visible Presence which would once again be restored to His temple. In this way, through a Jeremias, and an Ezechiel, the idea of new life as created through death took a new hold on the minds of the people, and gained also a purer significance than before. For they had been brought to discover that it was through the suffering and death *of the faithful themselves* that they were to be made acceptable to God and to enjoy true life in the light of His face.

And even then, in the Apocalyptic Books, appeared the dawn of the idea of a last and still more perfect Exodus, in which the People of God should have to "pass" outside the confines of this world of flesh and blood, so as to come, in the light of the resurrection, before Him Who sits between the Cherubim in unapproachable light.[19]

Thus, in the light of the Mystery, Christ appeared to the authors of the New Testament precisely as being the fulfillment of the figure of the Suffering Servant, as in His death and resurrection He accomplished the true and permanent Exodus. Did not Jesus Himself say: "the Son of Man has not come to be served but to serve," "and to give his life as a ransom for many?"[20] And at the Transfiguration, when He was going to Jerusalem to prepare for His passion, had not the disciples heard Him talking with Moses and Elias who "spoke of his *exodus* (this is the Greek word) which He was about to fulfill in Jerusalem?"[21]

Now we can grasp the general idea which accounts for the whole economy of Biblical lessons in the ancient Church. The whole Bible was to be read just as in the Synagogue, but in such a way that the readings from the New Testament fitted into a framework already arranged to point towards those acts of God, central to Hebrew history, by which He created His people through death and suffering. And in this way, the readings both from the Old Testament and the New went to show that the suffering and death which were finally capable of producing the Mystery of the new birth into the resurrection were those of Jesus Christ.

But to say this is still not to give a full view of the richness and the living unity of the Christian synagogal service. In order to grasp something of its qualities, we need to consider what is the most perfect example of this service that we still retain,—the first part of the Good Friday service. In this, the reading of the Passion is prepared for by the readings about the slain Paschal Lamb from the Exodus and the reading from Osee of the prophetic promise of a life to be given through death. And in this same service also we see two complementary characteristics of the ancient Christian synagogal service, which show us how the readings were to be understood by the people.

Between the readings the people are to break forth into songs which are, as it were, jubilant acts of faith in the saving Mystery proclaimed in the readings; as, for example, the Canticle of Habaccuc,

---

[19] of which, in a typically Jewish idiom, St. Paul was to speak later on in one of his Pastoral Epistles (I Tim. VI, 16).
[20] Matt. XX, 28.
[21] Luke IX, 31.

through which we worship the great Theophany in which that God Who wounds and slays shows Himself as the One Who also cures and brings to life: "In wrath, O God, remember mercy," and the Psalm "My God, my God, why hast Thou forsaken me?"—in which we conclude by a complete surrender and a quiet expectation of God's saving mercy.

And, secondly, after a silent prayer in which everyone, according to the use of the ancient Church, is to exercise his "kingly priesthood," the "high priest," that is, the Bishop who is presiding, or his delegate, says the Collect, so giving the final clue to the meaning of the reading which prompted the psalmody and the prayer, and making us ready for the new and more complete disclosure of the Mystery which will be given in the next reading.

In this full and coherent form, represented by the first part of our present Good Friday service, we can see how the Word is to be received in its permanent actuality by the hearts of the faithful which are open to receive the energies which, even in our time, the Mystery still has ready for them. And we can also see how, for this purpose, the faithful, led by the Church, are not to read the Word of God blindly as it were, or merely by some light of their own minds, but are always to read it in the light of the Mystery.

Moreover, now we can understand how much there is to deplore in the present state of the *Missa Catechumenorum*. In the first place, the whole ground-work has been shaken out of place by the almost complete disappearance of the readings from the Old Testament. Then, the suppression of the *lectio continua,* the full and continuous reading of the books of the Bible (which is still kept in the Eastern Liturgies) has by now obscured the complete and unified significance of all the lessons which made the Mystery the key to the whole of sacred history. Again, the fragments of psalmody which still remain in the first part of the Proper of the Mass are too often broken and disconnected to permit us to realize that this psalmody is meant to be a living apprehension by our faith of the Mystery as it is proclaimed in the lessons. And finally, the Collects are too often displaced, and so deprived of their meanings; the connection between them and the readings has disappeared; they no longer come as the conclusion to the personal prayer which has been fostered by the readings and the psalmody, and they have, therefore, lost almost all of their point.

Only in a shortened form, in the Masses of the great feasts and a number of Sundays and some at least of the Lenten Masses, can we catch a glimpse of what the first part of all Christian liturgy should be, in something of its original unity and richness:—the hearing of God's Word by God's People, the heralding to the faithful assembled in Christ of the saving Mystery of Christ. Let us hope that the work of scholars in this field will soon enable the Church to restore here the fullness of Catholic tradition.

CHAPTER NINE

The Eucharistic Celebration: From the Jewish to the Christian

FROM what has been said in the preceding chapter, it is already evident that, of Itself, the Word of God tends to evoke thanksgiving, not only as a normal response to it, but also as the natural product of it. For it is always through man himself—and not only in the incarnate Son of God—that God reveals Himself to man. Therefore, as a recent book has rightly insisted,[1] we cannot separate God's Word from the response to it. This truth, as we have seen, was clearly indicated by the fact that the readings of the synagogal service and, still earlier, all the proclamations of the Word of God to the People of God, have always been connected with the People's prayer and praise. Later on, indeed, we shall have to bring out still more the importance of the fact that, in the use of the Psalms, the answer itself was considered to be the Word of God on men's lips.

But this acknowledgment by man of the truth and goodness of God's Word—an acknowledgment which is a natural response to the proclamation of the Word—is not the only thanksgiving to be found in the synagogal service. We have already seen (in the example of Esdras) how, just at the point when in former celebrations of the Qehal Yahweh the sacrifice would have been offered, there was pronounced instead a solemn thanksgiving by the head of the people. In this thanksgiving, the whole story of the redemption of Israel as proclaimed in the Bible was summed up in praise, the people thus created by God were dedicated anew to Him, and a petition was made

[1] Thornton, L. S., *Revelation and the Modern World*, London, 1950.

115

for a future and final intervention of God by which He would accomplish the work He had begun and Himself bring to perfection the offering of the People.[2]

Now these characteristics of Esdras' prayer endure as conspicuous features of the worship of the synagogues and prepare directly for the worship of Christians. Let us therefore distinguish them with more precision and see how they appear in the Jewish liturgy. First of all, the thanksgiving is pronounced not by anybody, but by the head of the people and their divinely appointed representatives. Secondly, the thanksgiving comes as the culmination of the whole service, after the Word of God has been heard, at the point where, in more ancient times, the sacrifices of the covenant had to be offered; and the thanksgiving makes explicit reference to these sacrifices. And thirdly, as to the content and form of the eucharistic prayer, the thanksgiving itself, we can observe three features: 1) the way in which it embraces in a single view all that God has done in the course of history for His People as being the single act of the one God, and, particularly, the way in which this prayer unites a commemoration of creation with that of the redemptive intervention by which Israel was brought out of Egypt; 2) the very strong expression of the fact that the people, acknowledging by their praise that all that it has and is comes from God, not only must "give thanks" to Him for all His gifts in a more or less solemn fashion, but also, through this very thanksgiving, is to dedicate its whole life and being to its Creator and Redeemer; 3) the very characteristic way in which the prayer ends by asking God Himself to achieve what He has begun, that is, clearly to make that new intervention in history which will be the New Covenant promised by Jeremias and Ezechiel, in which the law of God will be written in the very hearts of His People. Let us now follow, therefore, the development of this type of eucharistic prayer in the Jewish liturgy as it was to be known and carried out by Our Lord Himself.

The morning service of the synagogue, the commemoration of God's action on behalf of His People throughout their history, centered on the *Shema Israel*, that is, a passage from Deuteronomy:

"Hear, O Israel, the Lord our God is one Lord.
Thou shalt love the Lord thy God with thy whole heart, and with thy whole soul, and with thy whole strength.

[2] See Nehemias, IX.

And these words, which I command thee this day, shall be in thy
  heart:

And thou shalt tell them to thy children, and thou shalt meditate
  upon them sitting in thy house, and walking on thy journey,
  sleeping and rising.

And thou shalt bind them as a sign on thy hand, and they shall be
  and shall move between thy eyes.

And thou shalt write them in the entry, and on the doors of thy
  house.

And when the Lord thy God shall have brought thee into the lan l,
  for which He swore to thy fathers, Abraham, Isaac, and Jacob:
  and shall have given thee great and goodly cities, which thou
  didst not build.

Houses full of riches, which thou didst not set up, cisterns which
  thou didst not dig, vineyards and olive yards, which thou didst
  not plant,

And thou shalt have eaten and be full:

Take heed diligently lest thou forget the Lord, Who brought thee
  out of the land of Egypt, out of the house of bondage.

Thou shalt fear the Lord thy God, and shall serve Him only, and
  thou shalt swear by His name. . . ."[3]

The president of the assembly introduced this summary of the
Word of God with this versicle:

"Praise the Lord, worthy of all praise,"
to which the people answered:
"Praised be the Lord, worthy of all praise forever."
Then the president exclaimed:

"Truly right, faithful and unshakeable, just. and trustworthy,
lovable and pleasing, precious and full of delight, reverend and
magnificent, assured and proved, useful and salutary, is that
promise in our favor, always and forever."

Then he proceeded from the thought of the Word which had
been proclaimed to the actual thanksgiving, saying:

"His ministers stand in the high places and reverently proclaim
with a loud voice the order of the living God, the King of the
world, all beloved, all elected, all powerful. All perfectly and rev-

[3] Deuteronomy VI, 4-13.

erently fulfill the commandment of their Creator, and all in holiness opening their mouths dedicated to psalmody and canticles,
praise and exalt, magnify and worship, sanctify and glorify the
name of the Almighty, the great King, tremendous and all-powerful, the Holy! Everyone in his own rank performs the service of the
heavenly kingdom and they excite one another to magnify the
holiness of their Creator in joy and gladness. All of one accord
pronounce the holy words and say reverently: Holy, holy, holy, the
Lord Sabaoth! All the earth is full of His glory. The Ophanim
and the holy Hayoth fly up with a great voice before the Seraphim
and answer in their turn: Blessed be the glory of the Lord in the
place of His dwelling."

In the same way, in the *Shemoneh Esreh,* the eighteen prayers in
which the expectation of Israel is renewed every day, the president says:

"We will hallow Thy Name on earth as it is in heaven, according to what has been written by Thy prophet: And they cry to
one another, saying":

And this time the whole assembly answers:
    "Holy, holy, holy is the Lord Sabaoth,
    All the earth is full of His glory!"
Then the president adds:
    "Facing one another they say":
And the faithful answer:
    "Blessed be the glory of the Lord in the place of His dwelling."

But it is perhaps not in the worship of the synagogue that we find
the most typical and complete thanksgiving or eucharistic prayer of
Judaism, but rather in the liturgy for meals. This fact could, indeed,
have been conjectured from the very text of the Schemah which we
have just quoted, and also from the constant parallel between creation
and redemption which was made in giving thanks, as we have seen
in the great prayer of Esdras. For creation has been spoiled by evil,
and God intervenes in history in order to re-establish His work in its
primitive goodness. And since the life of man has been poisoned by
sin even to death, the work of purifying him from his sin is like a new
creation, a rebirth from death. This is the reason for the insistence,
in every mention of the saving acts of God in behalf of His people, on

the fact that by means of these acts He has brought His People to the land flowing with milk and honey so that they could eat and drink and peacefully enjoy the life that God has given. The coming out of Egypt is like a return to Paradise. But since this is true, we see also that to eat is a sacred action for man because it is like being created anew, since all life comes from God. And, more especially, to eat the bread and to drink the wine coming from the soil of the Holy Land is to be created by God in a new holiness. What distinguishes the true Israelite in his eating from the Canaanites and all idolaters, is that he knows and acknowledges that food and drink are God's gifts; to him they are no longer the products of natural agencies tainted by sin; they are the gifts of the grace of his Redeemer, Who is also the Creator of all things.

We can, therefore, appreciate both the force and the deeply Jewish character of the thought which is expressed in one of St. Paul's Pastoral epistles: "For every creature of God is good, and nothing is to be rejected that is accepted with thanksgiving. For it is sanctified by the word of God and prayer."[4] This means that, through the Word of God and through thanksgiving which is Its reflection in man's heart, everything is restored to its original and holy condition of creaturehood, in its double relation to God and man. This truth implies first that, in acknowledging through a thanksgiving, the truth and the reality of the Word of God, man discovers anew the original meaning of creation, as a link of love between God and man. But this sentence of St. Paul's implies even more: it implies not only a perception of this by man's mind, but a real event that is brought about by thanksgiving. The Word of God, accepted by the People of God and coming back to God from the lips of men giving thanks, actually sanctifies the creatures over which it is pronounced. This thanksgiving is somewhat like Adam's giving of names to all creatures at the beginning. Man, through the Word of God and his answer to that Word which proceeds from the Word itself, is made the priest of creation, and he re-consecrates it to its Creator.

And here we can grasp a most important point in Jewish thought. Our Latin Ordinary of the Mass says, in describing the action of Our Lord in consecrating on Maundy Thursday: *gratias agens benedixit*. This phrase well emphasizes the double aspect: the God-ward action, *gratias agens,* from which follows the world-ward action, *benedixit*.

[4] I Tim. IV, 4-5.

But we must realize that these two Latin words are used to translate only one single word, the Greek *eucharisteo* which itself is a translation of the Hebrew *barak*. To the Hebrew mind, to *bless* anything and to pronounce a *thanksgiving* over it are not two actions but one. It is the *thanksgiving*, that is to say, the acknowledgment of God's Own creative Word made over the things which that self-same Word had created, which fills these things with the heavenly blessing. And from this fact follows the character of consecration which was ascribed to the thanksgiving, to the *eucharist* as pronounced over a meal, and, more especially, to the Word of God as it echoed from man's heart in that prayer.

It is only with all these ideas in mind that we can understand all the implications that the Book of Leviticus had for Jews. All its regulations meant to them the acknowledgment through God's Word that every creature is sacred, and that no creature can nourish the true life of man unless he explicitly recognize in it the gift of God. More especially, and explicitly, the Passover meal—from having the primitive significance common to all agricultural feasts connected with the return of Spring, of a partaking in the energies of nature in their circle of renewal after death—took on for the Hebrew a new meaning, that of the deliverance from Egypt, as marking the new creation and the new and sanctified life which was to follow it for the people.

And here we see that the problem of the relation between the Christian Mystery and the pagan mysteries cannot be fully solved except in reference to a still higher problem and to its solution. This higher problem is that of the relation between the Jewish rites, especially the liturgy of Jewish meals and most especially that of the Passover, to the sacred meals characteristic of all primitive agricultural forms of worship. What began as a half-magical adoration of the powers of nature, as seen in their perpetual alternation of life and death, becomes, in the Jewish rites, through God's Word and man's thanksgiving, the highest act of faith, the recognition by man of God's intervention which has once and for all renewed man and the world, which has condemned idolatry and redeemed man at once from the bondage of idols and the slavery of death. Nor does this mean that the ritual should cease to be as active in this new form as it was supposed to be in the primitive agricultural religions. But its action is no longer that of magical tricks which have been captured by man when the gods were not on guard; its action is that of the very

Word of God now making man once again Its cooperator in the great work of creation.

Let us notice that we have already, in the course of these observations, found in Judaism and its religious meals at least three of the four elements which remain as the integral and constituent parts of the Christian Eucharist: the sacrifice, understood as primarily self-dedication in the acknowledgment of God's absolute power over man and all things; the memorial, and, of course, the thanksgiving. But the element of the communion also, as we defined it in a previous chapter, was no less conspicuously present in these Jewish religious meals.

Let us observe, on this last point, that the Passover meal, although it was certainly a sacrifice of the whole nation (since all the Paschal lambs had to be slain at the same time and the same place), was nevertheless eminently a family meal. Moreover, it was first of all the life of the family in its living unity which this meal was to nourish. And these facts, of course, are connected with the fact that the whole people of Israel was seen as the development of one single family, proceeding from one father, Abraham.

But all during Jewish history, it was always possible for a guest or for a slave, brought into the family to partake of its Passover meal. And the condition for such participation was that he be voluntarily added to the family, and then his participation in the Passover meal became a consecration of this bond of adoption. But a very striking feature of the late development both of Judaism and of its celebration of religious meals (of the Passover or any feast-day or sabbath) seems to have been the tendency to make the religious meal not so much the bond of a natural family, as of a spiritual one. That Jesus should have held the supper of Maundy Thursday with his disciples seems to have been the general practice at that time of other rabbis with their disciples, and, more generally, of all kinds of pious communities, the *habouroth*, as they came to be called. Could not this practice be related to that teaching so characteristic of the prophets that it is not the whole of Israel which is God's true People, but only the faithful "remnant"? And so the communion of the Church, founded on faith in the Messias Who had come, seems to have been prepared for by the communion of those faithful Jews who took their meals together in order to wait together for His coming.

But in any case, with all these considerations before our eyes, it is to the liturgy of these sacred meals, as it was performed either in pious families or in faithful communities where the eschatological expectation was most ardent, that we are now to turn in order to discover how the Christian Eucharist arose from the Jewish.

Before the meal itself began, there were all kinds of hors d'oeuvres to be taken by each participant as he arrived, or with some one or two friends. But even here nothing was eaten without a blessing, given in that eucharistic form so characteristic of all Jewish blessing. This was especially true concerning the cups of wine which already were being passed around, for which the blessing was: "Blessed be Thou, O Lord our God, King of all eternity, Who didst create the fruit of the vine." That 'first cup'[5] of wine which is mentioned only in St. Luke's narrative, embarrassing so greatly exegetes who are ignorant of the Jewish liturgy, was evidently one of these. And the words of Jesus in this passage are an obvious allusion to the blessing just mentioned: "For I say to you that I will not drink of the fruit of the vine until the kingdom of God comes."[6]

Then, after a preliminary washing of hands with scented water, the community meal began; and it was felt so deeply that everything to be done after this point was an action of the whole community, that no new guests could be admitted after the first rite. This consisted in the solemn breaking of bread by the head of the family or the president of the community, accompanied by the blessing: "Blessed be Thou, O Lord our God, King of all eternity, Who didst make the earth produce bread." It is at this point that Our Lord, before He distributed the bread to all the members of the community according to the familiar rite, must have added: "This is my body which is being given for you; do this in remembrance of me."[7]

As we have already indicated, following a very pointed remark of Gregory Dix, those rationalist exegetes who, like Lietzmann, carry on lengthy discussions as to whether it is or is not very likely that Christ by these words should have created a new rite for the future, completely lose the meaning of that sentence. Far from needing or not needing to create a new rite for future use, Our Lord was only performing once again a very ancient rite which, even without Him, His disciples would certainly have gone on performing so long as they lived together. What Our Lord intended by these words was to give

[5] Luke XXII, 17.
[6] Luke XXII, 18.
[7] Luke XXII, 19.

new meaning to this old rite. Now once again an historical fact, a divine intervention of God into man's history was to invade, as it were, a human ritual. Through these words, the true Lamb of God, like the Servant of the Lord in Isaiah's prophecy, gave His life as a ransom for many. And afterwards, therefore, it would not be the fruit of this earth only that the disciples were to eat, but the true bread of heaven given them in the flesh of the Word made flesh.

But the meal went on. Jesus, according to custom, blessed with the ritual blessings every dish brought to the table after the breaking of the bread (somewhat as, in Christian antiquity, the Bishop blessed the oil and the fruits of the earth after he had consecrated the Bread of Life). In the meantime, the cups of wine continued to be passed around, each blessing his own individually as before the beginning of the meal. But, when the meal finally comes to an end, the last cup was to be blessed very solemnly by the father or president, and this blessing was the eucharist, the thanksgiving *par excellence*.

This rite was prepared for by a whole series of rites which still remain as so many constituent parts of the Christian Eucharist itself. First of all, with the coming of darkness the lamp was brought in. It was, and still is in Jewish families, the task of the mother to light the "sabbath lights" or the "festival lights," so we may suppose that Mary once more performed that religious duty. The rite of the *Eucharistia lucernaris,* now kept only in the Easter Vigil service, the solemn blessing of the lamp at the beginning of the sacred vigil, finds in this Jewish custom its origin; and we know that in primitive Christian communities it was a feature of every celebration of the Eucharist on Saturday nights, as it had been of every religious supper in Judaism. At the Last Supper, then, Jesus in His turn once more pronounced the blessing: "Blessed be Thou, O Lord our God, King of all eternity, Who didst create the lamps of fire" (that is, the stars).

Judas could not have gone out before this moment, since St. John noticed at this point that, by contrast with the now lighted room, it was dark outside.[8] After the lamp had been lit and blessed, incense was brought in, and, as we know, in Our Lord's time was actually burned to purify the air for the great action to follow. In Jewish families today, incense is still brought in at this point and, although the custom of burning it has disappeared, the father still says what Jesus Himself certainly said: "Blessed be Thou, O Lord our God,

[8] John XIII, 30.

King of all eternity, Thou Who didst create perfumed spices."

After this burning of incense, a second washing of hands was customary. Ordinarily, it was the task of the youngest member of the community to wash the hands of everyone else, finishing with. the oldest or the most important person present. We can understand, then, how it was St. John, who probably was the youngest, who noted the fact that Jesus Himself unexpectedly took up the basin and towel and washed not only the hands but the feet of the disciples. Our Lord performed, in other words, what was the work of a slave, in order to place Himself, as He said, as the Servant of the Lord amongst His own. And we can also now understand how it was that Peter, whose feet were washed last of all, was the one to protest, and that it was at his protest that Jesus, having carried out the rite, gave His explanation of what He had done.[9]

After this, the supper now being considered as finished according to St. Paul's statement,[10] the last cup was brought to the president. Wine had previously been poured into this cup and mixed with water as prescribed by the Jewish ritual. The president then said: "Let us give thanks," adding in the case of a great and more solemn assembly, "To the Lord our God." The others answered: "Blessed be the name of the Lord, now and forever."· The president continued: "With your agreement (everyone was then to make that bow of acquiescence which is still prescribed at this point in all Christian rites), we shall bless Him Who gave us to partake of His own goods," and the others added: "It is through His goodness that we live."

Then the officiant alone said, or rather sang, the great eucharistic prayer which we shall now quote in full:

> Blessed be Thou, O Lord our God, King of all eternity, Thou Who dost feed the whole world by Thy goodness, Thy grace, Thy mercy and Thy tender compassion. Thou dost give to all flesh its food, for Thy mercy endures for ever. Through Thy great goodness, food has never failed us: may it never fail us, for the love of Thy great name, for Thou dost provide for and sustain everything that has life; to all Thou doest good, and Thou dost provide with food every creature that Thou hast created. Blessed be Thou, O Lord, Who givest this food to all things.
>
> Blessed be Thou, O Lord, because Thou hast given to our fathers as an inheritance a vast, good and desirable land; and because Thou

[9] John XIII, 1-10.
[10] I Cor. 11, 15.

hast brought us, O Lord, out of Egypt, and delivered us from the house of bondage; and also for Thy covenant which Thou hast sealed in our flesh, for Thy Law which Thou hast taught us, for Thy statutes which Thou hast made known to us: for the life, grace and mercy which Thou hast poured out on us, and for the food with which Thou dost feed and sustain us always, every day and at all times and hours. For all this, O Lord our God, we give Thee thanks and we bless Thee. Blessed be Thy Name from the mouth of all the living, now and forever, according to what is written: Thou shalt eat and be filled, and Thou shalt bless the Lord thy God for the good land which He has given thee. Blessed be Thou, O Lord, for this food and for that land.

Have mercy, O Lord our God, on Israel Thy people, on Jerusalem Thy city, on Sion the dwelling of Thy glory, on the Kingdom of the house of David, Thine anointed, and on the great and holy house which has been called by Thy name. O God our Father, feed us, maintain us, sustain us, support us, relieve us, and grant us soon, Lord our God, that we should not need the gifts of men or their alms, but only the gifts of Thy helping hand, which is always full, open, holy and giving freely, so that we might not be ashamed or confounded forever. . . .

Here we notice once more the link between the creation and the Passover, and we see how the redemption of Israel from Egypt was interpreted as a new creation of the people, how the life to be found in the promised land was seen as a restoration of primitive life, in its holiness together with its joy of thanksgiving. And we can understand how it was that Our Lord was to insert just at this point, when the prayer passed from a commemoration of the past to a pleading for a new intervention of the saving God, His announcement of the new and definitive Passover. Then He could conclude with the prayer for the rebuilding of Jerusalem and the restoration of the house of God, to be brought about in the resurrection of His own body, and give the cup to His disciples, saying: "All of you drink of this: for this is My blood of the new covenant, which is being shed for you and for many . . ."[11]

Thus in the final thanksgiving of the preparatory covenant, Our Lord established the beginning of the new and eternal one, through His self-offering which was consummated the next day on the Cross.

[11] Some scholars suppose that the last part of the eucharistic prayer as we now have it was altered after the fall and final ruin of Jerusalem. But certainly the prayer for eschatological fulfillment, in this or another way, was already included in this eucharistic prayer in the time of Our Lord.

And when the disciples met again to break the bread and bless "the cup of blessing,"[12] as St. Paul still calls it, following the technical terminology of the Jewish liturgy, they knew that the risen Lord was again with them, that in His apostles He was now again re-enacting what He had done once for all, that in Him, through them, the almighty and all-creative Word of God was nourishing with the true bread of heaven the new "Qahal," the new family of God, and so making one body of all those who had now eaten the one bread.[13]

Here we see how the Christian Mystery, in its very ritual celebration, proceeds directly from the proclamation, the *kerygma,* of God's Word in its fullness in Christ. Through the thanksgiving of men, now performed in man by the Word of God Itself, in the proclamation of Christ's death, as St. Paul says,[14] the human life, the human world by which man must be nourished, is consecrated and sanctified so that it becomes, in the thanksgiving itself, the human body of the eternal Word. It becomes that body in which God's love is not only revealed but incarnate and poured forth through death to be a well-spring of divine life for men, so that all of them may become one Body in Christ, to the glory of the Father.

From all that we have said, we can already see how clearly the pattern of the Christian Eucharist, not only as a whole but in all its organic details, developed from the pattern of the Jewish eucharist. And we can, therefore, understand also how completely futile it is either to go to parallel rites in contemporary paganism for an explanation of the Eucharist and a sacrificial interpretation of the Cross itself, or to try to understand the meaning of the Eucharist and the Cross apart from the complete sacred history and religious pattern in which the Word of God chose to come to men. For all the antecedents of the sacrificial meal and of its inner significance, as well as of the *synaxis* of readings and prayers which lead up to it, are Jewish. And most characteristically Jewish is the element that connects the ritual meal with the proclamation of the Word,—I mean the Eucharist strictly speaking.

The Mystery, in these distinctive aspects of it, so well emphasized by Brilioth, is only the consequence of the fact that the Word of God has come to man to perform, of Itself, in man his thanksgiving.

Why—to use again the terms of the first definition of the Mystery

---

[12] Matt. XXVI, 28.
[13] I Cor. X, 16.
[14] I Cor. XI, 26.

that we gave earlier, following the lines of Brilioth's study—why is Christ present with His Church in the Eucharist? Why is her action also His? Why, finally, is the action which she performs nothing other than the saving act which He Himself once and for all performed on the Cross? These three questions have the same answer: in Christ, the Word of God Himself now makes His own the thanksgiving which man makes over the world in which and by which he is to live; the world itself, therefore, is now filled by the Word incarnate; the Word conforms to Itself all the men who receive it. Finally, as a result of all this, the Church, in all that she does and in all that she is, is nothing less than "the fullness of Him Who is completely filling up all things."[15]

To conclude this central section of our study, let us now review all the aspects of the Mystery which have been successively disclosed to us, so that we may see their unity and their continuity. This, at the same time, will be the best method of getting at the deep and most permanent truth contained in Dom Casel's affirmations, while disengaging them from opinions of secondary importance, the soundness of which can no longer be taken for granted.

The Mystery is, first of all, God Himself in His deepest nature which is so unfathomable by man's reason, but which He has revealed to us: that is to say, the Mystery is basically the divine *agape*, the creative and redemptive love which is pure gift, which does not seek any good in what it loves, but makes it good because so loved.

Thence, the Mystery is the one and great design of God for the world, for man, of adopting man as His child so as to reconcile all things to Himself in the Body of His Son. Here, properly speaking, is the Mystery of divine wisdom which seems madness to man's wisdom, because it transcends all created wisdom, even that of the Principalities and Powers, to whom the Mystery of God was only to be revealed through the Church.

Consequently, the Mystery is also the realization throughout history of that great design which comes to its fulfillment in Christ and His Cross. And therefore the Mystery is Christ, or the Cross, inasmuch as in the Cross we find the key to the Scriptures, the goal of all human history as "recapitulated" through God's intervention.

As the Mystery has thus been realized in Christ, just because

[15] Eph. I, 23.

Christ is Himself the all-creative Word of God through which the Mystery was proclaimed, so it has now to be proclaimed to us by the Church which He has sent, and realized in us by means of that proclamation. And this is the Mystery seen as "Christ in you, the hope of glory", that is, the Mystery in the sacramental order in connection with the apostolic *kerugma,* as both are united through the Mass.

Finally, therefore, the Mystery, in the Son of God made man and in His whole Body, is at once God's Word and man's thanksgiving or eucharist to God, the thanksgiving which itself arises from the Word, as it were echoing God in that living *eikon* of Him which is creation.

This means that the Mystery brings creation once more to its principle, through the coming of its Creator to it. And this is the reason why the Mystery found expression in the ritual pattern in which man had projected his relation to creation, with his craving for union and obsession with death which are, as it were, the vital knots by which man's being is tied to the being of creation as it now stands. But the Mystery breaks through that unchangeable relationship of finite beings enclosed in an unbreakable cycle, by the coming of the living God, and from the narrow circle of his bondage, it sets man free in *agape,* the fullness of divine life.

CHAPTER TEN

The Anaphora—A Note on "Epiclesis" and "Verba Consecrationis"

Our task in this present chapter is to study the way in which Christian tradition has embodied in its Eucharistic Prayer the Mystery which it received in the pattern of the Jewish eucharist. Obviously, the new leaven could not be put into the old paste without transforming it. But just as the New Testament cannot be understood, even in what is most radically new in it, unless we begin with the Old Testament and take advantage of the whole unbroken Jewish tradition, so it is also with the new Eucharist. For it gave full meaning to the lines of the old eucharist already laid out by divine providence, as they now met in their great focus, the Cross; but the new Eucharist did not change these lines.

The first thing that strikes us when we look at our own Mass with these lines in mind, is that the Preface is not in the least a kind of introductory prayer, a remote preparation for the essential act, but an integral part of that act, and one which gives us the right clue to the meaning of it, because the Preface is the direct expression of thanksgiving.

In this connection, we must notice how we have been misled by a word which is always being mistranslated, as well as by relatively recent changes in our rites which throw us off the right path. First, we think of the word "Preface," as it is used here in the Mass, as if it meant what we generally understand by that word. It seems to us, therefore, that the Preface merely introduces the Sanctus, itself a preparatory song, and that after the Sanctus what we should call serious business really begins,—the great Action which is to be accomplished in that "secrecy of mysteries" which has been talked about so much since the XVIIth century.

But "Preface," in this sense, is not at all the meaning of the Latin word *"praefatio."* It has by now been clearly demonstrated that the word was borrowed from the pontifical language of the old Romans. And in this technical terminology, the word means a prayer said in a loud voice (*praefari*) by the priest to accompany a sacrifice and to consecrate it by explaining its meaning and its intention.

It is, therefore, simply nonsense to suppose that our "Preface" is intended merely to introduce the Sanctus—which is, of course, a canticle indeed most suitably placed—or to suppose that the Sanctus is intended only to create the reverent atmosphere in which the sacred action will afterwards be carried out.

For, in fact, we possess extant examples of the Christian Eucharist Prayer coming from antiquity in which the Sanctus is absent. Such is the case in the Eucharistic Prayer of the famous *Traditio Apostolica* of Hippolytus of Rome. Moreover, in that text we have not only the essential line of thought of our present preface, but also some of its most characteristic phrases. And in this text it is quite evident that what we now call the Preface is of one piece with the whole Canon, or *Anaphora,* and that it gives to the whole Canon its leading idea, in the thanksgiving which the Preface formally expresses. This idea runs through the whole *anamnesis* (that is, the commemoration of creation and redemption), it blossoms out in the sacrifice offered to God and in the prayer for the communion of the worshippers in the good things that God has given them, and it is formally expressed once again in the concluding words of the Great Doxology, after the prayer has been offered for the consummation of the Mystery. Some scholars have been so struck by the perfect continuity of the *anaphora* in the liturgy of Hippolytus that they have even supposed that the introduction of the Sanctus might have been a later feature of the Christian Eucharist, and that originally it did not include the Sanctus, any more than did the Jewish eucharist, as we have seen it, which was carried out at meals.

But it seems unlikely that the Christian Church would have borrowed new details from the synagogal service centuries after it had separated from Judaism and had become deeply immersed in Greek culture. We may rather suppose that both types of Christian Eucharist existed from the first:—one closely and exclusively following the Jewish form of eucharist, and perhaps carried out, as the Jewish meal had been, apart from the *synaxis* of readings and prayers (it is certain that the Christian Eucharist was sometimes performed in this way in ancient times); the other type combining synagogal worship and the community meal, not only by simply having the meal come after the readings, but also by blending the eucharistic prayers of the synagogal worship with the form of eucharistic prayer proper for meals. We might even ask whether such a combination could not already have been tried out by Jewish pious communities, previous to its use in the Church.

In any case, what is certain is that the eucharistic aspect of the Mass is fundamental and is not a special feature which appears only in a merely introductory prayer. Rather, we can see here how the very sacrifice of the Mass is to be understood through the eucharist (thanksgiving), and (along the lines so well observed by Brilioth) how the sacrificial interpretation of the Cross itself can be said to have been the direct result of the Jewish meal.

For in the eucharist, in the thanksgiving which is the response awakened in man by the Word of God, the divine love which this Word expresses is reflected in man's heart. And just as the Word produces in creation the reality which it expresses, so the thanksgiving educes through the sacrifice the reality which it has formulated. Creation is an objective projection of the Word of God; and so the sacrifice which embodies man's thanksgiving in answer to that Word is an objective projection of It also. But this can only come about because in Christ God's Word and man's thanksgiving are made one by the incarnation. And now we can see how the Cross is the focus, properly speaking, of the whole Mystery. For in the Cross the new creation is fulfilled by the Word made flesh; that means first that God freely pours His own genuine love into man's heart by the Spirit.

But that means also that the new man, the Adam Who is Christ, fulfills in the Cross the thanksgiving of man to God. Finally, we can now see how in Christ the fullness of God giving Himself to man meets with the fullness of man offering himself to God.

When we have come to realize that Thanksgiving, in the Christian Eucharist, is not one element of four, but rather one which embraces the other three and also the Mystery itself (in the strictest sense given to the word by Brilioth), then the next point to clarify precisely is how the thanksgiving includes above all the *anamnesis,* the commemoration.

We have already seen how the form of Jewish eucharistic prayer proceeds from creation to redemption in history and how this was the point at which the proclamation of the Mystery in Christ was to be inserted, just before the prayer for the consummation of the work already begun. The older types of Christian Eucharistic Prayer all keep this outline, often disclosing—with a new wealth of detail, the vision of sacred history which is now to find its goal and center of unity in the Mystery of Christ and His Cross. The catholicity of this acknowledgment in thanksgiving of the divine Word and of Its redemptive work in the new creation is notable especially in texts like the *anaphora* of the eighth book of the *Apostolic Constitutions,* or that of St. Basil. By "catholicity" we mean here that unity and wholeness of the view of human history which sees it as achieving its end in the saving Cross.

Let us follow this development through the very beautiful text which is ascribed to St. Basil (but is probably much older, at least in the parts we shall quote).

We find, first of all, the preliminary dialogue with the faithful which, as we have already seen, introduced the Jewish eucharist. But it is most remarkable that here, as in all Christian liturgies, before the invitation to "give thanks," the celebrant says this new exhortation: "Sursum corda," to which the people answer: "Habemus ad Dominum." This insertion seems to mean, as was implied from the first in the Church, that, as the eucharist was no more that of an Israel "of the flesh" but of the spiritual one, this thanksgiving was no more to be limited to the visible gifts, but to be concerned with the Bread of heaven of which these visible gifts had become the *symbola,* that is, not only the image in the modern meaning of that word, but also the vehicle.

Then, after the dialogue, the celebrant begins what we should now call the Preface in our restricted application of the word:

> Master and Lord, God the Father almighty, Thou Who art to be adored, truly it is just, right and worthy of Thy excellent holiness to praise Thee, to sing to Thee, to bless Thee, to worship Thee, to give thanks to Thee, to glorify Thee, O God truly One; and also to offer to Thee with a contrite heart and an humble spirit that reasonable sacrifice, for Thou hast given us the knowledge of Thy truth. Who, then, should know how to exalt Thy power, to proclaim all Thy praise, or to make known, O Lord, in all times all Thy wonders?

In this first paragraph, we see how faithfully the idea is retained that the Mystery is first of all the knowledge of a divine secret, revealed by grace, and concerned with the ineffable God and His inscrutable wisdom in the conduct of the world: the truth of what He is and of what He does. Then we pass to the next aspect: the Mystery as being God Himself, as He is revealed to us in Christ. But before we go on to this aspect, let us notice two more points: first, how faithfully this prayer retains expressions so typical of Judaism about God's "ineffability"; and, secondly, how clearly this initial mention of the "reasonable sacrifice" as St. Paul calls it, implies that what is to be offered together with Christ's sacrifice is the sacrifice of ourselves. The prayer then continues:

> . . . Master of all things, Lord of heaven and earth and of all creation, visible and invisible, Thou Who dost sit on the throne of glory and search the abysses, eternal, invisible, incomprehensible, inexpressible, immutable; Father of our Lord Jesus Christ, our great God and Savior, our hope, the image of Thy goodness, the express seal of Thyself, O Father; living Word, true God, eternal Wisdom, Life, Sanctification, Strength, true Light, by Whom the Holy Spirit has been revealed: Spirit of Truth, Gift of our Adoption, pledge of our inheritance, earnest of eternal goods, life-giving virtue, source of sanctification, by Whose strengthening all intelligent and spiritual creatures serve Thee and direct to Thee the eternal hymn of glory!

Then comes the Sanctus, after the mention of the angels, as in the synagogal liturgy. Let us notice the meaning of this idea, as it was understood by the ancient Church. The spiritual world of the faithful angels is that world in which the Word has been from the first faithfully echoed in perfect thanksgiving. This has not been true of our own world, since Adam followed the perverse suggestion of the already fallen Prince of this world, Lucifer. Our world was marred then, in so far as it did not follow the example of the angelic world. The redemption is seen, therefore, as God's intervening to bring back the human world to the state of the angelic one. Thus the Fathers interpret the incarnation as the act of the Shepherd who leaves the ninety-nine faithful sheep in order to seek and find the lost one and bring it back to the fold. The fold is the whole of God's spiritual creation; the ninety-nine sheep are the angelic worlds; the one lost is this world of ours. This Eucharist, this thanksgiving which men perform through the redemptive incarnation, is seen, therefore, as bringing men back to

the ranks of the angelic choirs, and enabling men, finally to take part
in the angels' own unceasing eucharist.

> For all creatures serve Thee, and Thou it is Whom Angels, Arch-
> angels, Thrones, Dominations, Principalities, Powers, Virtues and the
> Cherubim with their innumerable eyes, all celebrate: Thou it is Who
> art surrounded by the Seraphim with six wings, two covering their
> faces, two covering their feet, and two flying, while they cry to one
> another with constant voice and ceaseless praise; singing the hymn of
> triumph they acclaim Thee, they implore Thee and they say:

> > Holy, holy, holy, the Lord Sabaoth,
> > heaven and earth are full of Thy glory,
> > Hosannah in the highest.
> > Blessed be he who comes in the name of the Lord,
> > Hosannah in the highest.

Here we may pause for a while to consider a change that had
taken place in the Sanctus from its usage in the synagogal liturgy, a
change the more striking since it can be observed in all Christian
liturgies. In the synagogal liturgy, the common practice is to conclude
the Sanctus, the cry of the Seraphim from Isaias[2] with the passage
"Blessed be the glory of the Lord in the place of His dwelling," from
Ezechiel.[3] This last verse is connected with the prophetic vision of
the glory of God borne on the Cherubim (the *Ophanim* and the
Hayoth which we have seen mentioned in the Jewish liturgy). It
seems that at first the Sanctus was accepted in this form in the Christian liturgy, since it can still be found in a prayer from the *Apostolic
Constitutions*.[4] But soon the change began to appear from "Blessed be
the glory of the Lord in the place of His dwelling" to "Blessed be he
that cometh in the name of the Lord," together with "Hosannah,"
the cry of victory.

The verse from Ezechiel was understood as a praise of the *Shekinah*, the mysterious presence of God with His People which had been
localized first in the tabernacle, then in the Temple: this presence
concerning which the rabbis after the exile, under the influence of
Ezechiel himself, taught that where two or three were gathered together to read the Bible, this *Shekinah* stood in their midst. But this
presence is seen to be superseded now by the revealed presence of God

[2] VI, 3.
[3] III, 12.
[4] VII. 35.

in Christ, through Whom the eschatological expectation of Israel is satisfied; and therefore the verse from Ezechiel gives way to the acclamation with which the people greeted Jesus as He came into Jerusalem.[5] But we must not forget that this second acclamation is itself borrowed from Psalm 117, and probably from the liturgy of the procession that brought the Ark of the Covenant to its enthronement in the temple. Here, therefore, the idea of the Advent, in Christ, of that Kingdom of God which was the expectation of Israel, is placed together with the parallel idea that Christ Himself is the true *Shekinah,* the true presence of God among His own. Did not Our Lord Himself implicitly say as much when, evidently alluding to the rabbinical saying which we just quoted concerning the *Shekinah,* he said: "Where two or three are gathered in My name, there I am in the midst of them"?

After the Sanctus and its concluding sentence, then, the Eucharistic Prayer of St. Basil's liturgy goes at once to the praise of God in His creation, but creation described in such a way as to prepare for the redemption through the incarnation:

Thou art holy in all Thy works, for it is with full justice and a rightful sentence that everything happened to us. Having created man from the clay of the earth but graced him with Thy likeness, O God, Thou didst put him in a paradise of delights promising to him, if he observed Thy commandments, immortality and the enjoyment of eternal goods. But after he had disobeyed Thee, O God, his Creator and, seduced by the serpent's subtlety, had been subjected to death by his own fault, in Thy just sentence, O God, Thou didst drive him out of paradise into this world, sending him back to that earth from which he had been drawn, but preparing for him, in Thy Christ, the salvation of a new birth.

Then, without any break, we come to the history of redemption.

For thou hast not ever turned from Thy creature, neither didst Thou forget the work of Thine own hands, but in many ways Thou hast visited us in Thy merciful goodness. Thou hast sent Thy prophets; Thou hast accomplished wonders by Thy saints who have been well-pleasing to Thine eyes from generation to generation. Thou hast spoken to us by the mouths of Thy servants the prophets, announcing through them Thy coming salvation. Thou hast given us the Law to help us; Thou hast commanded the angels to be our

[5] Matt. XXI, 9; Psalm XVII, 25.

guardians. Then, when the fullness of time had come, Thou hast spoken to us by Thine own Son, by Whom Thou didst create the worlds, He Who, being the brightness of Thy glory and the express image of Thy substance, upholding all things by the word of His power, thought it no robbery to be equal with Thee, God and Father, but, Himself God from all eternity, appeared on earth living the life of man. Taking flesh from the holy Virgin, He emptied Himself, taking upon Him the form of a servant, conforming Himself to the body of our weakness in order to conform us to the image of His glory. And since by man sin had come into the world and death through sin, Thine only Son, He Who is in Thy bosom, God and Father, He Who was born from a woman, the holy Mother of God and ever Virgin Mary, He who was made under the Law, has been pleased to condemn sin in His flesh, so that those who died in Adam should be brought to life again in Himself, Thy Christ. Having lived in this world, giving to us the precepts of salvation, he set us free from the seductions of idols and brought us to know Thee, God and Father, thus acquiring us for Himself as an elect people, a royal priesthood, a holy nation: having purified us through water and sanctified us through the Holy Spirit, He gave Himself as a ransom to the death which kept us captive, sold as we were under the reign of sin. Having come down through the Cross to hell, so that he should fulfill all in Himself, He delivered us from the pains of death; risen again on the third day and opening to all flesh the way of the resurrection from the dead, since the author of life could not be submitted to corruption, He has become the first-fruit of those who have fallen asleep, the first-born from the dead, to be Himself above all things, having the primacy over all. Ascended to heaven, He sits at the right hand of Thy majesty in the highest, and it is He Who will come to render to everyone according to his works.

Here we see how the eschatological expectation has been transformed, because of the fact that Christ has come and His Cross is now accomplished. The prayer for a future and more perfect deliverance is no longer as it were opposed to a commemoration of past blessings: for in this very commemoration all our prayers for the future are so well granted in advance that their realization itself is a part of the commemoration.

At this point, when the thanksgiving has been developed to include the fullness of the Mystery, we find an explicit commemoration of the Lord's supper itself. This brings us back to the central act of the Mystery, but not in such a way as to separate it from the whole; for the remembrance of the Supper and the Passion immediately calls forth, briefly but fully, the whole *anamnesis*. This is one of the two ways in which Christian liturgies have supplemented the Jewish eucharist by an explicit commemoration of the divine intervention which transformed it on Maundy Thursday. The other way, the same today as it was in the time of Hippolytus, is that of the Roman liturgy. In this liturgy, the express commemoration of our Lord's words and actions on Maundy Thursday is inserted into the full exposition of the Mystery, so that the *anamnesis* is developed in a single and continuous life, with no coming back for a second mention.

Some scholars infer from very archaic liturgies, like those of Addai and Mari, that possibly the most primitive type of Christian liturgy had neither of these explicit mentions, but only an implicit commemoration of the Lord's Supper, expressing, in the eucharist over bread and wine, the fullness of the Christian Mystery, and not merely the creation or the prophetic redemption from Egypt.

Here, then, is the end of St. Basil's *anaphora* in its most ancient formulation (altered in the Byzantine Middle Ages).

> He left us that memorial of His saving Passion which we have laid before Thee according to His precept. For, on the point of going to His voluntary death that is forever memorable and vivifying, on the night in which He gave Himself for the life of the world, taking bread in His holy and all pure hands, and offering it to Thee, God and Father, giving thanks He blessed it, broke it, and gave it to His holy disciples and apostles, saying: Take, eat, this is My body broken for you in remission of sins. Likewise, taking the chalice of the fruit of the vine, and having mixed it, giving thanks, He blessed it and hallowed it and gave it to His holy disciples and apostles, saying: Drink you all of this, this is My blood, that of the New Testament, that which is poured forth for you and for many, in remission of sins. Do this in remembrance of Me, for every time you eat of that bread and drink of that chalice, you proclaim my death and confess my resurrection. Therefore we also, O Lord, remembering His saving Passion, His life-giving Cross, His three days in the tomb, His resurrection from the dead, His ascension into heaven, His enthronement at Thy right hand, God and Father, and His glorious and awe-inspiring second coming,—we offer what is Thine, from what is Thine, to Thee, in all and for all.

After this, instead of the prayer of supplication which we found at the conclusion of the Jewish eucharist, there comes a general commemoration of the Mother of God, the saints, the faithful living and departed, the prayer asking that all together through the Eucharist may be brought into the unity of the Mystery. The great doxology, through which the first impulse of the Eucharistic Prayer, as it were, returns once again, finally establishes once more within the thanksgiving all the fullness of the elements of memorial, sacrifice, and communion which had been, so to speak, developed from that thanksgiving itself.

When we have reached this point in our study, we are perhaps in a good position to consider what answer can be given to the great question which has so long divided East and West: that is, what is the exact moment when the Mystery is to be understood as accomplished in the Eucharist, when the bread and wine are, in consequence, consecrated as the Body and Blood of Christ?

From what has been said already, it is clear that the consecration, the offering of the sacrifice, is the effect of the thanksgiving seen as a single whole and understood always, not only as being the perfect answer of man to the Word of God, but also as that answer now made one with God's Word *par excellence,* since Christ Himself, in giving us the word of the Cross, performs the one perfect Eucharist, thanksgiving, of mankind. It must, therefore, be said both that the Eucharist is consecrative because it embodies God's final word: "Take and eat: this is My body"; and also because through its prayer of thanksgiving, Christ in a single act offers Himself to the Father while He gives Himself to us as our food. These two explanations complement each other, and each supposes the other. Apart from the prayer of thanksgiving, the Eucharist disappears. But the prayer of thanksgiving has no meaning except as an answer to God's Word which is prompted and created by that Word Itself.

The tendency, then, either to reduce the consecrative action merely to a central prayer considered apart from the whole single Eucharist, or to reduce this action to a few words of God in Christ, distinct from the prayer of thanksgiving, is simply a tendency to disintegrate the Christian Eucharist and to lose its deeper meaning.

True enough, it cannot be disputed that a distinct *epiklesis,* as the East has it, coming after the express commemoration of the Holy Supper, is a later addition which more or less disfigures the primitive shape of the Eucharist. The solemn and express repetition of the words and gestures of our Lord on Maundy Thursday is certainly an older feature of the rite. A truly complete and well-balanced view, perhaps, is the only means of reconciling Eastern and Western theol-

ogies. It rises above the debate to a common agreement that there is
no eucharist except by means of the Word of God in Christ as it came
to its fullest expression on the eve of Good Friday; and also that the
Word of God in Christ achieves the perfect sacrifice and gives us the
heavenly food for divine life only because, in Christ Himself, this
Word finds its echo in the perfect thanksgiving of men.

It remains for us now to apply to the Canon of our Roman rite
as it stands today what we have discovered in Christian antiquity,
seen as itself springing from Jewish tradition. We took a liturgy like
that of St. Basil to begin with because its general line is unbroken, and
it parallels the Jewish prayer strikingly from beginning to end. But we
can see this paralleling very clearly in the Roman Canon also, at least
when we are not distracted by later insertions which more or less interrupt the continuity of that general line. The only difference is that
the terse brevity of the Roman rite gives us often simply a passing
allusion to something which St. Basil's liturgy fully develops. But
when the latter has already been studied, the former can easily be
grasped in the fullness of its implications.

First, let us notice that, although in the Roman rite, the Preface,
as we now call it (meaning especially the first part, which still is sung,
going as far as the Sanctus), is much shorter than in St. Basil's liturgy,
the fact that this Preface can undergo a series of changes in the course
of the liturgical year enables it to emphasize in turn each chief phase
or aspect of the full economy of the one Mystery. Ancient sacramentals, like the Leonine, exhibit a much greater variety of Prefaces than
we know today, having a different one for almost every Mass. But in
any case, the prayers *Te igitur* and *Hanc igitur* with *Quam obla-
tionem,* coming after the Sanctus and pursuing the same line of
thought as the Preface, above the more recently inserted commemorations (of the living, and of the saints in the *Communicantes*),—these
prayers make the transition from general and special motives for
thanksgiving to the commemoration of the Lord's Supper. From
there, in the *Unde et memores,* the *anamnesis* expands to include the
resurrection and the ascension, and then proceeds to offer back again
to God His own gifts,—the sacrifice proceeding from the thanksgiving.
In this way the Word of God returns to Him in the answer of man;
God is loved by His own love shed forth in our own hearts. Then the
Supra quae and *Supplices te rogamus,* in very beautiful and certainly
very ancient formulae, express the idea that the Christian sacrifice is

the perfection of all the ancient sacrifices, and that the Christian eucharist itself finds its perfection in man's joining the perpetual eucharist offered in heaven by the faithful angels. The downward and upward aspects of blessing, through God's Word and man's thanksgiving in Christ, are emphasized simultaneously by the *Supplices* which invokes both the acceptance of man's sacrifice and the descent of God's grace. And after the second interruption (by the final commemorations of the faithful departed and once more of the saints in the *Nobis quoque*), both downward and upward aspects are very finely united once more in the benediction of the *Per Quem haec omnia*, leading to the great doxology of the *Per ipsum et cum ipso and in ipso*.

But these explanations themselves raise one more question. How can we justify the insertion of all these intercessory prayers, in this Western Eucharist, prayers which break up the Canon and which seem themselves to be the broken parts of a different continuous prayer? We must say, first of all, that this continuous prayer, or group of prayers closely connected, was one which developed, as can be seen from the last part of St. Basil's *anaphora*, from the final section of the Jewish eucharistic prayer. These intercessory prayers inserted into our Canon are, in origin, a developed and detailed form of the prayer for the eschatological attainment of the fullness of the Mystery, through the perfection of the *communio sanctorum*.

The fact that these prayers have, in the Roman Mass, been broken into at least two parts and inserted at different points into the Eucharistic Prayer properly so called, seems to be a result of the still earlier practice of reciting this Eucharistic Prayer, from the Sanctus to its conclusion, in a low voice. It seems that the deacon, in what was probably the first stage of this development, utilized the silence of the priest in order to get through the reading of the list of names (much more lengthy at that time), stopping only during the narrative of the Institution (what we now call the words of consecration), and resuming his reading afterwards. At a later time, when a priest was celebrating without a deacon, he would insert the diaconal prayer wherever he could into his own *prex sacerdotalis*, as we find Eastern priests doing today when they have to celebrate under the same circumstances. And so we got the puzzle which our present Roman Canon actually is.

But this explanation only raises a further difficulty: How did the custom of singing the Canon in full come to disappear? We can infer from the *ordines romani* that at least in Rome the Canon was sung until a very late period, in the same tone which we still use for its first part. But it can be noticed everywhere, even before the Middle Ages, that priests commonly tended, while the choir was singing the Sanctus, to say quickly what the choir was singing more or less elaborately, and to go on with the priestly prayer in a low voice. Similarly, in the East, the early development of the answer of the people to the introductory invitation "Let us give thanks to the Lord our God" may have been responsible for the fact that even that part of the Eucharistic Prayer which precedes the Sanctus and which we still sing in the West, was from early times merely said, except for its conclusion. Of course, as in the West, while the Sanctus was sung, the priest resumed his saying of what followed in a low voice. But even now, in the East, he still sings the narrative of the Institution, and the sacrificial words also, which correspond to the last part of our *Unde et memores* and are accompanied by an elevation both of the bread and of the chalice. Then while the choir again sings, the priest again speaks in a low voice, up to the great doxology which he sings in full, awaiting the *Amen* of the people.

In the West, on the other hand, although the first part of the Preface is still sung, everything that follows the Sanctus is only spoken in a low voice; rubrics, however, still prescribe that the priest wait until the choir has finished singing the Sanctus before he says the narrative of the Institution, which prescription may perhaps indicate that this narrative continued to be sung, for some time at least, as it still is in the East.

What are we to think of these developments? We must acknowledge that they have been due to very trivial causes, and those not too edifying: on the one hand, to the tendency of all choirs to make a greater and greater display of their voices; on the other hand, to the tendency of most priests to compensate by dispatching their own *liturgia* at the highest speed possible. We should not necessarily want to have the Canon once again sung in full (with the intercessory prayer and its long list of names then removed to a place where it would not interrupt anything), but we could perhaps at least wish that the central narrative and the great doxology (*Per quem haec omnia . . .*) might once again be sung by priests of the Roman rite in the *tonus praefationis*. If the Sanctus were sung by the choir after what is now the Preface, and the Benedictus between these two other major parts of the *prex sacerdotalis,* then the whole canon would again appear in its continuous line of thought, fully recovering the exultant and triumphant character which now is conspicuous only in the shortened Preface.

CHAPTER ELEVEN

Ministries in the Mystery: Ordinations
and the Mass

O NE most remarkable feature of both the Jewish and the Christian eucharist (thanksgiving) is that, however solemn and public it is, it is always performed by a single man. We have not as yet emphasized this characteristic, but it is time to do so now. The eucharist, of course, is the concern of the whole liturgical assembly. It is not performed until that assembly has been asked not only to pay attention to it, but to assent to it; and it is concluded by the very solemn Amen of all the people. But yet, only one man "makes" the Eucharistic Prayer.

In the Old Covenant, it was the head of the family, or, in the communities of pious Jews who were expecting the Messias, the spiritual leader who was to say the eucharist. (Let us notice the fact that this substitution of spiritual leader for head of a family brings out the Jewish idea of the teacher as a father, an idea which prepares us to see how the primitive Church could easily think of Jesus as at once the Word and the Son of God.)

But in the New Covenant, it is the bishop, or the priest whom he has designated when he is not present himself, who is to say the Eucharist. Let us remember the phrase of St. Ignatius: "Let no Eucharist be accounted valid except that which is ratified by the bishop." But what is it that assigns this *leitourgia* to the bishop, making it so definitely his work that nobody can perform it in his stead except those co-workers whom he himself has endowed with the power to do so? There is no doubt that the answer is: because the

143

bishop holds the place of our Lord amongst us. Not only is he considered the "locum tenens" of Christ, but it is Christ Himself, personally, Who is considered as being present and as acting in and through the bishop, so that what the bishop does, Christ does. And, consequently, whenever and wherever the Eucharist is performed in the Church, there is always but one single Eucharist, that of Christ Himself.

But how is it that the bishop's Eucharist is to be considered as Christ's own Eucharist? And why is it so important that there should be no other Eucharist but Christ's one Eucharist in the New Covenant? The answer to the first question is that the bishop is the *apostolos* of Christ: he whom Christ has sent in such a way that He Himself is in him. And the answer to the second question is that Christ is the *apostolos* of the Father, He whom the Father has sent so that He Himself is in Him. This is to say, finally, that the great point of the Christian Eucharist is that in it the thanksgiving of man is one with the Word of God: it is the Word of God made man Who now out of man's thanksgiving makes the Mystery: "Christ in you, the hope of glory."

We have just stated, in a nutshell, one chief aspect of the Mystery which we will now develop point by point.

To begin with, let us consider once more the Old Covenant. Why was the saying of the great and solemn eucharist the special function of the father of the family, first of all, and then, at the dawn of the New Testament, the special function of the teacher? We can say that the answer lies in the fact that, in the old dispensation, the growth of the People of God came about through the agency of human generation. The faith of Abraham brought forth a people to God by means of his natural descendants. But this dignity of human fatherhood was, in fact, completely dependent on the Word of God which had not only called Abraham and given him his promised son, but also from the very beginning of creation has called man into being in Adam. And so the perception began to grow among the Jews that it was the spiritual father, as having, so to say, conceived spiritual sons through the Word of truth, who was fitted, rather than the physical father, to perform the eucharist.

Here we are still in the realm of types and figures. But when the fullness of time had come, then also came the reality. Then was made the first and only Eucharist which expressed more than a pious wish on the part of fallen men. For in the Eucharist of Jesus an answer to the Word of God is at last given in full actuality, an answer which in perfect thanksgiving, in perfect acknowledgment of God's love for man, gives back this love of God by a complete surrender of man. And such an answer is given in the Eucharist because it is Christ's own thanksgiving, the thanksgiving which led Him to the Cross. Thus, the Word of God Itself made man creates in man the perfect response to that Word.

All Christianity, then, comes into existence in order that this response should become not only that of the Head but also of the whole Body, in order that the Eucharist of Christ should become the Eucharist of the Church. But this wonderful uniting of the Word of God and the thanksgiving of man could not come about if the one God-Man did not Himself offer His own sacrifice in the Church. The unity achieved in Christ between God and man could not be useful for us, so to say, unless a similar unity were achieved between Christ and ourselves. But this unity is just what Christ intended, and what, at the Last Supper, He prayed His Father to bring about: "That all may be one, even as Thou, Father, in Me and I in Thee; that they also may be one in Us, that the world may believe that Thou hast sent Me. And the glory that Thou hast given Me, I have given to them, that they may be one, even as We are one: I in them and Thou in Me; that they may be perfected in unity, and that the world may know that Thou hast sent Me, and that Thou hast loved them even as Thou hast loved Me."[1]

We can now understand, then, what is the distance between the covenants, and how their difference goes along with the capital difference between the way of growth of the People of God in its preparatory phase, and the way by which it is to attain "the measure of the fullness of Christ," in its ultimate phase.

In the New Covenant, there has been given once and for all in Christ that fullness which was only looked forward to in the Old. It has been given not for a brief moment only, but so that all men may be filled from this fullness, so that the Church herself may be described as "the fullness of him who is wholly fulfilled in all."[2] The People of God, therefore, is now no longer to develop by means of human generation which multiplies and also separates, but by a way

[1] John XVII, 21-23.
[2] Eph. I, 23.

of reconciliation and "recapitulation." We were all born *from* Adam; the Jews were all born *from* Abraham; but we are now all to be born anew *in* Christ. We are all to be taken up into the one Eucharist of the one Christ, to be reconciled through His Blood, in his own Body; to be reconciled among ourselves as well as with the Father.

It is essential, therefore, to the accomplishment of the Mystery in the Church that it should be dependent upon a ministry through which Christ Himself, in that unique conjunction of divinity and manhood which is achieved in His single Person, should be permanently present to make of each and every eucharist His single Eucharist. Here precisely is the function of the apostolic ministry. Through the apostles and those men whom the apostles sent in their turn as they had been sent, Christ is always here present among us to speak and to act. Even though they are sinners as are we, the Word of God in Christ is still active on their lips just as it was on Christ's lips, because it is always the same Word; because, in a Judas as well as in a Peter, the Word is not said except by Christ Himself, Who is the living Word of the Father.

We might well pause here for a moment to consider the significance of this point which we have just brought out. It means that in Christianity there is only Christ; nothing more or greater could be thought of. The purpose of these "last times" in which we live, therefore, is that men may be taken up into Christ, that their lives may be plunged, as it were, into His saving Cross. From Adam, the human race has come by multiplication and division, to sin and to death; but in Christ the new mankind is to be born anew to holiness and unity in the fullness of God.

This is the clue to the significance of the apostolic ministry and of the fact that only a man who has validly received the divine commission through the apostolic succession can validly perform the Eucharist. Any other eucharist is empty of reality, because empty of significance; it is not Christ's own Eucharist. This is to say, not only is such a eucharist not the Eucharist as Christ instituted it, but—and this is the cardinal point—it is not that self-same Eucharist which He performed.

From this fact follows the importance of ordinations in the Church, and first of all, of course, of sacerdotal ordination, as directly connected with the Eucharist, with the proclamation and perpetual reality of the Mystery in the Eucharist.

Scholars have seldom pointed out how peculiar to Christianity is this characteristic of the special ordination of priests and the great importance attached to it. Yet there was nothing exactly like it either in the cults of ancient Rome, nor in the mystery religions, nor even in the worship of the Jews.

In the ancient Roman cults, the priestly functions were generally attached to the elected magistrates of the city. The man who had been regularly nominated to office regularly offered the sacrifice; when he went out of office, he left his priesthood as well.

In the pagan mysteries, the old families generally kept the priesthood for themselves, just as the Aaronic priesthood was hereditary among the Jews. The cult of the Syrian goddess, and perhaps that of Isis also, admitted initiates into its priesthood as to a second and higher initiation. But it does not seem that the carrying out of the rites by non-initiates was thought to be invalid, but only to be unlawful. Non-initiates were considered to be encroaching on someone else's rights in such a case, but not to be doing something with no effect whatever. Alcibiades was persecuted so relentlessly for performing a parody of the Eleusinian mysteries just because the people were persuaded that in doing so he had unlawfully touched something of the awful essence of the mysteries. The reason for this was that, as in all these pagan rites, it was the rite itself—as we have already noted —that was all-important. Whenever anyone said the right words, and performed the right actions, the thing then worked by itself, just like a magic trick. And, as we have said, these rites indeed were magic tricks, at least in their beginnings. This fact gives us the reason why the few professional priesthoods known among the Romans were actually not priests, but rather boards of experts who could whisper to anyone the correct formulae and actions when a rite was to be carried out,—they did not need to carry it out themselves.

We might indicate in this connection that, contrary to Protestant opinion, it is just at this point that the temptation to think in terms of magic is always a danger to the Christian idea of the Mystery. For it becomes mere magic when men forget in practice that the whole efficacy of the Mystery depends upon the fact that to the eyes of faith it is always Christ Himself Who performs the Mystery. To quote once more that famous sentence of St. Augustine's: "When Peter does it, when Judas does it, it is always Christ Who does it." And this, precisely, is the meaning of ordination. Protestants, therefore, in omitting ordination altogether, or in refusing to acknowledge in ordination the real transmission of a sacred power, do not thereby remove the temptation to think of the sacraments as magic; rather they make the only possible alternatives those of a magic conception of sacramentalism or of a completely empty one. Their idea that a sacrament is valid whenever it is performed as Christ performed it, whoever the man may be who carries it out, does not resemble the primitive Christian idea in the least. Although Protestants do not recognize this fact, theirs is rather, a prejudice borrowed from the degraded nominalist theologians of the Middle Ages. Some of these had already been led to believe that the sacred words "This is My Body" said by anybody, priest or layman, over any piece of bread would consecrate that bread just as surely as does the priest in carrying out the sacred liturgy. But such an idea was certainly a purely magical notion, and completely foreign to Christian tradition.

On the other hand, to believe that the divine words are operative only when they are used in the liturgy of the Church by the man who has been appointed to carry out this liturgy by Christ's own Word through the channel of the apostolate,—this is ultimately to believe that the Word of God retains its divine power only when it remains God's own Word, personally spoken in Christ for mankind.

And here we see also how close is the connection between the commission given in ordination to perform the Mystery in the sacramental rite, and the commission to preach the Word given also in ordination. For it is always the Word of God which, by means of the holy and apostolic ministry, maintains the one reality of the Mystery ever present and active in the Church.

One first consequence of this truth is that the whole significance both of the apostolic ministry and of the Mystery in the liturgy is gradually lost sight of when we separate the two offices of the priesthood,—of preaching the Word and performing the sacraments, especially the Eucharistic consecration. Of course, a priest does not always have to celebrate Mass when he preaches, nor always to preach when he celebrates Mass. But the fact that the Church does not allow him to perform the Eucharistic consecration, even in the most private form of celebration, without first going through the service of readings and prayers, should remind him of the impossibility of separating the Word from the performing of the Eucharist without a fatal disintegration of Christianity.

We must acknowledge, in this connection, that the Protestant reformers, especially Luther, were correct in their primary intuition of the fact that the Word and the Sacraments are never to be separated, and that the Word comes first inasmuch as it operates through the sacraments themselves. But the Reformers were wrong in so far as they did not see that the true Word of God is not present merely because someone repeats the material letter of it, but because God Himself is present in His Son, His Son Who is present in those men whom He has sent just as He has been sent by the Father. The Protestant reformers' failure to understand this truth forced them to the alternative we mentioned above: to consider either that the sacraments were operative by reason of the magical action of a word that could be spoken by anyone, or that the sacraments were external rites empty of reality because they were reduced to the status of a purely human word with no creative activity of its own.

And here we have a good opportunity to bring out one most important point in the liturgical theology of the Mystery. If the Mystery is present in the whole Mass, in the readings of the Bible as well as in the Eucharistic Prayer properly so called, it is often asked: Is no distinction, then, to be made between the two parts of the Mass? Certainly there is. But how is this distinction to be made? Here is the great point. First of all, we can say that the presence of the Mystery in its reality is coextensive with the whole proclamation of the Word in the Church, reaching out from its solemn reading in the liturgy to include every Christian's reading of the sacred words or repeating them to himself in meditation.

But we should also never forget the fact that the Word of God is divine only in so far as it is one, not with the unity of an abstraction, but with the living unity of a person, the Person of the Son of God made man. And we must remember also that the Son of God gave Himself to us on the Cross as He did nowhere else, in that action which was also the perfect surrender of Himself to the Father. Therefore we can meet the full creativeness, the full, actual and personal reality of the Mystery in the Church, only when Christ Himself performs the Eucharist which remains forever the meeting-place of God's Word with man's thanksgiving,—when Christ, that is, performs the Eucharist through those members of the Mystical Body through whom He Himself has arranged to be personally present, in that action in which the Church herself re-acts His own central action. Because the Mystery is so fully present here, it is not, of course, absent from the rest of the Mass or from the whole life of the Church and of all her members. But it is present throughout the Church's life inasmuch as everything else in that life is both a preparation for and a consequence of the Eucharist itself. The Eucharist properly so-called, the *prex sacerdotalis* which is the special *leitourgia* of the bishop or of the priest as his representative is, therefore, both the fount and the focus of the whole liturgy and of the whole life of the Mystical Body in a way which is absolutely unique, to which nothing else can properly be compared. The Mystery is everywhere in the Church, and especially in the performance of the liturgy, but it is really and fully present, in the wholeness of the one action performed by the one Christ, only in the Eucharistic Prayer.

All this having been said, we can now see how closely interrelated are the sacerdotal ordination and the Eucharistic celebration. When our Lord said: "Do this in commemoration of Me," with the added statement that He had sent the apostles as His Father had sent Him, He gave to the Twelve both the power themselves to celebrate the Eucharist as His own Eucharist, and the power to provide for that celebration until His coming again at the end of the world. It is, therefore, normally within the Eucharistic celebration itself that the ordinations of the sacred ministry are to be performed; and the Church hardly ever dispenses with this traditional usage, at least for the sacerdotal ordination. To be more precise, it is most significant that the traditional moment for the ordination of priests is just before the Gospel, that is, just before that point in the celebration of the Mass when the Word of God is to be proclaimed in the fullness of Christ. No less significant is the fact that, in the subsequent celebration of the Eucharist, the newly-ordained priests take their part in the celebration as it were within the bishop's own celebration. This usage, always kept in the West for the Mass of ordination, strikingly manifests the fact that, in all the Eucharists performed by all Christian priests, there is only one Eucharist which is that of Christ Himself continued in and through the apostolic ministry. The celebration by the priests of the second order of priesthood adds nothing to the celebration of the bishop; it is only his one celebration which extends itself through them to all parts of his flock.

We must however acknowledge the fact that concelebration, the practice of many priests together celebrating as one, is probably not a primitive one. For, if we mean, as we do now, by concelebration a common celebration in which all the priests present do and say the essential rites and words, recent scholarship has shown that this practice is definitely not primitive.[1]

It is certainly a legitimate hope that the practice of concelebration be allowed in the West as freely as in the East. But such a wish must not blind us to a most important idea, nor make us disregard a usage which is still quite according to law in the West, is more ancient than the use of concelebration, and has, perhaps an even deeper significance.

What is the exact significance of concelebration? It is that the Eucharist in its inner essence, the Mystery of the Cross, is not multiplied by the multiplicity of celebrations. Just as there is only one celebrant, Christ Himself, in all the priests, so there is, in fact, only one Eucharist in all Masses, because the one single Mystery fills the Church and the world for all time: the Mystery of what was once and for all accomplished on Golgotha.

But the fundamental idea that it is only One who always says and does the Eucharist in the assembly of all the people, that is, that it is Christ Who performs the Eucharist in the Church, is perhaps shown most clearly by the primitive type of celebration, that is, when only one priest, the bishop or his representative, says and performs the *prex sacerdotalis*. If the bishop could always assemble his whole flock for his own celebration, there would be no need for a communication of his apostolic powers to other priests. It is only because it is impossible to practice for the bishop to preside at the *synaxis* at all the times and in all the places needed by his flock, that it is necessary for him to associate with himself priests of the second rank as cooperators in his work. But when, in the ancient Church, there was need for more than one celebration in one place, what was the general custom? The priests would first watch the bishop perform the first and fundamental consecration, up to the breaking of the consecrated bread. Then each priest took a piece of the *fermentum,* that is to say, a portion of the bread consecrated by the bishop himself, and went to the place where he was to consecrate for those Christians who had not been able to join in the bishop's own Eucharist. And there, in his turn, he said the *prex sacerdotalis,* mingling with the sacrament which he was consecrating the Bread already consecrated by the bishop to show that they both were one.

[1] See the special number of *La Maison Dieu* published on the subject in 1953.

Or if a priest could not conveniently attend the episcopal celebration, he would wait with the portion of the bishop's flock committed to his care, so that the bishop's acolytes could bring, from his own hand, the *fermentum,* before the local celebration began. But there was never more than one celebration on any one day at any one altar; and it would have been looked upon as rank presumption for a priest either to celebrate where the bishop himself had celebrated, or to celebrate in his own place before the bishop had given him or sent him the *fermentum.*

Even though we cannot return to all these usages, full of significance as they are, yet we can learn from them a very clear lesson, i.e., the inner and essential unity of the Eucharist through the one Eucharist of the one bishop.

Let us not forget that, even today, on the two most solemn occasions for performing the Christian Eucharist, that is, Maundy Thursday and the Vigil of Easter, the Church strictly forbids all private celebrations and obliges every priest to attend the Mass of the bishop or the local superior (pastor) on these days and to receive Communion from his hand. If such a procedure were to offer God a poorer worship or give less reverence to Our Lord, could the Church actually prescribe it just at the times when the Eucharistic celebration ought to be the fullest and the most expressive of the whole ecclesiastical year? It is unthinkable. And no less unthinkable would be the supposition that the procedure which was that of the apostles and of all the Fathers of the Church, of the Church of the martyrs and of the primitive saints, could be less good than our own practice today, centering on private celebrations. We cannot even maintain that our contemporary usage has a long unbroken tradition in its favor. Until the end of the eighteenth century, the law or usages of the great religious orders strictly forbade private celebrations on great feasts. On such days everyone, priests as well as laymen, were to attend the superior's celebration and to communicate at his hand. And, more recently still the ceremonial for conclaves (until the first conclaves of the twentieth century), forbade the Cardinals to say any private Masses; they were to attend one and only one Mass each day, that of the Dean. And similarly, all through the nineteenth century, in most European countries, when retreats were held for the clergy of any diocese, the bishop himself was the only one to say Mass each day. This, in fact, is what the Roman Pontifical still prescribes for a diocesan Synod.

This point leads us to a further one which will carry us into the next subject for our study. We have strongly emphasized the fact that the central focus of the celebration of the Mystery, the Eucharistic Prayer, is the *prex sacerdotalis,* the priestly prayer; and that this is the action not of an individual as such but of one single minister in the Body, because he can take personally, as it were, by virtue of the apostolate entrusted to him, the place of the Head of the Body. But throughout everything that we have been saying, and especially in the last points we have made, it must have been clear that, just as the Head does not exist for itself or by itself, but in and for the Body, so the apostolic ministry has no meaning apart from the Church. This is the point which we must now bring out; this ministry—which is entrusted only to the bishops as the successors of the apostles and to the priests as co-workers of the bishops—has not been given to these men for themselves, but for the whole People of God. A private celebration of the Mass, therefore, is not the ideal in any way, though such a celebration is certainly valid since the validity of the whole Mass depends only on the validity of the *prex sacerdotalis.* But we must go further. A private celebration may be lawful in special circumstances (though today in the West at least, the Church never allows it without a minimum of attendance); but no circumstances can blind us to the fact that, since the celebration is always intended for the whole Body, it loses much of this intended effect and significance in proportion to the absence of the members of the Body and their lack of actual participation.

Here we must return to that idea expressed by St. Clement which we found at the very origin of the Christian liturgy. As he explained it, the one liturgy of the whole Church is to be composed of the co-operation and union of all the "liturgies," that is, the "public services" of all the different members. For these "liturgies" all need each other in order to be complete, just as every member, the head as well as the feet, needs the whole body in order to live its own life in the body. There is, therefore, as St. Clement explicitly tells us, not only the great leading liturgy of the bishop, but also the liturgy of the deacon, and even the liturgy of the laity. None of these liturgies is to encroach on any other, but neither should any of them dispense with any of the others.

We can now see, then, that in the view of the primitive Church, the layman was not meant in the least to be merely passive throughout the celebration. We should not so much think of the hierarchy as a structure which towers above the separate structure of the laity; we should, rather, think of the hierarchy as including the laity in the one building, including them, it may be, on the lowest level, but for that very reason on a most basic level. But it would be still more in accord with the ways of thought and expression common in the ancient Church to reverse this image. The hierarchy is a hierarchy of ministries (services); according to Christ's word, he who is the high priest among his brethren should be the man who, like Christ Himself, stands out more perfectly than anyone else, as the Lord's Servant. The Fathers preferred to say, therefore, following the Scriptures themselves, that the basis of the whole building of the Church is the apostles, with their successors the bishops. And the most numerous stones, those without which no building could be built at all, those which provide the meaning for the foundation itself, these are the laity. "The laymen, what are they?" an angry bishop once grumbled to Newman. And the great Cardinal answered, "Well, without them the Church would look rather foolish!"

This truth is perfectly illustrated by the way in which the Fathers commonly compare the hierarchy of the Old and the New Covenants. In the Old Israel there were the high priests, the Aaronic priests, the levites, and then the lay people. We might think that the high priest would be compared to the bishop, the Aaronic priests to Christian priests, the levites to Christian deacons and the lay people of the Old Covenant compared to the lay people of the New. But such a comparison is absolutely never to be found either in the writings of the Fathers or in the ancient liturgical texts. The comparison is always made in quite a different way. There is always the analogy of high-priest and bishop, and the analogy of levite and deacon. But then we meet with the startling analogy made between the Jewish priests and Christian laymen. This analogy is, of course, explicitly or implicitly, borne out by an allusion to the "royal priesthood" mentioned by St. Peter in his First Epistle, when he is speaking of the whole community of believers. For to the mind of the Fathers, we can truly say that there were no laymen in Christianity, in the sense attached to the word in the Old Dispensation. In the New Dispensation all the baptized are priests, *hiereis,* all are consecrated and fit for sacred actions. Let us remember here the vision of the temple, in St. John's Apocalypse, in which the outside court which was the place for laymen in the Old Covenant, has been abandoned as no longer needed. This truth does not mean in the least, of course, that all hierarchy has been abolished, as the Protestants wrongly understood it; for the apostolate, the distinctive feature of the New Testament, is the basis for a hierarchy which is even more essential to the People of God than was any kind of hierarchy to the Jewish people in the Old Testament.

But before we enquire further what this does mean, let us notice the place which the Fathers assign to the co-workers of the bishop, the priest, the "presbyters," *presbyteroi* of the New Testament. They are always compared to the "seniors of the people" in the Old Testament, that is, to the councillors of the high priest who sat with him in the Sanhedrin, and who in Greek-speaking Judaism had already been actually called *presbyteroi*.

And let us not imagine that these expressions were characteristic only of an archaic period in the history of the Church and were soon to be laid aside. For up to the end of the Patristic period the word *hiereus* or *sacerdos* is never applied to those whom today we still call "priests" (a word derived from *presbyteroi*). *Hiereus* or *sacerdos* in a wide sense was applied to all Christians. In a restricted sense, as meaning the high priest only, (*archiereus*, or *sacerdos magnus*), these words were applied only to bishops, or if occasionally extended also to "priests" of the second order, it was always only inasmuch as these priests were considered to be performing the function of a bishop, a high priest, in his behalf and in his stead.

This use is perfectly clear in the very ancient liturgies for ordinations which have been preserved for us in the *Apostolic Tradition* of St. Hippolytus. The prayer for the consecration of a bishop speaks only of sacerdotal functions. The prayer for the ordination of a "presbyter" speaks only of his administrative functions, of being a councillor to the bishop and an assistant dispensing him from administrative routine in order to leave him free to preach the Word and perform the Eucharist.

And even today, this use of images borrowed from the Old Testament, and the same explanation of the fundamental relation between the bishop and his priests or presbyters, is still to be found in the Roman Pontifical in the consecratory prefaces for episcopal consecration and for priestly ordination respectively, and also in the preceding admonitions. And we could also cite various other similar expressions now used in the Church, not so striking as this example, but still very remarkable. The hierarchy of Cardinals, for instance— Cardinal bishops, Cardinal priests—is always called in Latin *Cardinales-episcopi, Cardinales-presbyteri,* but never *Cardinales-sacerdotes.*

What does all this signify, then, for our understanding of the hierarchy of the Church and of its relationship to the liturgy? The basic idea is that, whatever your place in the Christian hierarchy, whatever your function in the Body, you are a sacred person, and what you are to perform is sacred. The *prex sacerdotalis,* which is the nucleus of the Church's liturgy, properly belongs to the high priest, that is to the bishop, alone, although he can delegate it to any of his "councillors," the *presbyteroi,* since they are his "co-workers," and he can delegate at the same time the powers to preside at the assembly where this *prex sacerdotalis* is to be performed. But all the members have to pray, each in his own way, in conjunction with that central prayer, as all the members have to offer the bread and wine over which the Eucharist is to be performed, and, afterwards, to receive these again when they have become the heavenly food. To pray, offer and communicate, these are the essential functions of "royal priesthood" which are common to all the members of the Body, and these members are, in their own way, no less sacred than is the Eucharist itself of which they all partake. This truth will emerge more clearly at the conclusion of our next chapter.

CHAPTER TWELVE

Initiation Into the Mystery: Baptism, Confirmation, Penance in the Mass

As we have seen, the Mass is the *situs* of the Mystery, of its ever-active presence in the Church. From this truth flows the unique importance of the Mass, since it is not only the center of the liturgy, but, as the Eastern Christians call it, "the liturgy" *par excellence.*

But we must also consider how it happens (as Dom Casel most emphatically states) that the Mystery is present and active, not only in the Mass, but in all the sacraments. Let us say once more that the grace of Christ cannot be separated from His person, and that we cannot have His grace except by means of some actual participation in what He did on the Cross. Are we, then, to conclude that there is no essential distinction to be made here, and that the Mass is only one of seven chief ways in which the Mystery, remaining the same in itself, must be renewed for our benefit? Such a conclusion would be most startling, and in direct opposition to the great Christian tradition, which was well expressed by St. Thomas when he said that the Mass is, as it were, the source of the whole sacramental order since in it is contained the Passion of Christ, from which spring all the graces diffused through the other sacraments.

But such a question could not have been raised if we had not lost sight of what the sacraments really are, and of the way in which they are connected with one another so as to make a single and well-organized whole. The modern method of presenting the theology of the sacraments completely neglects their mutual connections, practically forgetting the profound thought of St. Thomas. We tend now to re-

157

gard the sacraments as seven parallel and absolutely similar channels through which the grace of God comes to us, the parallelism itself serving to bring out their apparent independence. But the difficulties raised by this view are innumerable, as, for example, when the distinction between the sacramental form and matter, which was made for the Eucharist and first applied to it, is to be used for the sacrament of marriage! And how many unsolved and insoluble questions are raised, when we try to look at the sacraments in this way, by the fact that the distinguishing and defining of the seven sacraments of the New Law was done so late in the history of the Church! How can we explain the fact that the Church waited for so many centuries before she became aware of the paramount importance of these seven parallel rites? The only answer to this riddle, and to others like it, is that the Church always had a perfectly clear idea of the importance of the seven sacraments, but did not define their number earlier than she did because, until the end of the Middle Ages, they had always been understood to be component parts of a single whole, centered in the Eucharist, a whole which certainly, in its primitive unity, was felt to be still more essential to the Christian life than we now think the seven distinct (and even separated) rites to be.

Let us try, therefore, to recapture the older view of the sacramental order, and we shall then see that while the Mystery is located in the Mass, it is not thereby excluded from the other six sacraments, since they themselves cannot be rightly understood apart from the Mass itself. As we have said already, the hierarchy cannot be separated, even in the abstract, from the Eucharist, for the Eucharist is the product of the apostolic ministry through which the Church itself is constituted. The power to perform the liturgical celebration of the Mystery is the very content of the Sacrament of Orders. We can say that the Church is able to perform the Eucharist because she is endowed with the power to keep and to transmit that "apostolate" which is the basis of Christ's own mission to mankind, and which He has given to her as He Himself received it from His Father. We can also say that since the Church herself possesses, as the very heart of her life, the power to perform the Eucharist, she possesses in consequence the power to do what Christ did; and this includes the faculty which He Himself possessed of giving what He had received, of "sending" in the same way as that in which He Himself had been "sent" by His Father.

In other words, the power the Church possesses to perform the Eucharist includes the power to endow some men with that power of personally representing Our Lord without which no Christian Eucharist could be performed. But the Eucharist is not to be performed in a vacuum, but for a collective body of men who are to take part in it actively as well as passively. The root power of the Church to perform the Eucharist must also imply, therefore, a power to adapt men of all kinds and times and places to take their part in this performance. The first point to clarify is that this reasoning from the Eucharist to Baptism is not mere abstract theory.

So far we have been emphasizing one basic aspect of the Mystery, the fact that it cannot be present in the Church, in her liturgy, except by virtue of the apostolic ministry, and, more precisely, by virtue of the function that is proper to that ministry, the *prex sacerdotalis,* the eucharistic *praefatio* or *anaphora.* This aspect of the Mystery is certainly basic, but the very idea of a basis implies that something is to be built on the base. And obviously the whole sacramental order, and the whole Eucharistic liturgy in particular, would be pointless if it were not to animate a Body, to communicate to the Body the life of the Head.

But to say this is still not to say enough. It is not only the representation of the Mystery which would lose all point without this purpose: the Mystery itself as it is revealed in Christ would also become complete nonsense. For the Mystery is simply the revelation of God's love, of the divine *Agape,* as it wishes to communicate itself. God's love is not in any way a desire like the *eros* of Plato, but rather a pure gift; but, as has been well said, if this love does nevertheless appear to us as being in some way desire, this is because it reveals itself to us as a desire for fellowship. Not only the content of God's revelation in the Mystery, but the very fact that God reveals the Mystery, means that He wants to establish a living fellowship between Himself and us. As God has revealed Himself to man in Christ, we could attribute to Him those words of the Angel to the Soul in Newman's *Dream of Gerontius*:

> I would have nothing but to speak with thee
> For speaking's sake. I wish to hold with thee
> Conscious communion.

The aspect which we have been studying until now of this wonderful communication between God and man is that of the Word

Itself, which takes the initiative in the dialogue; and we have seen how It has managed to reach man and to adapt Itself to him so as to call forth his answer. Now we are to see how this answer, while remaining inseparable from the Word which created it, is nonetheless the authentic answer of man as he really is. We are to see how man is meant to receive the divine image, not passively (how could an image of Him Who is Life itself be passive?) but actively; how he is to play his own part in the dialogue between himself and God.

The leadership of the high priest in the Christian liturgy as we have studied it, then, would become meaningless if it were not to validate and bear along with it the sacerdotal action of all those "priests" who, in their hierarchically ordered collectivity, are to make up a chosen generation, a royal priesthood, a holy nation. We must now recall what we saw at the beginning of our study. We saw that the liturgy, the Mass as it has developed from the *Qehal Yahweh,* was actually the People of God in the process of making itself. The Word of God summoned that assembly, not only to speak to God's People as if that People already were in existence, but to make the People by means of the convocation itself and hearing of God's Word in the course of it. And, as we saw, the sacrifice with which that assembly always ended, was always the bond of union which in fact constituted the People as such while dedicating it to its God.

Here is the deepest meaning of the word "sacrifice": *sacrum facere,* to make holy. What is the holy thing which is made, or the thing which is made holy as the final effect of God's Word proclaimed to the world? We can say that it is the People, for it is made a People in being made the People *of God.* This is precisely the conclusion reached by St. Augustine, in a chapter we have previously quoted from the tenth Book of *The City of God.* The sacrifice which is offered to God the Father in Christianity is finally the whole redeemed City offering itself to its Redeemer. For St. Augustine, this was the final and unavoidable conclusion of his great principle, his great and distinctively Christian definition of sacrifice: *Verum sacrificium est omne opus, quod agitur ut sancta societate inhaereamus Deo:* "Every work which has as its object our cleaving to sound fellowship to God is a true sacrifice."

But the great point for us to emphasize here is that the City of God builds itself out of materials from the city of this world. Not that one city is to be transformed into the other; there is a radical enmity between the two and no hope of a possible reconciliation. But the city of this world is, so to speak, the quarry from which the stones are to be taken and incorporated into the building of the City of God. No stone is to be made part of the divine construction unless it first be disengaged from that devil's construction which is the result of Satan's perversion of the creation of God. The first point for us to study now is the process by means of which this is to be done. And thus we shall see how the Mystery and its ever-active proclamation implies a process of initiation, the main phases of which are Baptism and Confirmation.

Here we reach a decisive point in the development of our study, a point which is so much a part of the essence of the Mystery that some capital aspects of the Mystery can only be understood in the light of it. And this truth is what we have just indicated: the Mystery must be proclaimed and performed not in a docile world, nor even in a neutral world which might be at least passively disposed to be informed by it, but in a world which is positively hostile.

Here is the final meaning of that unavoidable aspect of death which lies at the heart of the mystery of life. Here only can we understand fully the implications of those ideas of "reconciliation" and "recapitulation" by which St. Paul qualifies the Mystery.

It is obvious that the redemption comes not only to perfect creation, but also to cure it. But this is not enough. For creation must be cured, not of a mere loss, a merely negative infirmity. It has, rather, to be "reconciled" from a state of inveterate enmity. And this reconciling implies so complete a remaking that it is a "recapitulation," that is, a bringing back of the whole history of creation to its beginnings, without which this history could never be brought into the fullness of God. If creation is to be adopted completely in the one and only Son of God, it must be born again, and this rebirth cannot be accomplished except through death.

In the first place, the Word of God as it proclaims the Mystery to the world is to be seen as always verifying that prophetic sentence: "All day long I stretched out my hand to a people unbelieving and contradicting."[1] Did not Christ on the Cross, the Word of God's love to man crucified by man, fulfill that prophecy in a most dreadful way?

[1] Isaias LXV, quoted in Rom. X, 21.

Therefore, prior to our consideration of how the Word gets heard in the Qehal Yahweh, where it is received with faith, lovingly acknowledged in the loving unity of its whole design, as this was to be accomplished in Christ, we are now to consider the Word of the Mystery in the humiliated condition in which the divine wisdom depicts itself:

> Standing in the top of the highest places by the way,
> in the midst of the paths,
> Beside the gates of the city,
> in the very doors she speaketh, saying:

> O ye men, to you I call,
> and my voice is to the sons of men.
> O little ones, understand subtlety,
> and ye unwise, take notice. . . .[2]

And this again:

> Wisdom hath built herself a house,
> she hath hewn her out seven pillars.
> She hath slain her victims, mingled her wine,
> and set forth her table.

> She hath sent her maids to invite to the tower,
> and to the walls of the city:
> Whosoever is a little one,
> let him come to me.

And to the unwise she said:

> Come, eat my bread, and drink the wine
> which I have mingled for you.
> Forsake childishness and live,
> and walk by the ways of prudence.[3]

[2] Proverbs VIII, 2-5.
[3] Proverbs IX, 1-6.

And Jesus Himself gave the last touch to the picture: "Behold, I have prepared my dinner; my oxen and my fatlings are killed, and everything is ready; come to the marriage-feast. But they made light of it, and went off, one to his farm and another to his business; and the rest laid hold of his servants, treated them shamefully, and killed them."[4]

This primary aspect of the Mystery has been best brought out by Origen: the obscure, misunderstood, broken and humiliated form in which the Word must first appear to natural men in order to seek and find him, to touch his as yet unregenerate heart and so bring him to the faith. One permanent aspect of the Mystery of the Cross is that signified by Holy Wisdom's going out from the banquet hall where everything is prepared for the marriage feast, going out to find her guests; and this aspect is in its way no less important than the aspect which is later acknowledged in the light of love triumphant. As we shall see later on, the Mystery must be continually reenacted, in this "outer darkness" of the world, through the "witness"—as St. John was the first to call it—given to the power of the Cross by the sufferings and death of Christ's apostles and servants,—what we now call martyrdom. We shall see how this martyrdom is to be considered the final and perfect fruit of the participation of Christ's servants in the Mystery through the Eucharist. Suffice it for the moment to point out that it is only by means of this martyrdom that the Mystery keeps in touch with the unregenerated heart of natural mankind in order to bring it to what St. Paul calls "the obedience of the Gospel."

When, however, this witness has attracted a man and awakened in his heart, not yet the faith itself, but a desire for faith, it will first bring him into the assembly of God's People. And the only way by which he can be conformed to and associated with the fellowship of the Mystery will be to cause him to become an active member of that assembly and so enable him to do what every one of the members of the "royal priesthood" can do: that is, as we have already said, to pray, to offer, and to communicate. The Christian initiation, then, is precisely this taking of a man into the Mystery by fitting him to perform the actions of prayer, offering and communion through a conformation to Christ. This fact means that there is no initiation into the Christian faith other than an initiation into active participation in

4 Matthew XXII, 2-6.

the Mass. Here is what we must now try to understand by contemplating the Mystery in the means by which it disposes mankind itself for this participation, that is, for the performance of the Mystery under the threefold aspect of prayer, offering and communion. And this means is the way of Baptism and Confirmation.

Let us notice at once that in making this statement we repudiate the fallacy of treating the sacraments as seven parallel channels of grace, similar, but independent. On the contrary, according to the mind of the ancient Church, Baptism and Confirmation had no meaning except as milestones on the way to the Eucharist. So evident is this way of thinking that we often find the Fathers tending to use the word "Baptism" as a comprehensive term to cover the whole process of initiation, a term including, in the first communion of the neophytes, the Eucharist itself; they treat Baptism properly so called and Confirmation as only so many introductory steps toward that final action. This way of speaking supposes, of course, that the normal method of administering Baptism and Confirmation is to include them in a Eucharistic celebration. We can say, therefore, that to the ancient Church, the Christian initiation is nothing other than the Eucharist itself, but the Eucharist developed in such a way as to include in its one continuous movement, not only men who are already Christian, but men just coming in from the outer darkness who need to be adapted to the light of the banquet-hall, who need to be endowed with that image of Christ which alone can enable men to do what the Son of God does. Here, then, we can see how the Mystery, while it never ceases to be present in the Eucharistic celebration and there only, nevertheless fills Baptism and Confirmation also.

As Origen says so beautifully, when a man has been touched to the heart by the Divine Word, when the Word is no longer as it were like a perfume which he breathes, or even an intoxicating wine which he drinks, but rather like the living blood which will enable him to bleed to death on the cross,—then he is ready for Christian initiation.

First, he will be introduced to the bishop by his godfathers, the guarantors of the sincerity of his desire for faith and Baptism. Next come the preparatory "scrutinies," each of which includes, after an imposition of hands and a signing with the cross, the two constant features of a teaching on prayer and an exorcism. In the meantime, the catechumen is still admitted only to the entrance of the church each day, to take part only passively in the first half of the *synaxis*: the Lenten readings, psalmody and prayer.

In one of the final scrutinies, the initiation reaches a climax with the *traditio evangelii,* the "handing over of the gospel," in which the deacons solemnly carry in the books of the four Gospels and begin the reading of them, which is explained to the catechumen by the homily of the bishop. And from this "handing over" of the Gospel springs the *traditio symboli,* the "transmission of the Creed," in which the unity and the wholeness of God's design in the Scriptures will be revealed to the catechumen in Christ, and the *traditio orationis,* that is, the transmission of the Lord's Prayer, in which through faith the perfect filial answer is to be given to that Fatherly love which the Gospel has disclosed.

Until he has received these *"traditiones,"* as the Fathers say in very characteristic sentences, the catechumen cannot truly pray any more than he can truly believe, that is, accept the Gospel in the living way in which a Christian accepts it. In order to be able to do so, the catechumen must be born again. He must have undergone death to this world and to the life of alienation from God which he has led in it, and afterwards have been reborn to the life of a child of God through the resurrection of Christ. Only the man who is no more a child of the fallen Adam—but who in the second Adam comes down from heaven as a child of the Heavenly Father—can truly say the "Our Father."

This *transitus,* this passage through death to the life of a child of God in Christ, is itself our fundamental participation in the *transitus,* the Passover of Christ, the essence of the Mystery leading to life eternal through the death of the Cross. This means a struggle: the Cross itself is made of that struggle. For just this reason, the Church exorcises the catechumen as she takes possession of him; that is, she begins for him the struggle with the powers of Hell that alienate from God a child of Adam. But the catechumen must now fight himself, and the *redditio symboli,* the personal confession of faith in the power of the Mystery which the candidate for Baptism makes on the eve of his final initiation, is, as it were, his personal challenge to those same powers which have crucified the Lord of Glory.

In the very Night of the Resurrection, therefore, when the Church has assembled to wait for the dawn of Christ's coming in the full light of His triumph, when the catechumen has meditated on the whole of the sacred history which is brought to completion in the Mystery, —then the catechumen himself is to lie down on the cross in order to be made able to rise again in the power of the Spirit of Christ. For this purpose, he is led to those waters from which, in the beginning, all life had been brought. Like Christ Himself, he is to be stripped of all his garments. Then his body is to be anointed with oil like a wrestler's, for he is now to struggle to the death with that death which lies in wait at the very source of our life. Into this source he is to plunge again, so that his own history, like the whole history of mankind, may be "recapitulated" in Christ: that is, may be brought back to its beginning so as to find at last its fulfillment.

The catechumen goes down into the water; he plunges into it and disappears completely. When he emerges once more he will no longer be the same man. The dusty image of Adam which he carried before has now been blotted out. He is dead with Christ to the life of man which was spoiled by the devil. Now, washed from his sins, he is a new man in the new Adam. The priestly hand marks his head with holy Chrism, that is the newly-baptized is engraved with the *eikon,* the image of Christ Who is the *eikon* of the Heavenly Father. He is clad in a white garment, and he goes forward with a light in his hand: for now that he has regained that garment of immortality which was lost by Adam, he is no longer a child of darkness but a child of light. For it is no longer he—his old self—who lives in him; it is Christ who lives in him, the Man of the last times, the Man come down from heaven, the Son of God.

Then for Confirmation the bishop pours on the forehead of the newly-baptized that chrism which is, as it were, the sweet perfume of Christ, the divine unction of the Anointed One, the very Spirit of Life Who is the Spirit of Love, the Spirit of the divine *Agape* now poured forth from God's heart into this new Christian's own heart.

And now, through Baptism in water and of the Spirit, the new Christian has been conformed to the Mystery: the divine pattern revealed in Christ has been imprinted in him. Now he prays, now he can pray the "Our Father," for he is not only called, but he truly *is* a child of God in the only-begotten Son; and because he can pray, not only with his lips, but with his heart,—since the Spirit of God

Himself strengthens his weakness and witnesses that he is God's son—
he can also offer and communicate.

From the Baptistry, therefore, the new Christian now returns to
the church, where the celebration of the Eucharist has been delayed,
waiting for the perfecting of this new member in order to be itself
brought to perfection. Now he is one with his brethren in Christ, and,
through his godfathers, he himself offers the bread and wine;[5] and
when the high-priest, having asked the assent of the new Christian,
has performed the Eucharist, the neophyte will receive his offering
back again, now become the heavenly food. He has been made one
with the offering Christ, and he will be made one with the Victim
offered, as It now stands in the glory of Its immolation. . . .

Once we have followed this process of Christian initiation, we can
at last perceive the full implication of the "royal priesthood," in its
three sacred functions of praying, offering, communicating.

It is only the "character" of Christ, that is, an ontological conformation to His image, the unction of the Spirit, that gives to a man
born of Adam participation in Christ's priesthood. Thus having "the
mind of Christ," as St. Paul says, the new man can also have what
the Saint calls "the intelligence of the Mystery,"[6] or "the understanding of His love."[7] In other words, the neophyte certainly knows
how to pray in the sense that he has been taught to recollect himself,
silently kneeling, when the deacon invites the assembly to prayer, and
to rise, hear the *Collecta* prayed aloud by the bishop, and give it his
Amen. But he can also do something more: in that silent prayer he
is now able to contemplate in his deepest heart the Mystery which he
has found in the Bible readings just made to him and his fellow-
Christians, and therefore he is able to pray that this Mystery be fulfilled in himself and in the whole Body of which he is now a member.

Only "the Spirit searches all things, even the deep things of God,"
says St. Paul, but "now we have received not the spirit of the world
but the Spirit that is from God, that we may know the things that have
been given us by God."[8] And elsewhere he says: ". . . we do not
know what we should pray for as we ought, but the Spirit himself
pleads for us with unutterable groanings. And He Who searches the

[5] In the old Roman use, the neophytes did not offer personally, but through their
sponsors.
[6] Ephes. 3: 3.
[7] Ephes. 3: 19.
[8] I Cor. II, 12 ff.

hearts knows what the Spirit desires, that He pleads for the saints according to God."[9] But this is true only of the man reborn, in whose heart the Spirit of God has been shed abroad. Only such a man understands the love of God; only he has the "intelligence" of the Mystery; only he prays in the Spirit. But such a prayer is no less necessary to the Church, is no less an integral part of her liturgical prayer, than is the official formulation which is made publicly by the bishop or by the priest who leads the collective prayers in the bishop's name. For this official formulation has no other purpose than to prompt that prayer of the heart in which the Spirit is alive. Neither has it any meaning except as "collecting" those unheard and unutterable groanings of the Spirit. And we can boldly say that if they were not present in some way the Mystery would not be fulfilled any more than if there were no apostolic ministry validly to say the *prex sacerdotalis*. For the Mystery is proclaimed and performed through the apostolic ministry only in order to become the life of man reborn in Christ. And if there were no such *renati,* men reborn, or if they ceased to take part in the liturgical celebration, it would lack its full meaning, and, finally, lose its content.[10]

For the performance of the liturgy, considered as objective and divinely given, is not an end in itself, but rather has as its end the subjective apprehension of the Mystery by man. If this were not true, we should again fall into the error of thinking of the liturgy as the "official disposition of an external worship." But since the liturgy is not and could not be such an empty show, we must acknowledge the fact that the "royal priesthood" of the whole Body not only is as essential in its own way as the priesthood of the apostolic ministry, but is also the purpose of this latter. Nor should the use we have just made of the terms "objective" and "subjective" be considered to mean that there is no objective element in this "royal priesthood." On the contrary, it proceeds entirely from the objective gifts of Baptism and Confirmation: the divine "character" of Christ which is imprinted by these sacraments, and the gift of the Spirit demanded by that character itself.

The "intelligence of the mystery" which is given in prayer to the man reborn in Christ, being itself a reality, has as an immediate

[9] Rom. VIII, 26-27.

[10] Of course we do not mean that a private Mass is invalid, but that the Mass at large would lose its end if there were no People of God to make use of the gifts brought to mankind through the Mass.

consequence the Christian's power to partake effectively in the Mystery; since the "understanding of God's love" cannot exist without loving also in that very love. Therefore, as the newly-baptized can now pray, so also can he now offer. His offering is primarily the free offering of the bread and wine to be consecrated, together with all the fruits of the earth and of the labor of man, with everything that sustains man's life. This means, as the Fathers are never tired of repeating, that what man possesses that he can offer in the Eucharist is his own life from its very sources.

The unregenerated man cannot offer his life to God. Not only does he not know God, not only has the Mystery not been revealed to him, so that he can not understand the love which calls for his own love, but also he is alienated from himself. He cannot be God's possession because he is now in the grip of the devil. The man reborn in Christ, however, has been freed from this subjection. He has been set free, not for that freedom to commit sin which is a chain of bondage, but for the freedom from sin which makes him able to live to God, that is, to enjoy perfect liberty.

But let us note carefully at this point the fact that the offering of man, even of man now regenerated, would have no value unless it were made through Christ, through His Own perpetual offering. What man presents at the altar is properly only the material for sacrifice. But the sacrifice itself is only performed through the consecrative power of the Eucharist, of the *prex sacerdotalis,* in which Christ Himself takes man's offering and makes it His own, so that it is no longer man's bread and wine, but His Body and Blood. Only in this way is the immolation accomplished, and man himself in Christ appears before the Father, as His son, loving the Father in the same love with which the Father loves the Son.

The offertory, in other words, is not in itself the sacrifice: the Mass is not, as we too often hear it explained, our own sacrifice coming to be united to Christ's own sacrifice./In Christianity there is not and cannot be any sacrifice other than Christ's own sacrifice: no idea could be more opposed to the true spirit of the liturgy than the supposition that we could bring to the altar some sacrifice of our own, complete in itself, which we ourselves have made prior to our meeting Christ at the altar, and then add it to His own Cross. Nothing can be added to the Cross: we are only to leave our lives and ourselves in the hands of Christ so as to be taken into His Cross./While we are to "work out our salvation with fear and trembling," we must always remember that it is God Who gives us both "the will and the power to do so,"[11] and where are these gifts given us if not in the gift of the Mystery itself?

On the other hand, it is certain that the losing of oneself, the voluntary death which sinful man's offering of himself to God implies, would have no meaning, would be merely suicide, if it were to be attempted by man alone. It is only the Cross of Christ which gives life, and it is only through the divine power shown on the Cross that man can ever find life through death, can through his own death find the life of God.

Man cannot, therefore, attain to the full thanksgiving which perfectly echoes God's Word unless he is taken up by Christ, the Word made man, into that thanksgiving which He alone of all mankind can accomplish. And from this truth it follows that our own offering has no significance except that of an abandonment of ourselves through faith into the hands of Christ, so that we may be presented to the Father not only with Him, but also by Him and in Him.

But once again, when we have said all this, we must re-emphasize the fact that Christ's thanksgiving to God made in man's flesh, and its perpetuation amongst us by means of the apostolic ministry, would miss its primary purpose were we not, through it, to offer ourselves, our souls and our bodies, as a living sacrifice to God, as our rational sacrifice, holy and acceptable to Him. It is to achieve this purpose that Christ Himself ascended the Cross, and as long as we have not joined Him there, there is something lacking, as St. Paul says, in the sufferings of Christ, which has to be filled up, for His Body the Church.[12]

But both the sacrifice of Christ and our being joined to it have a further purpose. This is the completion of Christ's risen body by the full participation of all the elect in its eternal life, in its divine life given to men. And it is this further purpose which is, finally, not only promised but in some way already inaugurated by communion. When we communicate, we are as it were attaining in advance the ultimate end of Christianity: we are reaching that fullness of Christ completing Himself in the Church. Moreover, communion is so marvellously at once promise and realization of the final reality of heaven, that by communion, our life—the individual life of each of us, as well as

[11] Philip 2: 12-13.
[12] Coloss. 1:24.

the common life in the one Body—is even now in some way plunged into that love which will be its possession for all eternity.

We can conclude, then, by seeing what light has been shed on the question of the presence of the Mystery first of all in the Mass, and through the Mass itself in Baptism and Confirmation. We can say that within the perpetual celebration of the Mystery in the assembly of the Church, which finds its focus in the Eucharistic Prayer, a man is adapted by the Mystery, through the waters of the holy fount and the unction of the Spirit, to an active participation in the Mystery itself. A man is made a member of Christ and endowed with His Spirit by being once and for all reborn in His death and resurrection. And therefore he is made able to pray in Christ, that is to say, to receive the Mystery from the depths of God into the depth of his own heart; he can offer himself through Christ to the Father; and he can receive in himself the accepted Offering which has become the ever-living Body, so as to be made himself a member of that Body.

And this communication to a man of this new being, of this ability to take his part in a new and wholly divine life,—this communication is not something external to the Mystery: it is the Mystery itself inasmuch as in the Cross, in the power of Christ's blood, lies the power to "reconcile" all men together to God in His own Body, to "recapitulate," to bring back to its source the life of all men, so that it may attain to the fullness of God's own life.

A few words only need to be added concerning the Sacrament of Penance. After a kind of temporary suspension of the effects of Baptism in which sin excludes a man from the communion, the fellowship of the Mystery, Penance is precisely a reintegration of the sinner into that fellowship. This re-integration is accomplished by that same virtue inherent in the Mystery by which it conforms men to participation in the Mystery itself. It is for this reason that, in the public rite for the reconciliation of penitents as it still stands in the Roman Pontifical, we first see the sinners who have been excluded from the assembly, once again waiting at the door among the catechumens, for admittance into the *Qehal Yahweh*. Then, on Maundy Thursday, just when Christ is going to summon His Own to His banquet "for the remission of their sins," the bishop goes to the door of the church, takes the penitents by the hand and reintroduces them to their former places in the community, there to pray, to offer and to communicate once more.

CHAPTER THIRTEEN

The Expansion of the Mystery: The Blessings Flowing From the Mass (Nuptial Blessing, the Oil of the Sick, Consecrations.)

So FAR we have seen how four of the Sacraments—Ordination, Baptism, Confirmation and Penance—are related to the Eucharist, and how, in consequence, the Mystery is present and active through them, though always in dependence on its fundamental presence in and activity through the Mass itself.

We are now to study how this presence and activity of the Mystery is to be found in the other two sacraments, Holy Matrimony and the Anointing of the Sick, and also in all the sacramentals which imply some consecration of people or things. Those rites which we have been considering had to be understood as being preparations for or steps initiating men into the celebration of the Eucharist. Those which we are now going to study can be understood only if we think of them as various forms of that blessing which, as we have said, is so closely connected with the Eucharist that, to the Jewish mentality, they are not properly two things but only one.

Let us remember here Lietzmann's mistake, mentioned in an earlier chapter, which was so well brought out and explained by Cullman. Because St. Paul's eucharist is full of the Cross, it could not, according to Lietzmann, be reconciled with the joy and gladness of what he believed must be quite another type of eucharist — the agape-meal of the primitive Church. But his mistake lies in his not recognizing that the great motive for the Eucharistic joy and gladness of Christians is, precisely, the Cross. For the Cross is no longer seen as a sign of painful death and irretrievable loss, but rather

as the sign of victory through the resurrection. It is, therefore, through
the Eucharist of the Cross and for the Cross, that Eucharist through
which we offer ourselves and our own bodies as a living sacrifice to
God, that we are able once more to find, in the communion of the
Mystery, ourselves and all things which pertain to our life all now
filled with this very life of God. Once more, and now more than
ever, the Eucharist is in itself the great blessing, which restores creation to its primitive condition and fills it with that marvellous joy
which, as says the book of Job, made the sons of God all sing together on the first morning.

Since the blessing which is the counterpart of the Eucharistic sacrifice is thus a restoring of creation itself to its former goodness, it is
natural that it should first touch the continuation of creation, as it
were, in man and for man; that is to say, the natural process of
human generation. Human marriage, therefore, is to be taken into
the working of the Mystery by means of the Nuptial Blessing which,
like all the most important blessings in the ancient Church, is to be
given at the conclusion of the Eucharistic prayer itself (at the end of
the *Pater Noster*). And, as the formula of the Ritual says quite
plainly, it is no platonic union of souls which is here to be blessed,
but the sexual love of man and woman.

But this love is blessed in reference to its primary end: the pro-
creation of children. And we can say that it is through the blessing
of this primary purpose that sexual love itself is blessed. A man and
woman are to be blessed in their nuptial union because they are con-
curring not only in a multiplication of the sons of Adam, but also in
preparing new members for the Mystical Body and so working for its
completion. More expressly, it is the woman in her fecundity who is
blessed, for, as St. Paul says, "She will be saved by child-bearing,"—
a sentence which can be explained by his other saying, "Your children are holy."[1] What does this mean? It means that the love which
is to dominate in Christian marriage is no longer the love which is
basically that of want, of self-centered desire, but instead that same
sacrificial love which is working through the Mystery, the divine love
which does not seek its own, but above all seeks to give life and give
it abundantly. There is a mutual oblation implied in human love from
the first, when it is more than mere selfish desire, and this mutual
oblation is itself to be fulfilled in Christian marriage in a common

[1] Cf. 1 Tim., 2: 14; and 1 Cor., 6:14.

oblation of both lovers in a creative love which is animated by the divine *agape*. Thus, their mutual love will not be merely the association of two egotisms, but rather the true image of the love of Christ and the Church, and, through this, an image of the Mystery itself.

Here we can see how the Christian Mystery not only realizes on a far higher plane what was sketched by the sexual symbolism in the the fecundity rites of the pagan mysteries, but also brings sexuality itself into the sphere of the divine *agape*.

However, the blessing brought to the natural fecundity of human life, flowing from creation, is also to touch and transfigure the weakness inherent in human life since the fall. Modern psychology emphasizes the strange and fascinating way in which the will to love and the will to die[2] are interwoven in the recesses of the human heart. But that fact was guessed at by art and literature from the very beginning of civilization. Is it not clear to every man that life as it stands now, even when it craves for a full expansion of itself, cannot avoid tending towards death?

As the natural fecundity of human life, therefore, is taken up into the supernatural blessing, so also is its natural decay. Our Lord said of the illness of Lazarus: "This sickness is not unto death, but for the glory of God, that through it the Son of God may be glorified,"[3] when in fact Lazarus was to die—but to die in such a way that Jesus could say to Martha as they approached the dead body, ". . . if thou believe, thou shalt behold the glory of God." In precisely the same way, the Eucharist of His Cross takes our own infirmity and makes of it a way to life and resurrection.

Human bodies that have been struck down by mortal illness are to be anointed with *oleum infirmorum*, the oil that has been blessed by the bishop at the conclusion of the Eucharist on Maundy Thursday. Thus, they are to be prepared to go through the "way of all flesh," as the Old Testament phrase expressed it, to everlasting life. By this means, human infirmity, including human death, is—like human fecundity—not only to become an image of the Mystery, but also to be absorbed into it and to work towards its final fulfillment.

These two fundamental blessings, thus understood, furnish the

[2] Sometimes called the love instinct and the death instinct: but, strictly, this use of the word *instinct* is incorrect: man does not possess the tendency to respond to a particular stimulus with an unlearned technique to satisfy a particular need.

[3] John, 11:4. Note that the literal rendering of the Greek would not be "sickness," but "weakness" or "infirmity."

cue to all those other blessings given in what we now call the sacramentals, and which were regarded by the ancient Church as a fringe of the sacramental order itself. All such blessings have always been connected with the Mass; in ancient times they were for the most part actually carried out at that point in the Mass where the Oil of the Sick is still blessed today—and that is, at the end of the canon, before the words *per quem haec omnia,* which express exactly the universal blessing that is included in the Eucharist of the Cross.

But even when blessings are not so directly grafted on the Eucharist itself, the Thanksgiving par excellence, it is remarkable how all the great blessings of people or things in the Church's liturgy take on a Eucharistic pattern. The central blessing of the ceremony of Ordination, the blessing of the Baptismal water, the blessing of the Chrism for Confirmation, all show this typical pattern. Each of these blessings is introduced by the same dialogue as that which leads us to the Eucharist itself. And each is developed in the same exultant manner in a *Praefatio.* In the Blessing of the Palms on Palm Sunday we even find the Sanctus introduced as it is in the *Anaphora* or Eucharistic canon. But rather more interesting is the fact that in most of the other and more ancient blessings which have been retained in the Roman rite, we find not only the style, but also the continuous line of development of the traditional Eucharist, and we find this continuous line perhaps more carefully kept in these blessings than it now is in the Mass itself.

In addition to those blessings which are directly concerned with the sacraments themselves and those to which we have already alluded, we must mention, among the consecratory *Praefationes* retained in the *Pontificale Romanum,* those for the consecration of virgins, for the coronation of a Christian king, and for the dedication of a Christian temple.

The whole rite of the *Consecratio virginum* is a fairly recent composition, not without poetic qualities, but with perhaps too much of that medieval sentimentality in its very poetry which is foreign to the sober mind of Christian antiquity. But the *Praefatio* itself is very ancient; we even find in it some of the most characteristic phrases of the liturgy of Hippolytus. This Preface describes the way of life which is other and better than human marriage, the way in which the mystery of unity between Christ and His Church is presented less visibly, but may be achieved more effectively, and describes it in terms which perfectly illustrate the meaning of the ascetical and contemplative life in Christianity.

Again, the consecratory Preface for the coronation of a king expresses the Christian meaning of the active life in relation to the Mystery. Here we can see how the whole active life of man is to be christianized through an unceasing struggle with the powers of evil and through the ever-renewed witness which can be given through the passing kingdoms of this world to the enduring kingship of Christ.

As an example of the blessing of things rather than persons, the consecration of a church is outstanding in the fullness of its implications. In the Preface of this consecration, all the eschatological implications of the Mystery open out. We are given a vision of how this world is to be re-conquered by the Cross and to be made once more the house of God and the gate of heaven through the building up of the Church on earth. For the Church is to be the temple of God where He is pleased to dwell for all eternity, since the Church is the very Body of His Son. Moreover, in this Preface we see also how in the Church on earth we are already taking part in the perpetual eucharist, the perpetual thanksgiving of the angelic choirs, and in the eternal worship of the Father by His Incarnate Son.

We could continue to look at the most innumerable ways in which the Church, by the power of the Mystery itself, adapts all creation to her own growth and fulfillment. But we have said enough to outline the essentials of this process, and it will be more fruitful to answer, in the light of what has just been said, a final and most important question which is raised by the continual presence of the Mystery in the sacramental order, a presence whose focus is the Eucharist properly so called. How are we finally to think of this presence itself, of this presence of the Cross of Christ in particular? How is it possible for an action of the past already accomplished once and for all, to be perpetually re-enacted, and to be re-enacted in such a way as to be permanently actual with all its essential reality, though without any of its original circumstances and visible characteristics? No question, certainly, goes more deeply than does this one into the essence of the sacramental Mystery, and none is more difficult to answer. But some glimpse of the solution at least may perhaps be gained from what has been said earlier, and, in particular, from what we have just seen of the way in which the Mystery is to be applied to the whole life of man through the sacramental order.

For we can now see from our previous study that there are, in the final analysis, not one but two fundamental actualities of the Mystery, and that both are fully real, historical facts, each with its own set of concrete circumstances. The first actuality is what we might call the actuality of the Mystery seen in its source, in Christ as head of the Church. Here the actuality of the Mystery is that of the Cross of Christ, which was accomplished once and for all and can never be begun again, since it has already brought Him to His final glorification, to the state in which He is to remain forever. The second actuality is what we might call the actuality of the Mystery seen in its purpose, that is, in the whole body of Christ. Here the actuality of the Mystery is that of the Cross that the Church is to bear in the whole life of each and all of her members, until that Cross brings them all together "to the mature measure of the fullness of Christ."[4] And we can say that it is then that both actualities will be made one, for Christ Himself will be made all in all.

But precisely in order to attain that final end which is the consummation of all things in God, our own endeavors here and now must be caused to participate in what Christ did once and for all. Or, to put it more exactly, the "actuality" of what we do here and now must be derived from the actuality of what Christ did once and for all.

Here precisely is the place of the sacramental aspect of the Mystery. We can say that the Mystery is present in its fullness in the sacramental order in so far as, through the sacraments, what Christ did comes into contact with what we are, not only to enable us to do something similar to what He did, nor, to speak exactly, to give us by means of what He did the supernatural power to do the same thing again, but rather, in everything that we must do, to enable us truly to participate in that which He did once and for all.

For this reason, the way in which the Cross is present *in mysterio* is in no respect similar to that of a mere natural presence. If it were, it could not serve its purpose. It would constitute a third actuality of the Cross, in the fullest sense both historical and local, which would be neither the Cross *of Christ,* nor *our own* cross; whereas what is required is some way of being present which will enable the Cross *of Christ* to be efficacious in informing *our own* lives. The basic reality and efficacy of the Cross as Our Lord endured it in His temporal life on earth and as it enabled Him to pass to His life of ever-

4 Eph. IV, 13.

lasting glory—this basic reality and efficacy must be so made present as to inform our temporal lives and incorporate them into itself, thus bringing them to a similarly glorious end.

This is what is effected by way of the sacraments. They are such a *way* indeed, and nothing else. They bring the most wonderful reality to us, and they bring us to that reality. But theirs is not a static reality which could be dealt with, even abstractly, as something in itself, that could be regarded apart from Christ, the Head, and His body, the Church, and their unity in one flesh. Herein lies the reason why the sacramental order, even though its beauty outshines anything else in our present intermediate state of being, is to cease to exist when the reality which it heralds has been attained in its fullness. For the ultimate reality to which the sacramental order is leading us finally is the reality of the mystical but perfectly real identifying of us with Christ, of our lives with His life. And when that blessed reality is attained, there will be no room for sacraments any more.

The possibility of the sacramental order, and of the strangely mysterious transient reality which is its characteristic, depends ultimately on the absolutely unique relationship between Christ and the Church, between the Second Adam and the new humanity to be reborn in Him. Christ is, in some way, one individual member of the human race, and His earthly life is one among the innumerable individual human lives which make up the whole of human history. But to consider Him under this aspect only is to leave out precisely what distinguishes Christ from all other human individuals, what makes Him the Head of all mankind, and what makes what He once did the inexhaustible source of what now has to be accomplished by all men.

But even to say this much is still not to say enough. Christ is not only the Head; He is, in a certain sense, also the whole. As He Himself says in St. John's Gospel, He is the whole Vine of which, in which, we are to be the branches, not adding anything of our own to the Vine, but rather finding our own life only in living in It. What He did is to be the source of what we are to do; but more than this, what we are to do and the best that we can do is to allow Christ to pervade our lives so thoroughly that we do not live any more but He lives His own life in us. Everything that we can do does not add one single merit to the merits acquired by Christ's Cross, but has value only in so far as it identifies us so completely with the Crucified as to make His own merits ours.

This identification could not be accomplished so long as Christ led a mortal life like our own. But now that by means of His Passion He has attained to His Resurrection and lasting state of glory, now that He is the "Christ-Pneuma" (to use once more a phrase of St. Paul which was dear to Dom Casel), because He has been made life-giving Spirit, His Spirit can now dwell in us, can witness effectively in us to the fact that we are all children of God in the only Son, can imprint in us all the unique Image, the perfect *eikon* of the Father which Christ is Himself. This is what is now in the making, being brought about by the sacramental order, and it will appear as fully made only when, through Christ, God will at last be all in all.

But the sacramental order accomplishes this purpose only by truly fostering our own activity. For we can say that it is, finally, in that exercise of the "royal priesthood" which makes the whole body of the Church a "chosen generation" and a "holy nation" that the actuality of the Mystery is the actuality of the meeting of God's creative action with our created action: the meeting of the eternal life of God in the freedom of His boundless love with our mortal life, in order to make our life immortal in that same love which He sheds forth in our hearts.

From all that we have been saying, one conclusion must be clearly drawn. The multiform blessing that is poured on all human life, and through it on all the human world, is, to speak more exactly, a consecration, and a consecration by the imposition on everything of the sign of the Cross.

As we have already said, all the Jewish blessings were consecrations through thanksgiving, in so far as, by man's acknowledgment and acceptance of the creative Word of God, they restored things spoiled by human sin to their original conformity to that creative Word. And this can be said even more truly of Christian blessings. The blessing of the Christian Eucharist makes bread and wine, created things which are made to nourish human life, into the Body and Blood of Christ on which we feed to become His Mystical Body. And it can be said that, along the same lines, the blessings which are included in all the sacraments as being derived from that basic thanksgiving, the Eucharist, are to consecrate us, in everything that we are and everything that we do, as members of that same Body. And when the blessings are not directly those of people but of things, they are for the purpose of adapting these things to the life of the Mystical Body, so that Christ will be all in all.

On the other hand, this universal process which the Apocalypse calls "the marriage of the Lamb" (for any consecration of any creature to God is only carried out through that marvellous union of the Church with Christ),—this process cannot be accomplished in any other way than by His Cross. It is eminently true of Baptism, that in it we are united with Christ by being united to His death; and it is true also of the whole process of the assimilation of all things to Christ, and of all the aspects of this process as they are carried out by the sacraments or by sacramentals. If the divine Word is compared to a sword and the divine love to a burning fire, it is for the reason that nothing of this world, tainted by sin, can now be made holy except through some immolation. As we said before, nothing is in the city of God which has not come from the city of this world. But nothing can go to the city of God without leaving the city of this world; and such a transition always means, in some way or other, to die. The city of this world cannot simply become the city of God. All that it can do is to be broken to pieces in order to provide the city of God with its building-stones,—and this means death for the city of this world also. God blesses man and his efforts only by conforming him to His Son, and his efforts to His Son's Cross.

But this does not mean that God's blessing itself confers death, nor does it mean that death itself can confer this blessing.

On the first point,—it is one of the most striking features of the ancient Roman liturgy that it always insists on the unavoidable death which is implied in man's very life since the fall; but it only mentions this death in order to add immediately that what was the curse of man has now, by the Cross of Christ, been made his blessing, not only in Christ Himself personally, but in all those who follow Him. Thus we read in a Preface from the Leonine Sacramentary for the feast of a martyr:

> Vere dignum et justum est nos tibi semper et ubique gratias agere . . . per Christum Dominum nostrum: qui non solum debitum mortis antiquae quo idem non tenebatur exsolvens pro debitoribus repensavit sed martyribus suis contulit ut quod humana substantia contra voluntatem sui creatoris agendo contraxerat et praefixa lege fuerat solutura, dum pro testimonio creatoris sponte susciperent, fieret eis de reatu justitia et poena transiret ad gloriam . . .

"It is truly right and just that we should always and everywhere give thanks to Thee . . . through Christ our Lord, Who not only paid the ancient debt of death which He Himself did not owe for those who did owe it; but also granted to His martyrs that this debt, which human nature had contracted by acting against the will of its Creator and which was to be paid for according to preordained law, would, as they willingly accepted it on the testimony of the Creator, free them from guilt and enable them to go from suffering to glory."

In other words, the blessing does not make the Cross; it does not of itself produce death. Death is the product of human life itself in its present state. But what Christ brings to our lives, as to His own, is the power to transform what was a necessary condemnation into a free offering.

This truth also implies the second point we made above, that not only is it not the blessing which brings death, but that death does not of itself bring this blessing. Of itself, even if a man were ready to impose it on himself, death would not be a sacrifice but only a sterile suicide. The only death which is sacrificial, which is consecrative, is the death of Christ. Therefore, the natural process which now brings us to death can accomplish consecration to God in us as in Christ only when it is taken up into Christ. The Cross is our salvation, not because it is a cross, but only because, and insofar as, it is the Cross of Christ, the voluntary death of the living God by which He manifests His divine and creative love.

And this truth may, perhaps, help to solve a problem that touches the very essence of sacrifice. What is it that makes a sacrifice? Is it the offering, or is it the immolation? Is it the gift, or is it the death or destruction of what is given? If the question is put in this form, it cannot be answered, because such a formulation does not include a third and most important term, that is, God's own intervention. And when this third term is neglected, we also neglect the element that makes an immolation worthy of the name; that is to say, immolation is not any kind of death, but only a death which has as one of its essential qualities the divine intervention.

We can say, therefore, that the offering,—the offering of ourselves and of what pertains to us,—is certainly the nucleus of our sacrifice, as it is to be understood from the New Testament. Here, certainly, is the "spiritual oblation," the "reasonable sacrifice," of which the Apostle speaks. But this offering cannot be effectively carried out by our own effort, but only by God's intervention in Christ. The offering of the "royal priesthood," which is ourselves, can only be accomplished by Him Who is the unique King-priest, after the order of Melchise-dech. Moreover, it is only by His Cross that Christ fulfills His obla-tion and ours also. But His Cross is always the immolation which con-secrates, not because it is human death, but because it is human death taken up into Life itself. This is to say that death is essential to the blessing, but only as it is the life-giving death of Christ. And this truth brings us to a last and most important consideration concerning the sacramental order.

As we have already said, to understand rightly the actuality of the Mystery in the sacramental world, we must look at it as being the perpetual transition from the past but now once for all achieved actu-ality of our Lord's life-giving Passion, to the always actual Passion of His Body, the Church, which will be completed in glory only at the end of time. We have already said also that both actualities of the Mystery are finally to coincide. Then there will be no further need of sacraments, since the "mature measure of the fullness of Christ," will have been attained: the "Christ-Pneuma" will be everywhere present in His risen Mystical Body, the all in all. What we have just been saying should now help us to understand how the aspect of im-molation which is inherent in the blessing imparted by the sacraments to man and to the world is itself, therefore, linked to their own tran-sient aspect: it is the aspect of the sacrifice seen as something in the making. But through that very "making," the sacramental sacrifice which springs from the Eucharist and pervades, through the sacra-ments and sacramentals, the whole life and world of man, is already tending to the fullness of life in the resurrection.

We said above that the sacraments were never to be considered as some static kind of being, but rather as a way from Christ to us, a communication of what He did and is, to what we do and are. But now we must say much more: the sacraments are a way from what Christ has already become in the glory of His Resurrection to what we are to become in the same glory. The actuality of the sacramen-tal order, finally, cannot be measured by the merely transient actuality of this present world where we live and strive. Nor, in spite of the permanent achievement of what Christ did once and for all in His earthly life, is it this past actuality which gives us the final key to the actuality of the sacramental order. Only the eschatological actuality of the Mystery in its final development; only the fullness of Christ when His whole Mystical Body is complete, when the whole city of

God has been offered to the Father, when, in its final resurrection, God will be all in all; only this ultimate actuality of the Mystery can be what permanently sustains the actuality of the Mystery in the sacramental order. Through the sacramental order, we can say that the fullness of the Mystery attracts us to itself.

But we may object: how can a reality which is still in the future foster the actuality of what we are to do here and now? Does not the future seem even less capable than the past of providing any actuality for the present?

The answer is: what is future for us is not in this case future in itself. Let us repeat once more: in the risen Christ, in the "Christ-Pneuma," the fullness of our eschatological expectation is already realized: in Him is realized both the fullness of God and the fullness of His plan concerning creation. What we are expecting is only what He already is.

When we all come to His fullness, we shall not add anything to it, but shall find ourselves in it. Christ is the Vine, we are the branches. He *is* the Vine, the whole Vine: He does not need to become it. But *we* are to become the branches more fully and perfectly than we are now. St. Augustine described Communion to communicants as "the Mystery of ourselves," meaning that they were to discover their true selves in Christ.

Let us therefore keep in mind everything that we have been observing so far, in order that we may understand the full meaning of this last explanation, and say in conclusion that the actuality of the Mystery is simply the actuality of the risen Christ. As He stands in the glory of His resurrection, like the Lamb slain but glorious, He has found the way to hold for us and to communicate to us all the healing power and the life-giving reality of His Cross. More than this, in this glory of His resurrection, He already has and is everything which we are to have and to be in Him at the end of time. And it is this which He is already giving to us here and now in the sacramental order, by means of that very way of the Cross by which His loving obedience purchased all this glory for us, and by which our obedient faith is now to acquire it. In this last and radiant view of the Mystery, we must then hold to the best definition of it ever given by St. Paul himself: the Mystery is "Christ in you, the hope of glory."

CHAPTER FOURTEEN

The Mystery of the Liturgical Year:
The Easter Liturgy

LET US keep in mind the conclusion arrived at in the previous chapter: the Mystery brings us, ourselves, to the state in which Christ is now, by the way which He himself took to reach this state; and the Mystery is able to do this by reason of the fact that He Himself, in His victory which He has already won, can make us fight His own struggle,—for He Himself now lives in us more than we ourselves. Through His Cross, through His own Cross which we are to carry after Him because He will be carrying it Himself in us, we go to His glory. This is the main point that we are now to develop in more detail, by a consideration of the liturgical year, the Christian festivals.

What is their true meaning? More deeply, what actually are they? Is the liturgical year to be understood merely as a kind of high evangelical pedagogy? Is it merely a psychological device invented to make us meditate in turn on all the phases, all the events in the life and death of our Lord? Is it merely a system of readings, songs and prayers so arranged as to cause us to go more deeply each year into the meaning of the Word of God and enable us to understand it more fully? Nobody will, of course, deny that the liturgical year is all this; but is it nothing more?

Or can we suppose that the facts which the liturgy is commemorating from one end of the year to the other are in some way effectively revived here and now? The events which we bewail on Good Friday, exult in on Easter, glory in on Ascension Day and Pentecost,—are they happening again? The question is a natural one, for if the events

185

we commemorate have no special actuality on the day when they are commemorated, why should the Church try to nurture special feelings in us on each of these days? Why should she put us in some particular disposition of mind for one of these feasts rather than at some other time? If there is no actuality to the series of feasts such as we are supposing, what have we to say to those people who meditate on the Blessed Trinity at Christmas, on the Sacred Heart at Easter, or on the Nativity at Pentecost with no reference to the Feast, simply because the meditation book which they are using happens to have brought them to these topics on these particular days? Were not the Puritans really right after all when they rejected the whole liturgical year as being a baseless superstition?

But if we are not prepared to imitate the Puritans, or even the good people who pursue their private course of personal meditations regardless of whether it is Easter or Christmas, what shall we say about the liturgical year? What should we think? How are we to understand and explain the yearly bringing back to life of events which were accomplished in the past once and for all? In particular, how can we understand this revival of the Passion, which—far from needing to happen again and again in a cyclical recurrence of death and rebirth as did the *dromenon* of the pagan mysteries—was endured by our Lord precisely to free us from our slavery to what St. Paul calls *ta stoicheia tou kosmou* (τὰ στοιχεῖα τοῦ κόσμου) that is, the "elements" of this world as it now is, shut up in itself and closed off from the ever new freedom of divine love?[1] We have, it is true, already examined the way by which (through the Mass and the whole sacramental order which springs from it) we can all, in the one Christ, participate in the Mystery without its having to happen again. But besides the Mass itself and the Sacraments as connected with it, must we think that there is another way in which the Mystery is brought to life annually and in such a manner as again to go through all its historical phases?

Here exactly is the problem. How can it be solved? First of all, we can be quite certain that the idea of the reality, the always actual reality of what is celebrated in the liturgical festivals, is an idea as old in Christianity as are the festivals themselves. To be convinced of this fact, we need only to read once more the homilies of St. Gregory Nazianzen or of St. Leo the Great. On every page, these remind us

[1] Gal. 4: 3-11.

of the fact that in the liturgical year we are not only making a commemoration of the past but also actually living again the realities on
which we are meditating with the Church.

For example, in his 38th Oration, *In Theophania* (which he probably gave on the 25th of December, 379, to introduce the Christmas
festival in his church at Constantinople), St. Gregory Nazianzen
says: "Christ is born; give Him glory! Christ is coming from heaven;
go to meet Him! While He is on earth, ascend up to heaven. . . .
Darkness once more is dispelled; light dawns again. Once more
Egypt is afflicted by darkness while Israel again is illuminated by the
pillar of light. Let the people sitting in the darkness of error contemplate the great light of wisdom and knowledge. The old things
are no more; behold, everything is made new!"[2]

But St. Leo is still more impressive, for he does not use any rhet-
orical flourishes and we can clearly see that he weighs every word
that he uses. So in his first sermon for the Nativity (Sermon XXV, 1)
we find him saying: "Non solum in memoriam, sed in conspectum
quodammodo redit Angeli Gabrielis cum Maria stupente colloquium,
et conceptio de Spiritu Sancto tam mire promissa quam credita."
"The awe-inspiring conversation of the angel Gabriel with Mary, as
marvellously promised as it was believed, is given back not only to our
memory, but in some way also to our sight." And in his ninth sermon
on the same subject, St. Leo repeats (Sermon XXVIII, 2): "Licet
dispensatio actionum corporalium sicut aeterno consilio fuerat prae-
ordinata transierit . . . indesinenter tamen ipsum partum salutiferae
virginis adoramus." "Even though the succession of physical actions
is now past, as it was preordained in the eternal design . . . nevertheless we unceasingly adore that Birth from the Virgin who brought
forth our salvation."

Even more interesting than these are the statements of St. Leo in
his sixth and seventh sermons for the Epiphany: "Dies dilectissimi
quo primum gentibus Salvator mundi Christus apparuit sacro nobis
honore venerandus est et illa hodie cordibus nostris concipienda sunt
gaudia. . . . Neque enim ita ille emensus est dies ut virtus operis quae
tunc est revelata transierit . . ." "That day, beloved children, on
which Christ, the Savior of the world, for the first time appeared to
the Gentiles, is to be venerated with a most holy honor by us also. . . .
For that day is not past in such a way that the power of the work

[2] P. G. vol, 36, col. 312.

which was then revealed should be past as well."[3] And the next sermon makes some remarkable clarifications of the same idea: "Memoria rerum ab humani generis Salvatore gestarum magnam nobis dilectissimi confert utilitatem, si quae veneramur credita suscipiamus imitanda. In dispensationibus enim sacramentorum Christi et virtutes sunt gratiae et incitamenta doctrinae, ut quem confitemus fidei spiritu, operum quoque sequamur exemplo." "The remembrance of the things done by the Savior of mankind, dearly beloved children, is most useful to us, if these things we honor by believing, we take upon ourselves by imitating. For in the dispensation of Christ's mysteries there is at once the power of grace and the encouragement of teaching, so that He whom we confess in the spirit of faith, we may follow in the example of our work."[4]

To give these statements their full meaning, we must first of all go back to the chief points that have been made concerning the Mystery, together with the clarifications of them that we have been making in the last few chapters. Under one aspect, certainly, the Mystery is a historical fact, or rather a historical process, which has been accomplished once and for all and never can be begun again; and the center and summit of this process is the Cross. But this process has brought into existence for mankind and for the whole world, a reality which is to fill all time, for this process tends to make God all in all. To speak more precisely, the Cross of Christ, together with His entire historical life which ever tended towards the Cross, has brought forth the enduring fruit of Christ's resurrection and glorification. And in this state, the Lord has been made, as St. Paul says, "life-giving Spirit." That is to say, Christ is now the Second Adam, the heavenly Man, the ultimate Man, in whom all men are to die in order to live again in His own divine life. Therefore, through the power of His Cross, now triumphant because of His resurrection, all men are to undergo a cross which will not be some other cross, but rather their participation in His, so that they may become partakers also of His own resurrection.

This Mystery is what the Church proclaims; this it is that by faith now makes her life; and it is the hope of this final glory that is already made actual in *agape,* divine love. We can say that the Church proclaims this Mystery through the fact that she lives it; we can say with equal truth that she lives it because she possesses in the

[3] Sermon XXXV, 1.
[4] Sermon XXXVI, 1.

apostolate the effective power of proclaiming it. Is it not in the celebration of the Eucharist that the Church shows forth the Lord's death until He comes? But also is not the Word which the Church proclaims in heralding the Mystery the Word of the new creation: the word which is itself divine, and which is proclaimed by the Church with divine authority, because of the power given to the apostolate? Therefore, in the Church here and now, as in the beginning of the world, God speaks, and His Word is accomplished.

On these truths, of course, depends all the meaning and reality of the liturgical year. For the liturgical year, seen as a whole, is the great and permanent proclamation by the Church of the Word with which she has been entrusted. In the celebration of the liturgical year, therefore, the Mystery is proclaimed, communicated and participated in. Since the liturgy is, according to the fine phrase of Pius XI, "the principal organ of the ordinary magisterium of the Church," and as the liturgy is all set out within the framework of the liturgical year, this framework contains not only an expression of the Mystery but also the reality of the Mystery, working by faith through charity and tending toward its final revelation. For the Word of the Mystery cannot be so solemnly proclaimed by the Church without creating thereby what it proclaims.

But the real problem arises with the further question: how are we to understand in more detail the appropriation of different elements and phases of the Mystery to the different festivals and seasons of the liturgical year? Does the development of the Mystery adapt itself somehow to the development of the liturgical year? And if so, how, then, are we to understand this adaptation?

Before we attempt to proceed further, we must first bring out once more, from what has been said already, the unbreakable unity of the Mystery. It is true that certain of the Fathers, if not St. Paul himself, were inclined to speak of distinct "mysteries" under the one "Mystery." St. Gregory Nazianzen, for instance, says in a famous sentence: "How many celebrations (of liturgical feasts) for each and every one of the mysteries of Christ."[5] But the Fathers are always careful not only to place all these mysteries in the "mystery," but also never to isolate the actuality of one mystery from the actuality of the whole. (Dom Casel also insisted, at all times and rightly, on this

[5] Orat. 38, P. G. vol. 36, col 329 c.

point). Let us always remember that, to the mind of St. Paul, all distinct mysteries were fused into the one single Mystery. That Mystery itself included a very wide and comprehensive process. But in this process, no single phase could be isolated, no phase had any significance, let alone any possible actuality, apart from the whole. No one phase, therefore, could have a value by itself, nor be partaken of by itself. For to partake of the Mystery is to partake of Christ,—of Christ Who is the same yesterday, today and tomorrow; of Christ Who will re-enact in us everything that has been achieved in Himself, through His own action accomplished once for all. Even the Action *par excellence* which was the climax of His earthly life, that is, His Cross and with it the fulfillment of the Mystery, cannot be separated from the whole Mystery; it can only be distinguished, within the unity of the Mystery, as that to which everything tended which happened before, and from which everything proceeds which is to happen hereafter. Much less, then, could any other phase be isolated from the one Whole.

This truth, we must insist once more, was one about which the mind of Christian antiquity never hesitated even for a moment. The Paschal celebration, therefore, from Lent to Pentecost, involved one single vision of the complete Mystery, actualized for us in and through the risen Christ, the *Christos-Pneuma*. We learn, for example, from the *Peregrinatio Aetheriae* that on Easter Sunday itself the *whole Passion* was read on the Mount of Olives; and yet in Jerusalem, if anywhere, there could have been a strong temptation to try to reduce the Mystery to the historical development of the earthly life of Jesus, and so to isolate successive episodes in that development!

But from this example we can see that the early Christians did not understand the problem in the same way as we do. For them the actuality of the Mystery did not depend, as it seems to for us, so much on the possibility of bringing into some kind of present existence one of the phases of the earthly life of Jesus. As they saw it, the actuality of the Mystery was always our actual participation in the one and complete action already accomplished by Jesus, made present by our participation in His risen life, for the purpose of bringing to fruition in us all the virtualities of the final and perfect Kingdom of God.

But it cannot be denied,—and it could only have been by that false archeologism which we have always deplored, as does the Encyclical

Mediator Dei—that the Church, first in Jerusalem and then else-where, accepted a progressive extension of the celebration of the Mystery and a correlative specialization of the feasts and seasons. This tendency began with the perfectly natural desire to have a sort of concrete, and as it were factual, reproduction of the major events of Our Lord's life at the very places where these events happened; and this tendency led to distinct celebrations of the Lord's Supper, of His Death, and of His Resurrection. It is remarkable nevertheless that even today the liturgy of the Lord's Supper is suffused with the proclamation of His final glory; the worship of the Cross on Good Friday resounds with shouts of victory; and, on Easter Sunday, the exultation in the Resurrection expresses itself in the words: "Mors et vita duello conflixere mirando," "Death and life fought in a marvel-lous struggle"; while the Paschal season then just beginning, celebrates the Paschal meal with the *Ad regias Agni dapes.*

Later on, though quite soon after the establishment of the differ-ent celebrations of Holy Week and Easter Week, the Feasts of the Ascension and Pentecost began to assume a particular significance. And, at about the same time, another focus of the liturgical year appeared in the Christmas-Epiphany celebration. None the less, every Eucharist always proclaims the whole Mystery, always cele-brates the Cross and the eternal kingdom to which the Church is journeying by means of the Cross; so that the Eastern liturgy con-siders Christmas as a second Easter festival.

How, then, are we to interpret this development, the complexity of which is quite apparent even from what little we have said? How, more precisely, are we to understand such startling statements of the liturgy as those for Epiphany; "Hodie coelesti Sponso juncta est Ecclesia: quoniam in Jordane lavit Christus ejus crimina: currunt cum muneribus Magi ad regales nuptias, et ex aqua facto vino lae-tantur convivae, alleluia!" "Today has the Church been united with her heavenly Bridegroom: for in the Jordan Christ washed her from her sins; the Wise Men run with gifts to the royal marriage-feast; and, the guests rejoice in the water changed to wine, alleluia"—Or how are we to sing on Easter Day: "Haec dies quam fecit Dominus, ex-sultemus et laetemur in ea: This is the day that the Lord has made, let us be glad in it and rejoice?"

To answer these questions, we might first recall the fact that the wholeness of the Mystery does not imply any lack of a well-defined structure, a structure which we do well to consider again here. In God's design, the Mystery is characterized by an unbreakable unity; but, on the plane of its accomplishment in history, we need to recognize in it an entire and complex process, and even to distinguish two processes,—though the one in some way not only produces but includes the other. The first of these two processes is the "passage," the *transitus* of Christ through death to life. The second is our own *transitus,* our own "passage," the "passage" of the Church through death to life. These two "passages," these two "Passovers" are, however, only one, for the second is fully pre-contained in the first. The always-actual link between the two is the risen Christ, the Lord Who has been made life-giving Spirit, the heavenly Adam who communicates His radiant image to us who had first received the disfigured image of the first Adam. And the goal of the second "Passover" is that we should reach the goal of the first, that we should "all attain to the unity of the faith and of the knowledge of the Son of God, to the perfect Man, (εἰς ἄνδρα τέλειον) to the mature measure of the fullness of Christ."[6]

If what we have just said is true, it must also be said that there exists here and now a process of death and resurrection to which we are to adapt ourselves, a process which we must make our own. This process reproduces that of the historical life of our Lord. As St. Peter says in his Epistle, "Unto this, indeed, (to do right and yet suffer), you have been called . . . because Christ also has suffered for you, leaving you an example that you may follow in his steps."[7] But we can only follow these steps because He Himself, in His glorified manhood, is daily giving us His graces. These graces were acquired by His passion that was accomplished once for all; and they are given to us in such a way as to make of our own passion, which is leading us to glory, in a very real sense the "filling up in our flesh of what is lacking of the sufferings of Christ, for His body, which is the Church."[8] It is in this sense, then, that the Church can revive one by one the phases of the earthly life of her Head. Our Lord does not need to live on earth again and to die again,—this has been done once and for all. But the Church, His Body, must progressively, in all her members, pass through everything that He did. She can do so only through the permanent virtue of that "passage" as He Himself endured it. And

[6] Eph. IV, 13.
[7] 1 Peter II, 20-21.
[8] cf. Col. I, 24.

its virtue is hers by reason of the union which is always hers with Him Who now presents to the Father in heaven the sacrifice He accomplished in the days of His earthly life, while the Church herself presents the same sacrifice here on earth in the Eucharist.

Keeping this in mind, we can see precisely wherein lies not only the difference between the Eucharist itself and the Christian feasts, but also the connection between them. In the Feasts, as in everything else in the Church, it is the Eucharist which makes actual the presence of the Mystery. But the celebration, in connection with the Eucharist, of the various Feasts, brings about a development of the Mystery in us, in all the details of the process through which it developed for Christ in the past.

But here we face a final question, the answer to which will serve to bring out more exactly both the difference between the Eucharist and the liturgical year, and the relationship of analogy that exists between them. How can the Mystery which is accomplished in us in its fullness in every celebration of the Eucharist, also be set forth in the sequence of its historical process throughout the liturgical year—in the course of which the Eucharist is renewed daily—and be displayed over again every year?

The answer to this question requires that we consider the exact meaning which time has for Christianity. More exactly, what is the relationship between that cyclical time in which nature operates and causes man to operate, and that irreversible historic time in which God has intervened once for all and brought about a decisive change in man and in the whole human world?

If we consider the various ways in which we have to meet with the Mystery in our own lives, we can say that we first meet with its fullness once and for all in the process of Baptismal initiation; and, secondly, that we meet it again (or, to speak more exactly, the whole Church and every one of us in her meets it again) every day in the Mass; while, thirdly, during each of the years which have already passed, and during those that are still to come between the day of Christ's victory on the Cross and His final victory on the last day, the Church, and ourselves in her, must go through one and all the phases of the Mystery as they were once undergone by Christ, and as we now are to undergo them in our turn, in order to be wholly His. How, then, are we to think of the relationship between these three ways of meeting with the Mystery? How and why are we to meet the Mystery in these three different ways, and not simply in one single way?

The necessity for these three different ways of meeting the Mystery is a consequence of the very nature of time. Our created nature is so bound up with this created time in which all living beings live that our being cannot be taken up into the divine unless the time which is connatural to us is also in some way taken up. And, we might add, the natural rhythms of time, the days and months and years in which life develops, are not merely some external frame for time, but are of its very essence.

Thus, every man—every living creature on earth—is brought into existence by a process which is accomplished at birth once and for all, and can never be repeated. And, we might say, this process of human birth is itself a kind of death, since it involves the end of one mode of living and the beginning of a higher mode, the passage from one to the other being fraught with a kind of agony, both for mother and child.

And our lives, which have begun with this kind of "death," are made up of days which all begin with the "birth" of waking and end with the "death" of sleep. (Note here, the importance of our "unconscious" which many modern psychologists attribute to this analogy between the process of birth and the daily process of sleeping and waking). Moreover, while our days all go through this same cycle, they are all organized in larger and similarly recurring cycles, of which the years are the most elementary form. More generally, each of us must go through the periods of childhood, youth, maturity, and in each of them in some way be born anew, develop the potentialities of that period to the full, and in some way "die" to the perfection achieved in one period in order to begin afresh to work for the perfection of the next period.

When God became man, then, so that man (as the Fathers say) could in some way become God, His decisive intervention was not designed to interfere with this natural process of human development in time, with all its inner complexity, but rather to assume it. An incarnation which had not been an incarnation into our time as well as into our flesh would not have been a true incarnation at all. For, as our brief survey of the cycles of human life shows, our human life is organically bound up with time, and, as we have just said, the natural rhythms of time are not a detail added on to time, but of its essence. Time is not an abstract frame, uniform in itself, neither is it independent of the beings who live immersed in its flow. Only the modern idea of an artificial universe made like our machines has caused us to be convinced of these two related errors. To dispel them, we need only to go back and look at the real universe of God's creation, and to live once more the full life that we share with all living creatures in it.

In order, therefore, to assume our life and by His intervention to transfigure both it and the world in which we live it, God causes us first to pass through a new birth which follows that sequence so characteristic of human birth itself, of a kind of death introducing us into a new mode of life. And thus, through this new birth of Baptism and Confirmation, the Mystery takes possession of us once and for all.

But, in the natural order, a human being, once born of and in the material universe, is not independent of it but must daily nourish his life with food taken, like his own body, from this material world. In the same way, the man re-born in Christ must return again and again to that Mystery in which he has been re-created once and for all, in order to be nourished by It as It comes to him under the appearance of daily food. Thus the Mass of each day makes every day we live in Christ a microcosm of our whole Christian life, just as the natural day is a microcosm of our whole natural life.

And, just as our natural life also grows by means of large cycles of time, made up of many days, so does our Christian life. The liturgy, then, takes the natural year, the cycle of human life which is in harmony with the rhythm of the cosmos, and presents the great phases of the Mystery which we are to undergo throughout the year's recurring days, while, in the celebration of the Eucharist, it transfigures each of these days.

But this is not all. We have still to note the link which is, perhaps, the most necessary one between natural time and our Christian lives. The unique event of birth marks the beginning of the interrelated cycles of days and years in human life. But those cycles lead progressively toward another unique event, the event of death. As it is given to man to be born only once, so—in spite of the appearance of simple recurrence of one day after another, one year after another, in his life —it is given him only once to die. The same also can be said of the supernatural life as it is incarnated in our human lives. Our daily participation in the Mystery and the annual re-living by us of all its phases are not simply to continue in unending cycles of time. They are bringing us toward our own natural death. Now, however, when we come to die, we shall have been made ready for death, not only by the natural rhythm of created and fallen human life, but also by the supernatural rhythms of supernatural life as these are grafted on our natural living. Therefore, death will then be changed for us, as it was changed for Christ. It will not be the mere necessity of nature leading us from the state of living of fallen man only to destruction: death for us will have become rather a free offering, leading, through a transfigured death, to everlasting life. Having taken part in the Mystery along the lines of our natural life, we shall transform our natural death (as we saw above when speaking of the Last Anointing) into the life-giving sacrifice of Christ. For the death for which we have been thus prepared will be a death assimilated to the Cross of Christ; that is to say, it will bring us to the risen Christ Who came to His glory by means of His Cross, to the Christ Who dies no more, for in Him death has been swallowed up in victory.

To draw such parallels and to make this kind of identification between natural and supernatural life might seem at first sight to risk blurring a most important distinction which we made earlier in our study. When we were comparing the pagan mysteries with the Christian Mystery, did we not stress the vast difference between their ever-recurring cycles of birth and death, and the victory of divine life over human death once and for all accomplished by Christ? But the conclusion which we have just arrived.at, far from blurring the all-important distinction between the recurrence of the pagan mysteries and the unique victory of Christ can help us to define this difference more precisely.

The divine intervention in history obviously did not suddenly put a .stop to its natural rhythms. If it had done so, it would have only suppressed human history, far from transforming it and bringing it to fulfillment. What the divine intervention does, therefore, is to open up, as it were, those closed cycles of time, which up to that moment had been only revolving on themselves. These cycles—to use the same image—are now in a process of development into a larger and larger spiral, and this process will reach its term at the moment when the spiral of human history loses itself, or, rather, finds its fulfillment in God's eternity. This moment will come for each of us at our own death, inasmuch as our death will consummate our identification with Christ on His Cross, achieved through the Mystery. And for the whole universe this moment will come at the last moment of history, when Christ will come again and perfect natural life in universal resurrection. In the light of all this, we can now go more deeply than before into the distinction between the pagan mysteries and the Christian Mystery. Truth to tell, the reality of the pagan mysteries was not even capable of binding man to the ever-recurring cycles of nature, as it boasted.

Let us note, first, that the taking up of men into these ever-recurring cycles of birth and death did not seem to the pagans of the mystery cults, as it does to us, a devilish slavery from which Christ has set us free. To them it seemed rather "a beautiful dream with which to enchant oneself," to use Plato's phrase. For it was the only way known to the pagans of fulfilling the hope for man's divinization, that is the way of identification with the cosmic gods who were the only gods they knew, the gods who are called by St. Paul "those poor elements of the world," as opposed to the very Lord of the world. But natural man was not, in fact, capable of such an assimilation to a perfectly uniform cycle, always turning around on itself again and again. This was only the impossible ideal of Greek wisdom, the ideal of the divinization of man through his identification with perfect limitation. The sad reality was, of course, that through the apparently invariable and recurrent cycles of natural time, man progressed toward decay and finally death. Nor could natural humanity succeed in breaking through the cycles of natural time, which for each man never tend to an infinitely expansive, but rather to an ever diminishing spiral, ending in the immobility of death. We can therefore say that God's intervention once for all in Christ has reversed this deadly curve of human life-times, transferring it from a spiral closing in upon itself to end in death into a spiral expanding to lose itself in life, in the fullness of life in God. A universe perfectly circling around and round is only a dream of idolatry. The true universe—which is always both naturally and supernaturally the universe of God—from the very impulse of its creation by Him tends to open itself out to God. Alas, from the impulse given by sin, it has tended to close in upon itself and move toward death. But now, in the Cross of Christ, through death itself, it once again opens to God and to the fullness of life in Him.

In the sacramental world, therefore, the liturgical year leads us progressively to a full assimilation to the power of Christ's death through all the elemental details of our temporal lives, and so enables us to exchange a life born only to die, for a death which will bring us to life. Throughout our lives, we are to adapt ourselves progressively to the Cross, so that when we ourselves come to die, it may mean death only to self, but life in Him Who is unbounded Love.

* * *

We HAVE only now to apply all this to the whole liturgical year, as it has been elaborated by the Church throughout the centuries. Let us begin, then, with the nucleus of the liturgical year: the Paschal Triduum, from Maundy Thursday to the Easter Vigil.

In her Eucharistic celebration of Maundy Thursday, the Church, through her own offering, joins in that free offering of Christ which was accomplished by that historic action through which He brought salvation to mankind. The Church thus takes us into her own fundamental consent to the fundamental decision which is the origin of our salvation. And in doing so, she causes us to accept, with the acceptance of Jesus Himself in Gethsemani, all the sufferings which are bound up with our salvation, for us as for Him. But she causes us also to hail by faith that unspeakable joy of the Resurrection, in consideration of which (according to one reading of the Epistle to the Hebrews) our Lord Himself accepted His Cross.

Then, on Good Friday, while we are contemplating the salvific paradox of the Cross, the Church causes us to realize what could not be discovered by the "powers" who crucified the Lord of glory,—that in His Cross is our glorification. Here coincide, in an ideal way, our concern with the death of Christ accepted in all its realism, and the acknowledgment, through faith developing its energies in love, of the divine glory which is included in that death.

And then, in the holy night, the Church introduces us to the eschatological celebration of the Mystery considered in its final fulfillment. In the risen Christ made life-giving Spirit, she feeds our hope with all the substance of anticipated actuality, actuality brought by love to meet the expectation of our faith. Therefore the Easter Season, which opens with the Christian Passover, closes with the celebration of the Ascension, in the surge of that faith imbued with love which meets beyond the veil of death Him Who has gone to prepare a place for us with His Father, and Who, exalted at the Father's right hand, attracts to Himself by His intercession all those who follow Him on the royal road of His Cross. Pentecost comes afterwards like the anticipated inauguration of our final entrance into the Kingdom: we receive the peace which is found through hope at the summit of its striving, a peace which is both painful and joyful, because it is found in what St. Paul calls the "pledge" or the "earnest" of the Spirit.

The fact that the Easter season originally was, and still essentially is, the season of Baptism, shows us how realistically the Church views our mystical conformation to the life of Christ through the liturgical year. Through the process of baptismal initiation, we are given that basic reproduction of the life of Christ in our own lives which is the germ of the whole process of our association to the Mystery. But, as it is essential to the fulfillment of that unique participation by each of us in the death and resurrection of Christ which is Baptism to renew itself and, as it were, perpetually to refresh itself by participation in the Eucharist, so the season of Lent, by leading us all to the Paschal communion, is the way by which we each, year after year, may renew and refresh our own initiation.

CHAPTER FIFTEEN

The Mystery in the Liturgical Year: The Advent Liturgy, Christmas and Epiphany

I T IS NOT difficult to see how the principles which we studied in the last chapter may be directly applied to the Easter cycle. But what about the more recent and secondary cycle of feasts centered on Christmas and Epiphany? How may we interpret this cycle? How, in particular, are we to understand its actuality? Is it possible that there is a kind of second focus in the accomplishment of the Mystery, more or less independent of the first—that the Nativity is, as it were, more or less independent of the Cross? And can we then partake of the Nativity of our Lord as we partake of His Cross and Resurrection?

At first sight, we might be tempted to think that this was true; we might easily believe that the homilies of the Fathers, like that famous homily by St. Gregory of Nazianzen for the feast of the Nativity which we have already quoted, point toward such an idea. Does he not even say, further on in the same homily: "Today's feast is that of the Theophany or the Nativity. It may be called by either name. For God has appeared to us through the Nativity . . . so that He Who first gave us life, now gives us blessed life; or, rather, after we had fallen from that blessed life through sin, He restores it to us by His Incarnation. This feast, then, is called Theophany because He appeared then, and Nativity because He was born then. This feast is ours. Today we celebrate the coming of God to us in order that we should come to Him, or, rather, in order that we should come back to Him; so that, putting off the old man, we should put on the new man; as we were dead in the old Adam, so let us live in Christ, being born with Him, crucified with Him, buried with Him, risen again with Him."

But if we look more closely at this beautiful homily, must we not be struck by the fact that, though St. Gregory begins by speaking of the Nativity in almost the same phrases as those which might be used to describe the presence of the Mystery in the feast of Easter itself, yet, as soon as he tries to make his thought more precise, he goes from the Nativity to the Cross, or, more generally speaking, to the *transitus,* the passage through death to eternal life? In the very opening words of this homily which we quoted in the last chapter, a most characteristic sentence shows that St. Gregory was very far from meaning to draw a parallel between the Nativity and the Cross as though we were to partake of both in the same way; he says, "Christ is coming from heaven. Go to meet Him! While He is on earth, may you ascend up to heaven." In other words, we can now begin to see why Eastern Christians call Christmas another Paschal Feast: not that there could be two different Paschal mysteries, but that the feast of the Nativity, rightly understood, brings us to the one Paschal Mystery, the coming of man through Christ's death to the life of God.

Such a view of the Christmas-Epiphany cycle is borne out by all the Scriptures and all Christian tradition. It is only through a *participation in the death and resurrection of Christ* that we are to be *born* again in Baptism to a new life, and by no means through some fancied participation in His human birth. Nothing could be more foreign to the whole teaching of St. Paul and St. John than such an idea of participation in Christ's birth. It is *on the Cross,* in the Blood and water flowing from His side, that the Church is *born* of Christ through the sacramental order, as Eve was born of Adam. This is the teaching of St. Augustine and of all the Fathers (and of the modern Encyclical *Mystici Corporis*). Neither the Bible nor the Fathers ever mention anything like a new birth of mankind which would be a participation in the birth of the Son of God in our own flesh. For there is no Incarnation redemptive as such, that is, considered apart from the redemption won on the Cross. The texts of St. John or the Fathers which people have sometimes tried to use to prove what we are rejecting, i.e., to try to oppose a redemption by the Incarnation to the redemption by the Cross, can be used in such a way only if they are completely misunderstood. To the mind of St. John, the earthly life of Christ had no meaning except to go forward to glory through the Cross, to reach the glory of the Ascension through the exaltation on the Cross. To the mind of the Fathers, the Incarnation can only be called redemptive in one very definite sense: in the sense that it was an incarnation in a flesh which must undergo death, so that the death of Adam should die in the death of Christ.

But is there not some tradition of medieval mysticism that would transfer what might be said of Christ's historic Nativity to the so-called "birth" of the Divine Word in our souls? It is certainly true that there is such a tradition, and that it can even to some extent appeal to the authority of Origen, who often goes from one birth to another. But this tradition is not in opposition to what we have just said. Whatever may be our opinion about the above-mentioned analogy between the Nativity of Christ and what should rather be called our own nativity to the Divine Life, such an analogy cannot imply a connection between the two kinds of "births," much less a participation. All tradition unanimously holds that our re-birth to heaven is not a participation in Christ's birth to this world, but in His death and resurrection. One of the Prefaces for Easter in the Gelasian Sacramentary speaks most decisively on this point: in this beautiful text we do find a comparison drawn between Christ's Birth from the Virgin and our own birth to everlasting life. But this new birth of ours is not ascribed to any separate Mystery of the Nativity, but to the Paschal Mystery itself: "Mary exulted with joy at the birth of her Child, so the Church exults with joy in the Mystery through which her children are born," that is, the Paschal Mystery. It is not the Nativity of Christ as such, therefore, which causes the Church to sing of our spiritual re-birth as her children, but rather the Cross and Resurrection to which the Nativity was the necessary pre-requisite.

This fact need not trouble us, nor make us feel in any way at a loss to find some actual meaning, some permanent reality in the celebration of Christmas. For, however startling it may seem to us, the fact is that the idea that the formal object of the celebration of the Christmas and Epiphany cycle is the temporal birth of our Lord, is a recent view. It is not borne out either by the history of the liturgy or by the liturgical texts even as they stand today. We can easily see that this new modern interpretation must have made some mistake when we observe what happens to the Advent liturgy as soon as we accept this interpretation. In its false light, we must candidly own, the whole Advent liturgy is meaningless. From beginning to end, the Advent liturgy prays for the coming of Christ, for the fulfillment of our hope. But if the coming we have in mind is that of Christ's Nativity, how can we still pray for it? What meaning can such a hope have, since its object has already been fully realized in the past?

As against such a chimera, we must then acknowledge that the Advent texts themselves, taken in their most obvious sense, express not an expectation of the Nativity which has already happened, but of the *Parousia* which is still to come. We find there, not the hope of what is now called the first coming of Christ (for how can we still hope for it?), but the hope of His final coming on the clouds of heaven.

> The Lord Who is come, * come, let us adore Him!
> The Lord now is near, * come, let us adore Him!
> Today you will know that Lord is to come, * and in the
>   morning you will see His glory.
> Tomorrow the iniquity of the earth will be blotted out, and
>   the Lord of the world will reign over us . . .
> Tomorrow will be for you Salvation, says the Lord of hosts . . .

What meaning can any of these texts have if we try to interpret them in any other way? More generally, what could be more artificial, more unhealthy than these modern commentaries on Advent which try to make us act as if we were the people for whom Christ was yet unborn? How can we seriously beg of God that the Savior should be born to us, now that we know that He was born some thousand years ago,—when, indeed, the fact that He was born then is the first basis of our faith?

What, then, are we to conclude? Certainly not that we cannot make our own the expressions of expectation of the Patriarchs and Prophets as they are given us all through the Advent liturgy. On the contrary, what we have just said should make us all readier to utter their words with our own lips. We can do this because the human birth of Christ was not, in and of itself, the object of their hope. What were they hoping for? For the advent of the Kingdom of God, for the visible destruction of the powers of evil, for the abolition of sin and death, for the final manifest appearance of God to His people: "Oh, that Thou wouldst rend the heavens and come down!" This hope, this very hope, is what we still are expecting. The "first coming" of our Lord, His Nativity, far from satisfying our expectation, has brought it to the highest pitch of intensity. For our hope has been fed with the Bread of heaven, the "viaticum" par excellence, which is the flesh of the Son of Man; but this bread has been given us only to bring us to the Kingdom of the Resurrection, where flesh itself will become transparent to the Spirit, and where it will no longer be under a veil that we shall meet the Master, but face to face. If our ideas of our participation in the Mystery are deprived of this eschatological dimension, they lose all significance, for our participation is nothing other than our going, our "passing" in Christ to the reality of the future Kingdom, of the Kingdom which is coming to us in the King of eternity.

That such is the meaning of Advent, and therefore its perpetual actuality, is borne out by the texts for the Christmas liturgy as well. For chiefly they sing of the "Theophany"—to use St. Gregory's phrase, —the divine appearance of the King of glory. "The King of peace has been glorified. . . . He Whom all the world desires to see . . ." "Know that the Kingdom of God is at hand: I tell you the truth, I will tarry no longer." What is announced in those Christmas antiphons if it is not the final Kingdom, the *Parousia,* the "Showing-forth" in glory of the King of eternity, Who, by His appearance alone, will cause all wars to cease?

When we consider it in this light, the celebration of Christmas and Epiphany (the two feasts are so closely connected as to form but one celebration) reveals a significance, the majestic grandeur of which has been often overlooked, but the actuality of which cannot be questioned. This celebration is that of eschatological expectation: of the hope, the ardent prayer, for the *Parousia.* "Come, Lord Jesus. Come quickly!" This is the last word in the celebration of the Mystery: it nourishes in us the divine discontent, the holy impatience, should we call it, which must remain in our hearts when we have celebrated the Mystery as we should. From this point of view, it is easy to understand how it was that the Christmas-Epiphany cycle was introduced into the liturgical year at the end of the fourth century, when the Church of Constantine had become well installed in this world and was in danger of losing the fervor of its hope for the world to come. The purpose of Advent, Christmas and Epiphany is ceaselessly to re-animate in us that hope, that expectation. But how can they do so if we reduce their significance to a sentimental commemoration of the childhood of Jesus, especially when in it we see only what touches our hearts about all childhood, transmuted only by some aura of divinity?

Is this to say that the commemoration of the Nativity is not rightly placed at Christmas time? To say so would be a foolish paradox; for we should rather say that the Nativity has its place in the liturgy of this whole season of expectation only because it *is* a commemoration. For we have here an example of a most useful distinction, made by St. Augustine himself, between the feasts which are also "sacramenta" and those which are only *"commemorationes."* "Easter," he says, "is a *sacramentum,* because in it we not only *commemorate* the death and resurrection of Our Lord, but we also *celebrate* our own actual passage from death to life, from a mortal life to life everlasting. But the feast of Christmas, insofar as it *recalls* Christ's Nativity, is only a *commemoratio,* an anniversary."

In this connection, we can now try to weigh the exact value of that analogy, so dear to many souls from the Middle Ages on, between Christ's Nativity at Bethlehem and what they like to call, after Origen's phrase, the nativity of the Word of God in our own souls. We have already pointed out that it would certainly be more exact to speak of our nativity, our birth, to life in that Word of God. But to re-phrase it thus at once diminishes the strength of the comparison. Does it suppress all its value? We should think not; but we should say that it does show that the word "analogy" is not the right one to use here. It is rather by way of opposition than by way of analogy or parallelism that Christ's nativity to our mortal life and our own nativity to divine life in Him are to be brought together. This opposition, let us observe again, was clearly indicated by St. Gregory in the very first words of his homily *In Theophania.* For him, the descent of Christ suggested our ascent to the Father, His coming after us suggested our coming back to Him, and so on. And, clearly, this is what the Church has always had in mind in the celebration of the Nativity.

Certainly, a link exists between the Nativity and the *Parousia,* between Christ's first coming to us and His second coming to take us up with Him. But this does not at all imply the same kind of direct relationship as that into which we are brought with Christ's action by the Paschal Mystery, where what happened to Christ is what is to happen to us. The Christmas relationship is rather that of contrast between the Giver and the receivers; between Him Who made Himself poor and ourselves who are enriched by His poverty. What the Church sees in the Nativity is not that sentimental picture which is accessible even to an unbeliever. In the descent of God to man, the Church celebrates a reality which can be perceived by Faith alone: the beginning of the action which is to bring man back to God. And, finally, the intention of the Church in taking the Nativity to be, not so much the object of her celebration, as the occasion of it, is to call attention to the end of that *transitus* from its very beginning. Even, that is, in celebrating the beginning of the "passage" of God made man through the humiliation proper to sinful man, she proclaims the glorification of God Himself in the raising of man to His divine glory, through the same God made man.

How significant, in this light, is the fact that the Church never kept, nor took the trouble to find, the exact historical date of the Nativity, whereas she was always very much concerned with the coincidence of the saving Passion with the date of the Jewish Passover. For the celebration of the Nativity of the Savior, she has deliberately taken a symbolic date, that of the winter solstice, so as to show from the outset that her intention was not to indulge in tender feelings about the divine infancy, but rather to hail by faith the first dawn of the light bringing the "Day of Yahweh," that Day which we hope for, both with "fear and trembling," and with the exultation of victory.

Our celebration of Christmas, in other words, has nothing in common with those fruitless recollections of childhood which lull our nostalgia as fallen children of Adam. In the Birth of the second Adam, which seemed to be a purely earthly one, we acknowledge the coming of the Divine Man, Who, as the first antiphon of Epiphany sings, "was born before the dawn." In this first contact with the God of heaven, with Him Who cannot be seen by bodily eyes, but only by the eyes of faith, the Church seizes upon the promise, clings to the "earnest," of that Day when somehow even the eyes of the body will see Him as He is, in the glorified Christ. And in this way she also anticipates our own birth to eternity, our birth beyond death: the birth which will make us "sons of the Resurrection." The commemoration of Christ's appearance to the Wise Men, of the Baptism of Christ with its trinitarian Theophany, of the miracle of Cana which was the "sign of His glory,"—all these come right after the commemoration of the earthly birth of the Savior, in order to fix our gaze upon that heavenly birth through which we are to find Him again, not under any illusion of a past come back, but in the blessed actuality of Him "Who was, and Who is, and Who is to come."

From these facts, one conclusion must be drawn which at first sight may seem, perhaps, bewildering, but is nonetheless inevitable. This conclusion is that Advent, together with Christmas and Epiphany, far from being the first or introductory part of the liturgical year, is properly its end. Since the late Middle Ages, it has become generally customary to consider the First Sunday of Advent as the beginning of the Temporal cycle of the year. The custom of putting first in liturgical books the liturgy for this Sunday may have grown up more or less as a result of that faulty interpretation of Christmas which we have been endeavoring to dispel.[1] Even if this were not so, however, the arrangement of our liturgical books encourages the mistaken notions which tend to empty this whole part of the Temporal cycle of its theological meaning.

But, even today, the liturgy still shows striking marks of the more ancient way of understanding the liturgical year. Far from making a new beginning, Advent still comes in direct continuity with the last Sundays after Pentecost, which already are filled—note especially the last Sunday after Pentecost—with the idea of the second coming of Christ. In the Middle Ages, the Twenty-fourth Sunday was called Doom Sunday; it has been inferred, indeed, that the Sequence *Dies Irae* was composed for that Sunday, where it naturally leads into the Gospel of the end of the world, instead of for the liturgy for the dead, where it has no connection with either the Epistle or the Gospel. (It was not used formerly in the liturgy for the dead, nor is it used in the present Cistercian Rite).

Another very striking feature of the liturgical year, still present today, is that the annual reading of the Bible, in the *lectio continua* of Matins, does not begin on the First Sunday of Advent, but on Sep-

---

[1] To state the case more exactly, the older liturgical books did not distinguish, as we do, between the "temporal" and "sanctoral" cycles. These books simply took all the months as they came on the civil calendar, beginning with January, and put in each one the various feasts as they were assigned to special days, or as they generally fell on some one or other day of each month. When this arrangement was discarded for a more coherent one, it must have appeared illogical to begin the year with Epiphany and end with Christmas, or, since the connection between Advent and Christmas was felt to be so strong, to begin with Christmas and leave Advent for the end. It seems, therefore, that the present arrangement of our books is a compromise between the fact that the civil calendar begins with January, and the fact that Advent, Christmas and Epiphany form a whole season. This arrangement, then, is probably no more than an attempt to keep as close as possible to the civil year in ordering the Temporal cycle of the liturgical year, while at the same time, avoiding the separation of feasts that are intimately connected.

tuagesima, with the book of Genesis; and the reading goes on consecutively all through the following year, broken only by more or less modern modifications, the reasons for which are not always obvious.

Now, clearly, when we have regained this view of the whole, every new liturgical year makes us feel afresh the necessity to go again and again, every year of our life, through the whole course of the Mystery, starting with the first communication of God's Word to fallen man, in order to prepare ourselves for the final coming of the Kingdom. A full human life should year by year become increasingly synchronized with the rhythm of the liturgical year. Such a life would mean a more and more perfect preparation for the call of Christ to come and meet Him on the other side of our death and of the death of the world, in that other world of divine life to which He rose at His Ascension, and whence He is to come again in order to take us there with Him forever.

These considerations on Advent, Christmas and Epiphany, ought to lead us, in conclusion, to two meditations: first, on the meaning of the way in which the Church refers, constantly and basically, to the Old Testament in introducing us to the Mystery; and secondly, on the importance of eschatology for any real grasp of the Mystery.

We frequently hear criticisms of the Church for having retained so many readings from the Old Testament in her liturgy; of her using the Psalter as the main material of her own prayer; of her never expressing her ideas about the New Testament without constant references to the Old. Many people think, for example, that the Easter Vigil will never be truly popular so long as the four readings from the Old Testament—the only readings that remain of the original twelve —are kept; or so long as the *Exsultet,* or the Blessing of the Font, all preserve their references to the Exodus. Now that the New Testament has arrived, now that we have the Gospel, the full light which was only foreshadowed by the Prophets, why should we continue to burden ourselves with all these relics of what was merely a preparatory stage? Why not give people the full Gospel today, but nothing else? What are Abraham, Moses and the Prophets to us now that Christ has come?

Such reasonings, however sensible they may seem at first glance, actually betray a total and radical misunderstanding of the Christian Mystery. True enough, it is only in Christ that God's Word comes to us in its fullness; but to interpret this fact as if it meant that the

Old Testament was thereby rendered meaningless and useless is only to misconceive the meaning of Christ Himself. For if it is true that the Old Testament cannot be fully understood except in the light of Christ's coming, it is also true that Christ Himself cannot be fully understood except in the light of the Old Testament. To get rid of the Old Testament because Christ has come would be about as sensible as it would be to ignore the first words of a Latin or German sentence because the last word is the key word.

We must say, therefore, that what revelation takes over from the Old Testament in progressing to the New is not merely an external frame, still less a kind of scaffolding that is to be torn down when the building is finished. On the contrary, it is the basis, the foundation, the removal of which would bring the whole building down in ruins. For revelation is not made only *through* what we call sacred history, as if this were a kind of medium which could be separated from the message; revelation *is* that sacred history, and it cannot be separated from it without vanishing altogether.

What should we think of a husband and wife who, after a whole life spent together, could say to one another, "come, let us forget our common history; let us never think any more of our first meeting, of the circumstances of our falling in love, of our honeymoon, of the birth and childhood of our sons and daughters, of all our common joys and trials through the years. Let us get rid of all that dead past. It is merely a burden which prevents us from knowing and loving each other just as we are now. Let us suppress the past entirely and live only in the present, for then our love will be far clearer and deeper than it is?" Such conduct would obviously be senseless, for the mutual love of such a couple would die if their common past was forgotten and with it their knowledge of themselves and of each other. Little or nothing would remain of their present itself if their memory of the past could be blotted out. For we are not only what our history has made us; we are in some way that history itself, memory being the basis of personal conscience as well as of personal love.

And the same thing is, of course, true of our relationship to God. What He has done for us and with us in Christ is only the final product of what He began to do (I do not say, began to prepare, for it is not a matter of external preparation but of internal germination), when His first word was addressed to Abraham, or, rather, to Adam himself immediately after the Fall.

The Old Testament, therefore, is by no means to be thought of as a kind of elementary teaching which has no value when one has got to the core of the subject. What God has to say to man is not a sequence of propositions of increasing complexity, the last of which, once it has been grasped, could dispense with all the preceding ones. Through the whole history of revelation, God has only one thing to say to man; but this one thing, the Mystery, needs a long and progressive experience for its full reception. And, as is the case with all vital experience, the whole fruit of it needs to be gathered and kept faithfully in memory if it is to be useful. The Mystery is a reality we cannot grasp in its final form unless we understand it as a living product, which has developed from the seed of its first form, as that was sown by God. We cannot understand it if we think of it as a kind of logical deduction which, once attained, renders unnecessary any adverting to the steps by which it was reached.

That desire of divine love for man's fellowship, that struggle through which that love is to free man from his slavery to sin and death and bring him back to itself; that "passage" through which alone man is once more to receive life in the divine love, by means of freely accepted death; the fact that in this "passage" God Himself comes down to make with man that long and difficult journey which will bring him to the Kingdom:—all this, which describes the Mystery as it stands in the fullness of the New Testament, equally well describes its foreshadowing in the Old Testament. To speak more exactly, the description we have just given of the Mystery of the New Testament is properly the description of the great events of the First Covenant. It is only by means of a "spiritual" transposition that this description applies to the Sacred Covenant. But let us take note of the fact that the only way to express fully the significance of the New Testament is to take what was revealed in the literal sense of the Old Testament, but to take it with that added wealth of significance which is itself the product of what we might call the common experience of God and man taken as a whole.

Here we see the permanent value of that allegorical or "spiritual" exegesis of which the Fathers of the Church were so fond. And we see also that, however obsolete may be some of the ways in which the Fathers applied this principle of exegesis, the principle itself properly understood is beyond question. For it lies not only at the heart of all Christian exegesis, but at the heart of the Christian faith itself. Let

us repeat once more: the Old Testament is not a kind of incidental
or external shape of Christian teaching; it is inherent in the very
substance of Christian teaching. All the notions, all the realities involved in the Mystery cannot be grasped except by means of the
primitive realities of the Old Testament and the ideas arrived at by a
process of reflection upon these realities by those who had experi-
enced them fully

Have we not already seen, for example, that the Mystery as it is
first described by St. Paul, will certainly be mistaken for all kinds of
things completely foreign to its true nature if we do not see it in its
proper context of "wisdom" and "revelation," with all that these
terms imply of the whole development of religious thought in Israel?
The very innermost meaning of the Mystery comes out of all the ideas
connected with the Servant of the Lord (Isaiah 53), the ideas of the
freely willed suffering and death which redeems sinners from their
sin and brings them to true life. And these ideas themselves are only
a deepening, through the experience of exile and captivity, of the
fundamental experience of Israel, that is, of the Exodus,—the mysterious *transitus* of God through human history, by which through
separating man from his native soil and through seemingly abandoning him in the desert, God brought him out to reconciliation with
Himself in the Paradise regained.

Perhaps we can now begin to perceive the exact truth of what has
already been said: that revelation not only *took place* in the history
of Israel, but *is* the history of Israel. There is, therefore, no other way
for us to receive revelation than somehow to receive that sacred history. This is an obvious and natural consequence of the fact we have
continually insisted upon, the fact that the Word of God is creative,
and that therefore the revelation of God to us is our definitive creation: what creates our final and true selves. In this connection, we
may well use the axiom of biology,—that the process of ontogenesis
reproduces that of phylogenesis, that is, that the development of each
individual of a species goes through the same stages as did the whole
species during its whole evolution. For the process of history by
which the Mystical Body has been developed from natural humanity
at the call of God's Word is the process which every one of us must
undergo in order to become a living member of that Body.

We have said enough to show that there is no artificiality in so
interpreting the Old Testament as to apply it to the New. For such an

interpretation is of the very essence of the New Testament, which was not added on to the Old from without, but rather developed from within the Old under the continuous action of God's Word. The New Testament was not, so to speak, a sudden and unexpected action of this Word, but rather the evident blossoming of what had already been sown by the Word in the Old Testament. Even in the Old Testament, we can see how God brought about the revelation of new things by deepening and spiritualizing man's understanding of events that had already happened. It is characteristic of all the great prophets of the eighth and seventh centuries before Christ to proclaim a new message by means of a re-interpretation of the oldest traditions of Israel. What could come closer to the great New Testament revelation of *agape* than Osee's and Jeremias' revelation of *hesed?* But this revelation is given as only a new understanding of the old story of the redemption of Israel from Egypt, a new comprehension of it under the influence of new and deeper experience of the same underlying reality of God's love for men: "When Israel was a child I loved him: and I called my son out of Egypt."[2] The prophets therefore interpret the return from the Exile as a new Exodus, and they interpret it in this way so consistently that it is very difficult, for example, to give a date to psalms which speak of the first *transitus,* because they might have been composed either for a commemoration of the first Exodus or for a celebration of the return of the captives from Babylon. But we may go further, and say, rather, that the story of Exodus and of all the beginnings of Israel, as it stands now in our Bibles, is not so much a bare relation of historical facts as a reflection on that primitive history in the light of more recent events, a reflection which by means of this more complete experience had been enabled to discover what was only implicit in the primitive history.

We are finally, therefore, to see the Mystery as having not one but many successive realizations, each one having been not only prepared for by the preceding one, but, so to say, sketched in by it; each realization developing from the preceding one, and itself being the seed of the more complete realization to follow it.

The primitive Passover of natural humanity, that is, the spring ritual of a nature religion that knew only the false gods of fallen nature, was taken over and transfigured by the first Passover of the true God, His first "passage" among us at the Exodus.

[2] Osee XI, I.

But this transcendent saving action of God, objectively revealing the definitive pattern of the divine intervention, had to be assimilated, so to speak, by the subjective experiences of Israel. Israel had to discover that, on the one hand, the enemies of His People, on the other, its own Covenant with God, were realities not only of the external historical order, but also of the most interior personal experience. His People had to discover, that is, the meaning of personal suffering in the Servant of God himself, and the need for a law written not on tablets of stone but on the tablets of the human heart. And this was the first transfiguring development, or new realization of the Exodus taking place in the Exile and the return of the captives; a new realization which was itself a foreshadowing of the Death that would lead to life.[3]

But in this very experience of the Exile and the return, Israel was to discover its own utter inability to be, of itself, as a physical people, that Servant of the Lord whose offering should abolish death by means of dying and bring men to light, life and immortality. The apocalyptic expectation, thus aroused, of God's further intervention, was to be answered by God in the person of the one faithful Servant, Who would Himself—alone on His Cross as God had been alone in the night of the first Exodus—accomplish the definitive Exodus, so as actually to bring the people from darkness to light, from death to eternal life.

But once again God's transcendent intervention was not to stand alone, towering above our human weakness, accomplishing its work entirely without us. It was rather to be assimilated by us, so that the one faithful Servant should become the seed, the germ-cell of the faithful remnant promised to Israel, the Head of a whole Body. Therefore that body has now to make its own what God once did for Him in its Head. But now the two are one in God made man. It is, therefore, no longer an analogous experience which Israel has to undergo in answer to God's initiative, but the self-same experience: the new Israel has to enter into, to go through the unique and final *transitus,* the one "passage" of Christ through death to life. And this is the Mystery as we have it now.

Is this to say that we expect no further transfiguring realization of the Mystery? Far from it. Through our sacramental communion in the Mystery accomplished in Christ, we are tending towards its full

[3] See Ezechiel XXXVI.

accomplishment in ourselves, towards that death to ourselves and to the world of our unredeemed selves, through which we are to be brought to the world of the Resurrection, to God all in all in Christ, Head and Body.

This *transitus,* may we say, this "passage," this perpetual abandonment of what is behind in order to meet the coming Kingdom and the coming King,—this is not a detail but a central feature of the Mystery. This continual transfiguration is itself the Mystery. For the purpose of the Mystery is not to make us rest in any limited and temporal achievement, but to take us into the final Exodus from time to eternity, from the world to the Creator of the world.

In this truth we can see the permanent value and necessity of the Old Testament, and also the importance of the eschatological view in the Mystery. Both these lessons and their interconnection are the proper teaching of Advent.

CHAPTER SIXTEEN

Christian Mystery and
"Memoria Sanctorum"

THE CHIEF IDEA in the preceding chapters has been the actuality of the Mystery in the liturgy, or its actualizing through the liturgy, more especially through the celebration of the Mass and all the sacramental order whose source is in the Mass. But the most important aspect of what we have been attempting to explain is how the actuality of the Mystery is to be understood in what might be called the sacramental world. This actuality does not mean that the sacramental world is a world in its own right, standing by itself; nothing could be more calculated than such an idea to kill a true understanding of the presence of the Mystery in the liturgy. On the contrary, the sacramental world is precisely the meeting place of two worlds each equally real; and it is the reality of these two worlds, together with the reality of their meeting here and now, that makes all the actuality of the Mystery in the sacramental order. These two worlds are the world of Jesus' action on the Cross and the world of our own action here and now. But we have already seen that such a formulation might be misleading, since it might make us think that one of these worlds, and the one, in fact, which is the more real of the two, is only a world of the past. The truth is this: in the transient world of the sacraments two absolutely real worlds are brought into contact: our world of here and now, and the world to come where we are to live eternally. This latter is not only a world of the future, but the most actual of all worlds here and now as well, since it is the world of the risen Christ. The sacramental world is thus typical of these "last times" of history

215

in which we live, for the characteristic of these last times, as the New Testament strikingly points out, is a paradoxical juxtaposition of the world to come (already in existence in the *Christ-Pneuma*) and this world of ours. Let us add that what makes our time especially the time for salvation is this juxtaposition, since this enables us to pass from the world of here and now to the world to come, before the final coming of the eternal world destroys this temporary world together with all those who have not been willing to leave it behind.

The best illustration of this whole way of thinking is the liturgy of the saints, most especially the earliest form of this liturgy, the liturgy of the martyrs. The martyrs are men and women who have fully realized in their actual lives the presence of Christ and His Cross as it was brought to them through the sacramental Mystery. And they are also men and women who have accomplished, as we can see, that definitive "passage" by means of the Cross from the world of today to the world to come, the world of the Resurrection. The celebration of the "memory of the martyrs," as the ancient Church called it, is, therefore, the celebration in which the Mystery of the Head is fulfilled in the Body; it is the coming true, if we may use such an expression, of St. Paul's statement: "If we suffer with Him, we shall also be glorified with Him."

This interpretation of the cult devoted to the memory of the martyrs cannot be better studied than in a survey of the theology of one of the most famous martyrs of antiquity, St. Ignatius, Bishop of Antioch. Sometime during the first quarter of the second century, he was brought to Rome to suffer martyrdom, being able on his way there to visit a number of Christian Churches. During the last stages of his journey, he sent letters back to the Churches which had welcomed him, and also ahead to the Church of Rome, this last letter being intended especially to prevent the Christians of Rome from making any attempts to stop the execution of his sentence. All these letters of St. Ignatius are wonderful documents for showing the sentiments of the primitive Church: they make clear the central part played by the Bishop, the meaning of the Eucharist, the meaning of martyrdom itself. They give us a full and coherent view of Christianity, so deep and so pure that there are few Christian texts, apart from the New Testament itself, which can be compared to them. We shall try now to extract from these letters one of their central ideas, that is, the connection between the Eucharist and martyrdom. And afterwards we shall find a confirmation of this doctrine in authentic Acts of Martyrs transmitted to us from antiquity. The most impressive of these testimonies given by actual life to the theology of St. Ignatius is probably that of the Martyrdom of St. Polycarp, a Bishop of Asia-Minor, a friend and host of St. Ignatius, who himself suffered martyrdom sometime after he had collected, for the benefit of later Christian generations, the letters of his friend.

In the thought of St. Ignatius, the Eucharist is the great feast of divine *agape,* of divine love suffusing the hearts of men. It is, therefore, above all a feast of unity. It makes us one in Christ, one with the Father, one with each other. But it cannot accomplish this purpose unless it is celebrated in exactly the way which has been ordained by God in Christ,—that is to say, unless it is carried out in a hierarchical celebration led by the Bishop, surrounded by his priests who are one heart and one soul with him, with the service of the deacons and the unanimous participation of the faithful gathered round the altar. And then, in the Eucharist, all together partake of the flesh of the Lamb of God, and of His Blood which is, as St. Ignatius says in a beautiful phrase, immortal love itself. Thus all are made one body, and in such a way that their bodies are given a pledge, a promise of immortality. For, by that heavenly Food, they are made a living temple of God, Christophoroi, pneumatophoroi, theophoroi, that is to say, they bear in themselves the presence of Christ, of the Spirit, of God.

Against the Asiatic heretics already denounced by St. John the Evangelist, St. Ignatius insists that the Eucharist is itself a permanent proclamation of the reality of the Incarnation. If Christ had not borne our own flesh, that flesh could not have been freed from death in Him by the Cross, nor could His flesh now be for us a φάρμακον ἀθανασίας a remedy giving immortality.

We can, therefore, sum up St. Ignatius' idea of the effects of our participation in the Eucharist by saying that it makes Christ live in us; it nourishes our bodies with His crucified Body; it diffuses divine love in our hearts with His blood; and, finally, it assimilates our bodies to His own risen Body, so that the word of the Apostle is fully realized: "It is now no longer I that live, but Christ lives in me."

Now, martyrdom is a kind of carrying out in actual experience of what is grasped in the Eucharist by faith. This statement must be understood in a very full sense, as implying a mystical idea that is fully realistic; so strong are they that we might wonder indeed whether the expressions of this idea were not meant to be taken only as metaphors, if we had not the testimony of the ancient Acts of the Martyrs which leads us to take rather the most literal interpretation. In the martyr, the identification with the crucified Lord, which is conferred on us by the Eucharist and through which we are to attain to a participation in His resurrection,—this identification appears as now having become an actual reality. The martyr need do no more than surrender himself to that identification with Christ crucified which has been given him by the Eucharist. In the moment, therefore, when in actual fact the martyr himself is crucified, Christ reveals in him His risen presence. When the martyr suffers and dies, it is so truly Christ Who suffers and dies that the suffering is transcended, and the risen Christ is revealed in the martyr's very death. And this is true because, as St. Ignatius is fond of saying, the martyr is no more to be found in himself, but in Christ; and in Christ as He is now and forever: the immortal Giver of immortality.

As a consequence, there is to be seen in the writings of St. Ignatius, a very remarkable transfer of the whole terminology used for the doctrine of the Eucharist to the doctrine of martyrdom. The martyr is offering the sacrifice; he is himself the wheat of God, a living bread. This idea is fully realized in the martyrdom of St. Ignatius' friend, St. Polycarp, according to the description of eye witnesses. When the Bishop of Smyrna comes to the place where he is to be burned to death, as soon as everything is ready for the execution, he offers a prayer in the exact pattern of the Eucharistic prayer. Beginning with an exultant survey of creation, it goes straight to the redeeming love manifested on the Cross, asking it to bless the sacrifice which is now to be accomplished as a continuation of the Cross, a sacrifice which is to witness to an unbelieving world the power of life which springs from the Cross. And the Saint ends his prayer with a solemn doxology just as the flame is put to the pyre. (We can see here a fine example of those *ex tempore* formulae which were used by bishops in the first centuries, always following the ideal pattern of the Canon and strictly hieratic in style and development, while free in detailed elaboration). But the most remarkable fact about this martyrdom is that as the fire comes close to the saintly old man, all the bystanders are struck by the impression that he does not seem to suffer; his face appears as shining in a divine light, and, to borrow a most characteristic image from the narrative itself, he looks like a heavenly loaf being baked in the furnace of divine love. . . .

We can find this same idea, expressed in a more or less similar style and sometimes even more explicitly in almost all the Acts of the Martyrs. In many places it is formally stated that the martyrs experience what we should call a real presence of Christ at the climax of their martyrdom, and that this often occurs in such a way as to startle, not only the Christian witnesses of the martyrs' death, but the unbelievers as well. In many cases this presence seems to have been sufficient evidence to the unbelievers of the truth of the Gospel, and as a result of these martyrdoms, passers-by, soldiers, executioners, sometimes even the magistrate in charge himself, all are brought straightway to the faith. The letter about the martyrs of Lyons, for example, which was written only a few days after the event and was intended to make known to the other Churches how the martyrs had suffered,—this letter emphasizes the obviously supernatural way in which the frail woman Blandina had borne without a gesture or expression of pain sufferings which no strong man could have endured. But the most typical expression of the conviction common to many of these experiences is a touching story in the African *Passio Felicitatis et Perpetuae.* The young matron Perpetua, in prison only a few days before her martyrdom, gives birth to a child. She cannot help crying out in the pains of labor, and a soldier says to her with a mixture of pity and contempt: "What will you do when you are in the circus?" But she answers simply: "Then another One will suffer in me."

We can understand now why the Church called the day on which a martyr suffered, his *dies natalis,* his true birthday, and why She had a special celebration of the Eucharist on the anniversary of such a day, on the very place where the martyr was buried. Here may be found the final proof of what we have been emphasizing in our last chapter, that our birth to heavenly life in Christ has always been understood as a participation not in Christ's birth, but in His Cross and Resurrection. The martyrs were actually "martyrs," that is, witnesses, to the Mystery, to the reality of the communication of the Mystery to us through the Eucharist leading to the reality of our partaking of the Resurrection of Christ through the identification of our death with His.

On the other hand, the celebration of the Eucharist on the spot where the holy relics of the martyr were kept, and especially such a celebration on the anniversary day of his martyrdom, was considered at first to be a kind of permanent testimony to the actuality of the Mystery, and, more precisely, to the way in which that actuality both of death and of life in Christ has to be realized by us. But certainly it was more than this. Grafted on to the basic idea that the martyrs had already, in their very death, the pledge of their final resurrection, the idea also appears almost from the first that the martyrs in whose memory the Eucharist is offered will help us in some way to that same realization of the Mystery in ourselves. This idea finds a concrete form in that of the martyrs' interceding for us in Christ with the Father. But there is something in this idea which cannot be simply reduced to this element, something which had already been expressed by St. Paul in the wonderful phrase: "I rejoice now in the sufferings I bear for your sake; and what is lacking of the sufferings of Christ I fill up in my flesh for his body, which is the Church."[1] Might we not say that the positive efficacy for the whole Church of the re-enactment today of the Passion of Christ in the sacramental Mystery in some way depends on the full actuality given to it only by the full offering of the Martyrs? This is surely the only way in which we can understand St. Paul's phrase and the cult of the martyrs as seen in its fundamental connection with the Eucharist.

We must also connect with this idea one of the three ways which were used in the ancient Church for the consecration of an altar or a church, all three of which are now contained in the Dedication ceremony of the *Pontificale Romanum*. The Roman tradition held, in a very theological way, that a place became consecrated for the Eucharistic celebration simply by the first celebration that was held there. The Gallican tradition added various washings and anointings symbolic of a kind of baptism of space and time to make it fit for the Eucharistic celebration; but in the African tradition, the dedication of an altar or a church required that the relics of martyrs be brought to it. A place was understood to be consecrated for the Eucharistic celebration by reason of the fact that in that place the Eucharist had, so to say, achieved its final purpose, as witnessed by the holy relics. In an analogous line of thought, the time of the year when a martyr had consummated his oblation was consecrated to a festive celebration in which the remembrance of the martyr's victory was included in the great Christian *anamnesis* as an anticipation of the final consummation of all things. Was not that consummation itself

[1] Col. I, 24.

understood to be so fully realized in the Eucharistic celebration that it was, so to speak, attracted from the prayer for the future, to a place in the commemoration of the past?[2]

From all this comes an idea which we find expressed in many different ways in the writings of the Fathers, and especially in their homilies for the Masses *in die natali*. The Eucharist possesses what we might call the power not only of proclaiming, but of bringing about the object of our eschatological expectation, the Kingdom of the Resurrection, the fullness of Christ. But this power can only manifest itself in so far as, in the Eucharist, by the reality of our offering of ourselves, we fully consent to be taken up into the sacrifice of the Cross, so as to offer our own bodies "as a living sacrifice, holy and acceptable to God." We see, therefore, how it is that martyrdom is the fullest accomplishment of our "royal priesthood," and how it is that the liturgical celebration of the Eucharist achieves its full efficacy and reality only in this accomplishment.

This fact also explains why martyrdom has always been considered to be the full equivalent of Baptism for a catechumen, so much so as to render Baptism unnecessary. Since by martyrdom the catechumen's identification with Christ in His Cross has been realized as fully as it can be, including his coming to the resurrection, there would be no need for Baptism, for its fullest substance and its ultimate effects had already been brought about, though in a way different from the usual one.

And this fact also explains why the Church hesitated for so long to pronounce on the view apparently once held that as soon as a martyr had begun to suffer for Christ, he received the power to offer the Eucharist and to perform all the sacerdotal functions without any need for ordination. In this notion we see a confusion between the powers of the apostolic ministry of the high priest in the assembly of God's People, and the perfect correspondence to the work of that ministry by the "royal priesthood." But such a confusion was only possible as a result of a right feeling that martyrdom manifests perfectly the effect of the communication of priesthood from the Head to the Body. For only in martyrdom, we may say, does the Eucharistic celebration achieve its final effect of consecrating not only the Sacrament itself (which is only the means to a further end) but also, through the Sacrament, the whole reality of mankind.

[2] As we have seen in old Eastern liturgies, like that of St. Basil.

From this fact, we can understand the special importance that was soon given to the Bishop-martyrs above all. In them the Church could contemplate the perfect coming together of her own two aspects: the ministerial priesthood through which the very priesthood of Christ is always present and active in her by the apostolate; and the "royal priesthood" of all the members of the Church, which in the martyr perfectly achieves the purpose of Christ's continued presence through the sacraments, that is: His effectively becoming all in all by means of the effective and complete acceptance of His Cross. This union of the two aspects of the Church was soon perceived to be most especially true of the twelve Apostles and their martyrdom. For in them we can say that the apostolate achieves its perfect complement: as St. Gregory Nazianzen would say, the coming down of Christ to us meets with our rising up to Him, His coming after us to seek and find us meets with our coming back to be reconciled in Him, with the Father.

But the most important conclusion for us to draw from what we have been explaining is the relation between what we might call the sacramental world and religious experience, between the Mystery and mystical life, between the "objective" and "subjective" aspects of the same Christian piety.

From all the texts which have just been quoted, it is evident that the primitive Church possessed a very clear idea of a special experience of the divine realities which are brought to man by heavenly grace. In the descriptions of martyrdom which we have mentioned, we find the most ancient and primitive descriptions also of what is now called mystical experience. We need not hesitate to say that what St. Teresa of Avila describes under the name of "Spiritual Marriage" is precisely the experience of blessed identification with Christ so conspicuous in the martyrs. But it is remarkable how, in the most ancient texts of Christian hagiography, this mystical experience is always seen as correlative to the gift of sacramental grace. We might say that the mystical experience is simply a full realization in ourselves of the Mystery as communicated to us through the sacraments, and especially through the Eucharist. But we must also say no less emphatically that the objective gift of grace conferred by the sacraments was understood to lead us by its very nature toward that subjective apprehension. The life-giving Passion of Christ was understood to be present in the sacraments as calling for, inspiring, creating in us obedient and loving faith. And it was in so far as the Passion of Christ made present through the sacraments was met by our effective and real acceptance of the Passion in our actual lives, that the mystical experience was in preparation, as the final recognition of our identification, achieved by this way of sacrifice, with the risen Christ. This should suffice to dispel any temptation to oppose "objective" to "subjective" piety, as if there could be any subjective piety which did not proceed entirely from the apprehension of the Mystery as offered to our faith in the Sacrament, or as if there could be any extension of the Mystery to us which did not demand above all that we effectively hold ourselves ready for the reception of its living substance.

But there is a final point which must be stressed, and this is the fact that the mystical experience as such, as described in the primitive cult of the martyrs, though it is always placed in the closest possible relation with the Cross, is nevertheless, properly considered, always an identification with the *risen* Christ, with Christ as He is now. In the martyrs who suffer in a radiant gladness and have already transcended suffering itself, we can say that Christ is visibly apparent in so far as the Resurrection itself appears in their death. This fact, which is made so obviously manifest in the martyrs may serve to correct the tendency of some modern mystics to seek for mystical experience in a communion only with the suffering Christ. Certainly it is through identification, both mystical and supremely real, with *Christus passus*, that the mystical experience is to be achieved. But the mystical experience, if it is truly in continuity with that authentic experience which is acknowledged by the Church of the Fathers as the full Christian experience, must always be an experience of the risen Christ, as such. And is this not a final proof of our previous conclusion, that it is always a participation in the risen Christ, the *Christos-Pneuma,* which actualizes the Passion of Christ in the sacramental access to the Mystery? For, as St. Paul says, "Even though we have known Christ according to the flesh, yet now we know him so no longer,"[3] that is to say, though *we* still must be crucified in Christ, He does not have to be crucified again: "Christ, having risen from the dead, dies now no more, death shall no longer have dominion over Him. For the death that He died, He died to sin, once for all, but the life that He lives, He lives unto God."[4]

Since the martyrs were in some way "the saints" *par excellence,*

[3] 2 Cor. V, 16.
[4] Rom. VI, 9-10.

the saints from whom the idea of personal Christian sanctity was first derived, Christians soon began to ask whether there might not be some possible equivalents to martyrdom. If what makes of death a sacrifice is not the simple fact of dying, but the acceptance of death in the "fellowship of the Mystery" as the death of Christ, Christians might perhaps find a way of attaining to the sanctity of the martyrs if they accepted in this way their natural death when it came to them, even though they had not to suffer a death imposed on them by their fellow men. Almost from the first, this idea was accepted as true, and especially in the case of virgins consecrated to Christ. Virginity for the sake of the Kingdom of God was thought of as a kind of life-long martyrdom, since it implied a complete renunciation of the natural fruitfulness of human life in order to dedicate oneself more completely to the coming Kingdom. More generally, as we can see in Origen's *Exhortation to Martyrdom,* voluntary asceticism, which had first been considered as a preparation for martyrdom, began to be considered as its equivalent.

In the fourth century, when the opportunity for martyrdom had practically disappeared, the monk began to take the place of the martyr as accomplishing in his own way a freely-accepted martyrdom. But it is very important for us to see that the monk did not take the place of the martyr only by reason of his asceticism, but also because of the "charismatic," or, if we prefer the term, "mystical" character that was ascribed to the full development of his vocation. The primitive monk, to be truly a monk, must be a *pneumatpohoros,* a man in whom—because, like the martyr, he has consummated his offering of himself in the Eucharist of Christ—the *Christos-Pneuma* is to appear and to manifest Himself.

It is in this idea that we see the significance of the work undertaken at about the end of the fourth century by men like Gregory of Nyssa or Evagrius Ponticus, the work of building a theology of Christian contemplation considered as the basis of monastic spirituality.

We should not allow the philosophical materials which these men may have borrowed from Stoicism or Platonism to blind us to the fact that the purpose of their work was simply to nourish that realization in experience of the "I live now, no longer I, but Christ lives in me," which was the aim of St. Anthony's spiritual struggle as it was that of the martyrs themselves. Nothing could be further from the spirit of primitive monasticism than asceticism pursued as a goal in itself; and this is the reason why mystical theology developed very quickly as soon as monachism began to consider its own nature. Moreover, we must now acknowledge the fact that Christian mysticism was far from being a legacy to monachism from pagan forms of spirituality, either of the mystery-religions or of Neo-Platonism. The most primitive Christian mysticism was, and understood itself to be, the realization in experience of the Mystery, first to be obtained from meditation on the Scriptures, and then found in its permanent actuality in the liturgy. For the first uses of the word *mustikos* (μυστικός) in Christian literature are always in connection with a special understanding of the deeper meaning of the Scriptures, or of the reality in the liturgical celebration, which is accessible only to faith. Thus, even in writings so obviously influenced by Neo-Platonism as those ascribed to Dionysius the Areopagite, all the chief passages in which he defines the word *mustikos* (μυστικός) in connection with a special kind of spiritual experience, always refer to the knowledge of Scripture and to sacramental practice, so as to show that this special experience of the *mustikos* (μυστικός) is nothing else than the realization of the Mystery which is brought to us in these two related ways.

This fact also explains the remarkable way in which, in close connection with the primitive cult of virginity which developed into this monastic mysticism, the most important of all the cults of the saints came to be developed, that is, of course, the cult of the Blessed Virgin Mary. For Mary was to be venerated both for her divine Motherhood, which was the divinely given and supremely objective gift of God bestowed upon her in Christ, and for her virginity. And her virginity was seen to be the perfect example of Christian contemplative virginity, because it was so completely dedicated to the apprehension of the Mystery by loving faith that her whole life was the perfection of the martyrdom without bloodshed.

This truth was especially emphasized by the ancient Eastern Church in the two feasts of the Presentation of the Virgin in the Temple, and of her Dormition, or, as we say in the West, her Assumption. The first of these Feasts may have been connected with the legend, of dubious authenticity, that our Lady was actually cloistered in the Temple from her childhood; but this does not in the least diminish the intrinsic importance of the Feast. For, as can be seen from the Eastern liturgy, the legend itself was understood to be only the popular illustration of the fact that the life of the Virgin was from the first a life of total self-dedication to Christ, and, more particularly, to a contemplative faith in His Mystery as the source of the most absolute self-surrender. Here is the central idea that causes this Feast to be considered in the Eastern Church as the feast *par excellence* of the monastic life, considered as the realization of bloodless martyrdom. And here we can see the full flowering of the idea that such a virginity, through the death of renunciation of natural fruitfulness, is the means of attaining to supernatural fruitfulness in the Mystery. At the same time, we find here the only way in which the birth of Christ can be related to our own birth to divine life: not because it is a natural birth, but because it was, for Mary herself, the fruit of a perfect union with the Mystery of the Cross. We can, therefore, say quite truly that Mary is the Mother of divine life in us, while maintaining that divine life comes to us only from Christ's Cross, because Mary herself fulfilled her motherhood only in her spiritual union with the Cross.

Moreover, concerning the Feast of the Assumption, we can say that it is the Feast of that wonderful superposing of resurrection on death which was so conspicuous in the first martyrs and is seen here as achieving its perfection in the death of Mary. Had not that perfection its source in the perfection of Mary's bloodless martyrdom, of her contemplative "fiat" and her loving self-dedication to the Mystery?

To these remarks we shall only add two observations concerning the most ancient and the most recent of Mary's Feasts. The Feast of the Annunciation is as much a feast of the Christmas cycle as it is properly a "saint-feast." In this light, we can see it as the feast of the first proclamation of the coming of the Divine Word to us, the proclamation which itself effected that coming. In the ancient view, this feast was always understood as a celebration of the fulfillment of God's whole design: the fullness of times, the blotting out of the old sentence of condemnation, the return to Paradise,—these are its primitive themes.

As to the most recent Feast of the Immaculate Conception it is perhaps, when properly understood, the most eschatological of all feasts in its grasp of the Mystery. The perfect purity and beauty achieved in a human creature at the very beginning of the realization of the Mystery, achieved because of Mary's unique proximity to and cooperation with the Mystery,—this is, as it were, a living image of the purity and beauty which will be acquired at the end of time by the whole City of the redeemed, when all its members will have attained to such a perfect response to the Divine word, to such a perfection of their self-offering in the great thanksgiving of Christ to the Father, as was realized in Mary from the first. More than an image, in the impoverished modern sense of the word, let us rather say that Mary, immaculate from the very moment of her conception, is an earnest already given us of what the whole Church will be at the end of times, a pledge, so to say, of the actual possibility of man's attaining the perfect consummation of the Mystery as it is realized in Christ. And, still more, Mary is herself the perfection of that cooperation of mankind in the Sacrifice of Christ, in the work, that is, of its own redemption, which is the most powerful means of hastening the end of time, and the advent of the Kingdom of God "on earth as it is in heaven."

If we were to end this chapter here, we should, indeed, have given a general explanation of the whole cult of the saints as it is generally practised by Catholics today; but we should have omitted a most traditional part of this cult, the general neglect of which today may explain why our common apprehension of the Mystery is not now what it ought to be. For in the saint whom we are going to mention, that is, St. John the Baptist, we find both the permanent importance of the Old Testament and, linked up with the Old Testament itself, that eschatological impulse toward the final completion of the Mystery without which it cannot be understood properly or fully apprehended. Few facts in the history of piety are more startling than that of the great place which the cult of St. John the Baptist enjoyed in the devotion of Christians up to the Middle Ages, and yet the virtual oblivion into which this cult has fallen ever since. Obviously, there is nothing about St. John the Baptist to recommend him to a piety which feeds on tender feelings and delicate sentiments. A man who eats locusts and wears a camel's hair tunic and a leather girdle does not make a nice figure in a sweet painting of the Nativity! Nonetheless, St. John is a central figure in the whole economy of the Mystery, as is still shown by the place he has retained in the liturgy, and if we leave him out, we are in danger of losing the whole meaning of the Mystery itself. St. John was always regarded by antiquity as both the great martyr and the great ascetic. But he is above all, in his single person, the Old Testament acknowledging the New, and the New Testament proclaiming from the outset that the content of its "good news" is the coming, which was promised in the Old Testament, of that Kingdom which can only come from heaven. If we of today still had that devotion to St. John the Baptist which Our Lord Himself commended by his saying that no man born of woman was greater than St. John, then we should not fail to perceive that, as the Fathers said, *Novum testamentum in vetere latet, vetus in novo patet* (the New Testament in the Old lies concealed, the Old in the New stands revealed). In other words, St. John points to the fact that the New Testament already is implicit in the Old, so that the reality revealed in the New is only what was already on its way to us in the Old. Nor, if we had the ancient devotion to St. John the Baptist, could we forget that to believe in the Mystery, to accept it, is to know that the axe is already laid to the root of the tree, as St. John described it, and to act accordingly. This means that we are no longer to put our hopes on this world, but only on the world which is even now, though invisibly, present with Christ in the Mystery, where our life is hidden with Christ Himself in God.

This truth it is which brings us to the supreme lesson of the cult of St. John: that to be a true "friend of the Bridegroom," to be truly initiated into the Christian Mystery, is to adopt fully as our own that statement which shows the unique greatness of St. John: "He must increase, but I must decrease." Is this not, in effect, the radical need implied in any degree of realization of that phrase of St. Paul's which sums up what might be called the spirituality of the Mystery: "It is now no longer I that live, but Christ lives in me"?

CHAPTER SEVENTEEN

The Praise of the Mystery:
The Divine Office

W E HAVE now come in our study to that element which is the most comprehensive of all the elements of the divine liturgy: to that which makes, so to speak, the fitting atmosphere for the whole celebration of the liturgy. We mean, of course, the Divine Office,—the night vigil and the sacred day hours which are to fill with prayer the whole life of the Christian in the Church. It is, perhaps, most suitable that we should come to the consideration of the Divine Office when we have just seen, in the development of the cult of the saints, the import and the meaning of the ascetic tradition in the Church. For the Divine Office, as it is today, is probably the chief legacy of that tradition to the whole Church. Not that there had not always been, from the very beginning, a form of liturgical prayer to complete the Eucharistic synaxis, before the development of monasticism, but the two main characteristics of this form of prayer as we have it now—the fact that it is a sanctification of all the hours of the day, and of night itself, and the fact that it is essentially made up of the Psalter,—both come from the monastic tradition.

Our study of the permanent value of the Old Testament and of its basic use in the acknowledgment of the New, has, perhaps, prepared us to understand the striking fact that the prayer of the Church *par excellence* is still the Psalter. One of the fundamental aims of the first monks was to pray unceasingly; and to achieve this purpose they used the Psalms so constantly that—to borrow a beautiful phrase of Cassian—they did not seem so much to be reciting the Psalms as

229

to be re-creating them, for they said them from the heart as if they were extempore prayers.

We have already seen that to pray is the first of the three functions which belong to the "royal priesthood." It is not only in the temporal ordering of the liturgy of the Mass that prayer precedes the other two functions of offering and of communicating. Neither offering nor communicating could be carried out without prayer preceding, accompanying and following them. And therefore the Church has, as it were, enshrined her Eucharistic celebration in the unceasing action of her prayer.

But we have also seen that prayer, in the sense in which prayer is a fundamental activity of the "royal priesthood," does not mean any sort of prayer. It means a prayer that springs from a full understanding of the Mystery and, in the human words of our thanksgiving, carries our answer to the Divine Word of the Mystery. Therefore, as we have already pointed out, just as eucharist, that is, thanksgiving, is not only one aspect of the liturgical celebration but is so fundamental an aspect of it that everything is to be immersed in it, saturated with it,—so the whole life of Christians and above all Christian prayer, must take on the atmosphere of thanksgiving. But the saving perfection of human thanksgiving is realized only in Christ, because in Him man's answer to God's Word becomes identical with that Word Itself. And this is the basic motive for our use of the Psalter as our fundamental prayer. For the Psalter is also, in its way, a prayer of man which is at the same time the Word of God. If we wish, therefore, to give to God's Word the most faithful and most obedient answer in our prayer, we must use above any other that prayer which continues in the mouth of man to be the Word of God.

And precisely because the Psalter is the prayer inspired by God, it is also in its content the prayer of thanksgiving par excellence, the prayer which acknowledges God's Word in faith, accepts it with rejoicing, answers it by the most complete self-surrender. This is what makes the recitation of the Psalter as our *laus perennis,* our "perpetual praise," become formally the *laus mysterii,* the "praise of the Mystery."

And let us notice once more wherein consists the permanent value of the Old Testament. First of all, God has only one thing to communicate to man:—the mystery of His creating and redeeming love. He has, therefore, said this one thing from the very beginning, in a form so well adapted to the state of fallen man that its primitive significance could be progressively transfigured, but within the previous formulation. This formulation then, will remain, so long as we live in this transitory world, the indispensable basic expression of the Mystery, without which it would cease to find us where we are and to take us as we are into this transforming process. In the meantime, the whole meaning of the Old Testament, as we follow its development, is to awaken us to perceive that the basic expression of the Mystery in itself calls for ever deeper and wider realization. Herein consists especially the permanent value of the Psalter: it is a prayer which always takes, as its starting point, a former realization of the Mystery, but in its thanksgiving for these blessings always expresses the most daring expectation of a fuller and fuller realization. No other prayer is such a perfect acknowledgment of what God has done already as being the seed which will, as it were, blossom into the fullness of the future. Therefore, the Psalter understood in the full light of the Gospel should be above everything else the subject of our meditation, in order to nourish a prayer which springs from the complete understanding of the Mystery according to the laws of its own development, and produces the eager expectation of its final and full achievement.

Like all Jewish and Christian eucharistic prayers, the Psalter begins with a discovery of the whole world as the creation of God, as the product of God's Word, as being in itself the fundamental expression of God's Word to us, through which He is revealing Himself to us. It not only reveals His holiness, His awe-inspiring majesty, but also, in that very awesomeness, His *hesed,* His loving compassion for us men. For the whole world can be said to be present in the Psalter. Psalm 103 makes us contemplate in our praise the whole of creation, as we watch the sun, the image of God Himself and of His vivifying love, going through creation and filling it with life. Psalm 146 shows us at once the grandeur of the all-present God and His loving intimacy with man, as He reveals Himself in creation when it is seen in the light of His Word: He Who tells the number of the stars and calls them by name, is also He who heals the broken of heart and binds up their wounds.

For, just as does the Eucharist, this view of creation leads us to that sacred history in which He who has already been revealed in primitive creation, reveals Himself again. Psalm 18, beginning with the majestic law which manifests the Creator in the stars and in the succession of days and nights, goes on to praise the more explicit law which God gave to His own on Mt. Sinai, and concludes with the most intimate teaching of God as He reveals Himself to the very heart of man:

> The heavens declare the glory of God,
>   and the firmament proclaims His handiwork.
> Day pours out the word to day,
>   and night to night imparts knowledge; . . .
> The law of the Lord is perfect,
>   refreshing the soul:
> The decree of the Lord is trustworthy,
>   giving wisdom to the simple. . . .
> Let the words of my mouth
>   and the thought of my heart find favor
> Before you, O Lord,
>   my rock and my redeemer.

Thus, in praying the Psalms, we participate in the sacred history which is that of the Word of God seeking man and of the People of God created step by step through the progressive workings of the Word in us. This history is evinced in the Psalms primarily as the great struggle of God with the powers of hatred which have alienated God's creation from Him, man from His God, the people of earth from their Father in heaven. It sometimes seems to us that the Psalms are now obsolete because so many of them are songs of war. But it was precisely this aspect, perhaps more than any other, which caused the ancient monks to consider the Psalter as their prayer, as the proper prayer of any fully trained Christian. For although the struggle is transposed from the plane of external warfare with men to that of internal and spiritual war with the powers of evil, it can never cease on this earth, in the life of any Christian or in the life of the whole People of God. Far from it: progress in the Christian life, our progress in living in the Mystery, must be a progress in this war, until the Mystery is so entirely our whole life that death can come and find us ready for the only struggle which will end all our warfare.

But as the sacred history evoked in the Psalms is a warlike history, it is also the history which is dominated by the intervention of the "great Wrestler," of Him Whose "strong hand and outstretched arm" will rescue man in all his conflicts and bring him to the "peace that passes all understanding." This history is, therefore, what we might call the "theophanic" history, the history in which God Himself appears as being not only one actor in the drama with man, but as being, in the final analysis, Himself the great actor Whose intervention brings the struggle to its climax and to its final ending in victory. Let us observe, for example, the very typical Psalm 17:

> I love you, O Lord, my strength,
> > O Lord, my rock, my fortress, my deliverer.
> My God, my rock of refuge,
> > my shield, the horn of my salvation, my stronghold!
> Praised be the Lord, I exclaim,
> > and I am safe from my enemies.
> The breakers of death surged round about me,
> > the destroying floods overwhelmed me;
> The cords of the nether world enmeshed me,
> > the snares of death overtook me.
> In my distress I called upon the Lord
> > and cried out to my God;
> From his temple he heard my voice,
> > and my cry to him reached his ears.
>
> The earth swayed and quaked;
> > the foundations of the mountains trembled
> > and shook when his wrath flared up.
> Smoke rose from his nostrils,
> > and a devouring fire from his mouth
> > that kindled coals into flame.
> And he inclined the heavens and came down,
> > with dark clouds under his feet.
> He mounted a cherub and flew,
> > borne on the wings of the wind.
> He made darkness the cloak about him;
> > dark, misty rain-clouds his wrap.
> From the brightness of his presence
> > coals were kindled to flame.
> And the Lord thundered from heaven,

the Most High gave forth his voice;
He sent forth his arrows to put them to flight,
    with frequent lightnings he routed them.
Then the bed of the sea appeared,
    and the foundations of the world were laid bare,
And the rebuke of the Lord,
    at the blast of the wind of his wrath.
He reached out from on high and grasped me;
    he drew me out of the deep waters.
He rescued me from my mighty enemy
    and from my foes, who were too powerful for me.

We have given this long quotation because it demonstrates clearly that the struggle and the theophany described are those of the Exodus, the fundamental Passover. But this Psalm shows at the same time that the Exodus is used here as being an image of the struggle and theophany underlying the entire history of God's People, and especially of that final struggle which will bring us to everlasting peace.

But all through this history, as described in the Psalms, two contrasting aspects are always emphasized: the sin of man and the faithfulness of God; man's greatest infidelities only making more evident God's *hesed,* so that it is finally revealed fully as the love of a Father. So it is that the great historical Psalms, like 104 and 105, can take up the same story again and again, under either of these aspects, always concluding, however, with praise of that "mercy which endures for ever."

Moreover, from these two aspects of man's sinfulness and God's faithfulness is derived that feeling so characteristic of the Psalms, made up of the sense of man's unworthiness, of his sin which is to be acknowledged and confessed with the deepest humility, and of the sense of the greatness of God's love, which is always to be hoped for, which always gives man full confidence of final victory, as much in spite of himself as in spite of his enemies. As Psalm 102 so beautifully says:

Merciful and gracious is the Lord,
    slow to anger and abounding in kindness.
He will not always chide,
    nor does he keep his wrath forever,

Not according to our sins does he deal with us,
 nor does he requite us according to our crimes.
For as the heavens are high above the earth
 so surpassing is his kindness towards those who fear him.
As far as the east is from the west,
 so far has he put our transgressions from us.
As a father has compassion on his children,
 so the Lord has compassion on those who fear him,
For he knows how we are formed;
 he remembers that we are dust.

The realization of the Mystery in ourselves keeps us under the pressure of an unceasing conflict, in which we must at once suffer up to the last agony and at the same time hope with an unconquerable faith which is already triumphant. Both these motives and their paradoxical interrelation are so well and so frequently formulated in the Psalms as to render quotations almost unnecessary. "Save me, O God, for the waters threaten my life," cries Psalm 68, which is so often explicitly or implicitly quoted by St. Paul when he is speaking of Christ's Passion:

I am sunk in the abysmal swamp
 where there is no foothold;
I have reached the watery depths;
 the flood overwhelms me.
I am wearied with calling,
 my throat is parched;
My eyes have failed
 with looking for my God. . . .

But it will conclude with:

See, you lowly ones, and be glad;
 you, who seek God, may your hearts be merry!
For the Lord hears the poor,
 and his own who are in bonds he spurns not.
Let the heavens and the earth praise him,
 the seas and whatever moves in them!
For God will save Sion

and rebuild the cities of Juda.
They shall dwell in the land and own it,
    and the descendants of his servants shall inherit it,
    and those who love his name shall inhabit it.

In the same way, of course, is to be understood Psalm 21 which Our Lord took for His Own when He was dying on the cross: "My God, my God, why have you forsaken Me?" What bolder cry could be used by human distress?—Nevertheless the Psalm concludes:

I will proclaim your name to my brethren;
    in the midst of the assembly I will praise you;
You who fear the Lord, praise him;
    all you descendants of Jacob give glory to him;
    revere him, all you descendants of Israel!
For he has not spurned nor disdained
    the wretched man in his misery
Nor did he turn his face away from him,
    but when he cried out to him, he heard him. . . .

However, precisely because the struggle is now seen only as the occasion for the theophany, for God's coming down to His people, the prayer for deliverance becomes a prayer for the revelation of God's presence; and this prayer in turn, prompted by Him Who already is within us to pray better than we ourselves can do, blossoms into a hymn of exultant praise. So in Psalm 41-42:

As the hind longs for the running waters,
    so my soul longs for you, O God.
Athirst is my soul for God, the living God.
    When shall I go and behold the face of God? . . .
. . . Send forth your light and your fidelity;
    they shall lead me on
And bring me to your holy mountain,
    to your dwelling-place.
Then will I go in to the altar of God.
    the God of my gladness and joy;
Then will I give you thanks upon the harp,
    O God, my God.

> Why are you so downcast, O my soul?
>> Why do you sigh within me?
> Hope in God; for I shall again be thanking Him,
>> in the presence of my savior and my God.

In this expectation of the Kingdom, of the face-to-face companion-ship with the King, of the final fulfillment of the Mystery, we acknowl-edge the Mystery as already accomplished, the Kingdom as already come, the King as present, through the victory of faith, in the liturgical celebration. This acknowledgment is given surpassing expression in what have been called the "Psalms of the Enthronement," which were perhaps composed for a liturgical celebration of Yahweh estab-lished as the king of Israel in the Temple,—that is, the Psalms *Domi-nus regnavit* or *Cantate Domino,* from 92 to 98.

> Sing to the Lord a new song;
>> sing to the Lord, all you lands.
> Sing to the Lord; bless his name;
>> announce his salvation, day after day. . . .
> Sing to the Lord a new song,
>> for he has done wondrous deeds;
> His right hand has won victory for him,
>> his holy arm. . . .
> The Lord is king; let the earth rejoice;
>> let the many isles be glad. . . .
> The Lord is king; the peoples tremble;
>> He is throned upon the cherubim; the earth quakes. . . .
> The Lord in Sion is great,
>> He is high above all the peoples. . . .

We can see the same acknowledgment of future victory as already made present by faith in Psalm 117, composed for the transference of the Ark to the Temple; God is present with man, still in the midst of the struggle, on the way to final peace, and so man already feels the joy of that peace. It is for this reason, finally, that in the Psalms everything—the struggle and the expectation of victory, the sin of man and the mercy of God, our sufferings and our hope—flow to-gether into the great joy of the triumph and even now open to us, in the Mystery, the gates of eternity. So we sing in Psalm 99, *Jubilate*

Domino, what shall be the last note of our study, since it is the key-note of the whole:

> Sing joyfully to the Lord, all you lands;
>   serve the Lord with gladness;
>   come before him with joyful song.
> Know that the Lord is God;
>   he made us; his we are,
>   His people, the flock he tends.
> Enter his gates with thanksgiving,
>   his courts with praise;
> Give thanks to him; bless his name, for he is good,
>   the Lord whose kindness endures forever,
>   and his faithfulness, to all generations.

In order to achieve fully this "praise of the Mystery" through the constant recitation of the Psalter, it must be more than a mere *pensum divini officii,* a mere recitation of the Psalter, of its material. It must nourish the life of personal prayer, and itself be vitalized by that intimate apprehension of the Sacred Word which was so wonderfully realized in those monks of whom Cassian wrote that the Psalms had become as it were their own extempore prayers.

We can begin to understand how this personal apprehension of the Sacred Word was brought about if we consider how the Psalter was recited in choir in Christian antiquity, and was still recited in private throughout the Middle Ages. At the end of each Psalm, there was a pause for mental prayer—and it is probably to this pause that St. Benedict is alluding when he speaks in his Rule of the personal prayers of the monks which should be frequent and short, in order to bring their minds to God and not to leave them exposed to the dangers of idle thoughts. Like all the silent prayers of the faithful assembled, this pause was concluded by a collect, said by the monk presiding; in this collect the Christian application of the Psalms was summed up in a few words. From this usage have come to us three series of Psalter Collects, recently edited by Dom Wilmart and Dom Brou; they might illuminate our own use of the Psalter today, as they were found serviceable by the medieval monks who continued to copy them in their own psalters.

Let us take as an example the collects from the *"Series Romana"* for Psalm 109, the first for Sunday Vespers, and for Psalm 150, the last of daily Lauds in all the ancient uses. For Psalm 109 we read: *Ante luciferum genite, qui es ante principium totius creaturae, rogamus et quaesumus, ut sicut tuos inimicos pedibus ad dexteram Patris residens subjecisti, ita nos tuis officiis dignos habeas, ablata dominatione peccati.* "To Thee, begotten before the dawn, before any creature began to exist, we pray; and we plead that as Thou, Who art sitting at the right hand of the Father, hast made Thy enemies Thy footstool, so mayest Thou accept us, freed from the domination of sin, as worthy to give Thee service."

And for Psalm 150: *Armoniae nostrae suavissimum melos, qui nostri pectoris modulamina nunc flatibus nunc fidibus praecipis exerceri, praesta ut dum illa spiritali affectu concinimus, perpetualibus choris inserti, te cum sanctis omnibus conlaudemus.* "Thou Who art the loveliest melody of our choir, Thou Who hast commanded that the songs of our hearts should be rendered now by wind instruments, now by strings; grant that while we are singing with this spiritual desire, we may be admitted among the everlasting choirs and praise Thee together with all Thy saints."

This idea of the "unceasing" choirs of heaven, brings us to the second point of our study,—the application of an unceasing psalmody to the hours of the day and to the night vigil.

As we have said already, before the idea of the *laus perennis* was borrowed from monastic tradition, the Church had two hours of public prayer, at sunrise and at sunset, that is, Lauds and Vespers. Both these Hours still retain their original characteristic of praise, derived perhaps from the prayers of the synagogue which were said at the time of the morning and evening offering of incense in the Temple. Even today, morning and evening, together with the burning of incense at the *Benedictus* and the *Magnificat*, we recite at Lauds and Vespers the major hymns of praise from the Psalter. A very ancient tradition which has been retained by all Catholic rites except the Breviary of Pius X, gives as the invariable ending to Lauds each day the last three Psalms, 148, 149 and 150, in which are combined all possible motives for praise and all possible forms of it. A no less ancient tradition, which has been kept almost unbroken, reserves for Vespers the Psalms contained in what the Jews called the *Hallel*, that is, the Psalms used at the Paschal meal. These two chief "Hours" thus provide a most fitting frame for the Christian day illuminated by the

Eucharistic celebration. And their suitability is enhanced by the antiphons of both Lauds and Vespers, which usually take up the main themes of the feast or season. There is no doubt, therefore, that Christians who can join in the full prayer of the Church by means of only morning and evening prayers should use Lauds and Vespers for this purpose.

But the third, the sixth and the ninth hours of the day (about nine in the morning, noon, and three in the afternoon in our time-schedule), sanctified by both Christian and Jewish usage, should at least be consecrated by raising the mind to God in Christ, so that we fill the main stages of each day's journey with echoes of the Eucharistic celebration. The ancient monastic usage in the West for these times was to recite the Gradual psalms by heart—so reminding ourselves that no human work is worth anything unless it is accomplishing God's own work—or Psalm 118, which would bring the soul back to listening with obedient faith to the Word of God.

As to Prime and Compline, they were prayers which were added to sanctify the monks' going to work and going to rest, and Compline, especially as it stands in the ancient Roman rite, is full of the expression of that utter confidence in God which is the flower of a piety based on the Psalms. But the fact that today Prime and Compline have so frequently displaced the great fundamental prayer of Lauds and Vespers, even for the most liturgically-minded people, is a sad example of our lack of true traditional spirit. Where a sentimental appeal to our own pre-occupation with our work or our sleep is stronger than the appeal of the praise of God in the revelation of the Mystery, the spirit of the liturgy has certainly not been fully understood.

The Vigil also was a characteristic feature of the public prayer of the ancient Church, but only on the nights when the People of God was making ready for the great assembly of a solemn Eucharist, that is, the night of Saturday to Sunday, and the night preceding the great feasts. We have the formal witness of Tertullian himself that attendance at these Vigils, other than that of Easter, was purely optional, the practice of the more pious members of the Christian communities. The fathers frequently suggest, however, that all lay people, even those with families, should at least try to interrupt their night's sleep for a brief watch so as always to be ready for Christ's coming.

The ancient Vigil, as we still have it for Easter, was mainly taken up with long readings of Scripture, to be meditated on in silent prayer (like the readings at Mass), a silent prayer which was given form by psalmody and summed up in a *collecta*. It would certainly be well to try to restore such a Vigil Service to the faithful as a preparation for the Eucharistic celebration. It would serve to familiarize them once again with the Bible, as read in the mind of the Church, and it would once again arouse in them that watchful expectation for the coming of Christ which gives the final key to the Eucharist and to the life which is nourished by it.

The monastic daily Vigil, as it stands now in the Roman Breviary in a very shortened form, always gave greater room to the psalmody. Yet it always kept for this part of the Office those Psalms which are filled with recollections of Sacred History, those which are, in other words, most suited to be an accompaniment to the Bible readings and to the *Acta* of the Saints, together with the homilies of the Fathers. These Psalms are best able to carry us from meditative reading to that eucharistic prayer which contemplates the accomplishment of the Mystery in the history of God's People up to our own times. But, certainly, no part of the Office as it stands today needs a more thorough reformation than does Matins. If the Bible readings cannot return to the full *lectio continua*—a practice which was retained until very recently at least among the Carthusians,—it should at least not consist of the mere *incipit*, the beginning of each book, as is now the case, but rather of the central parts of every book, those that are the most essential to the full apprehension of the Mystery as it is expressed in the New Testament. The lives of the saints should be reduced to much more brief and sober commemorations; and the choice of readings from the Fathers should be completely revised, in order to provide a coherent commentary on Holy Scripture giving the full and traditional view.

What is most needed, however, is that all those, such as religious and clerics, who regularly use this Vigil, this "watching" prayer, should once again be awakened to its true significance. Then, when a more suitable form, along the lines we have just attempted to indicate, has been devised for the Vigil, those who use it would find for themselves, in silent prayer again introduced at its proper place in the Office, the right way to personal meditation, consisting simply in a quiet and deep assimilation of the formulae of the liturgy.

If all the Hours could be thus understood and prayed, then, in truth and not merely as a matter of abstract principle and official regulation, the Divine Office would be *the* prayer of the Church. For it would truly be, in its most essential parts, the prayer of all the members of the Church and, in all its parts, the prayer of the most fervent and most responsible members praying for the whole. Thus all Christian prayer would once again flow out from the Eucharistic celebration and flow back again to it, being in the full meaning of the term *perennis laus Mysterii,* the continual praise of the Mystery.

CHAPTER EIGHTEEN

"Liturgical" and "Non-Liturgical": The Spirit of Liturgy and of Devotion

W E CANNOT conclude our study without tackling the problem of the relation between liturgical life and our life in general: that is, first, between liturgy and our life of piety, and secondly, between liturgy and our life in the world of men. It is to these two subjects, therefore, that our last two chapters will be devoted.

But we must state immediately that the first problem, that of the relation between liturgy and spiritual life, is one which could not even have been raised in the ancient Church, or, if it had been raised, it would have been given no solution, for the terms of this problem would not have been understood. From what has been said already, it is clear that formerly the liturgy comprehended the whole prayer-life of the Church and of all Christians; and therefore, there was no problem. For the Christians of antiquity, the liturgy was not only a school of prayer, *the* school of prayer, but it *was* their prayer. In the collective prayer, each took his own part and so made it his own most personal prayer; thus a prayer which was nourished by that of the whole community brought back to the prayer of the whole community the spiritual fruit which each person had derived. The full reading of the Word of God, explained by the living tradition of the Church which spoke through the lips of the Bishop, led to prayer. This prayer was usually prompted and schooled by the psalms, and it was always finally summed up in the *Collecta;* but this summing up took place only after everyone had been given time to pray his own personal prayer, not apart from the whole Church, but at the height of his

243

communion with it. Then the Eucharist took the personal offering of the believer, and by means of the *Prex sacerdotalis,* i.e., the consecration, brought it into Christ's own sacrifice; and when that transfigured offering was given back in Communion, it was in order to take the Christian himself into the risen Christ. Then all the blessings of the sacramental order, which led up to or derived from these central actions of his spiritual life in the Body of Christ, filled the whole life of the Christian with the one and perfect Gift. Therefore his life was to be, with that of the Church herself, at once that continuous festival of the Christian year, and that school of asceticism which Christian life should be when the presence of the Mystery in it is understood as it should be. What could be added to such a way of life? Nothing, obviously. And therefore monasticism itself was then not so much a series of practices added to the common life of Christians in the Church, as a way to live that common life more fully and without any sort of hindrances.

But this state of affairs began to change when the liturgy, which had been for long a living practice, began to get fossilized; this happened simply because the Christian culture in which the liturgical forms had been elaborated was itself deteriorating. The process of fossilization continued until, at the turning point of the Middle Ages, that is about the end of the twelfth and beginning of the thirteenth century, the common people could not understand even the literal meaning of liturgical texts, since, except for the clerics and the intellectuals, Latin had become a dead language. But the learned themselves were at that period interested either in the profane and sentimental idealism of the "amour courtois"—a blend of manichean neoplatonism and sensual paganism—or in the intellectual world of averroist aristotelianism. One can imagine no climate more foreign to the spirit of the traditional liturgy. Therefore, the clergy and the intellectuals, far from being able to bring back the people to a true understanding of what the liturgy is and means, could only, even in their most well-intentioned efforts, block the way to such a return. If the two great mendicant orders, the Dominicans and the Franciscans, had not come into existence at that time, the final pagan outbursts of the Renaissance would have triumphed three centuries earlier than they did. But the Franciscans attempted, and in a way wonderfully accomplished, a Christianization of the world of the people, by giving a strong and evangelical stamp to the chivalric ideal which was already dominating that world. And, similarly, the Dominicans christianized Aristotle,—a no less remarkable achievement, which for at least two centuries was successful in keeping for the service of the Church the most brilliant and original minds of the age.

But these successes had to be paid for. Both Franciscans and Dominicans were too deeply immersed in the civilization of their time to be able to satisfy themselves with the traditional prayer and worship of the Church. They held to it as closely as they could,— the Franciscans with drastic abbreviations, the Dominicans by systematically reducing it to a position of honorable but distinctly secondary importance in their life. But both Orders now looked elsewhere to find the source of their spiritual teaching and piety. The Franciscans elaborated that type of piety which is focussed on the Manhood of Christ and on the purely human feelings that such a focussing could arouse. The cult of the Child lying in His manger-bed, the mysticism of the stigmata, both were natural offshoots of this new spirituality. The first Franciscans in no way realized the fact that the liturgy could hardly foster this spirituality or, except by means of radical changes, be made to harmonize with it. But this did not alter the case, and, whatever their conscious intention, the cleavage between liturgical and "popular" piety had begun and could only continue to widen.

The new departure was, perhaps, not so apparent with the Dominicans, more learned as they were than the Franciscans, and more consciously attached to the traditional ways of the Church. Nonetheless, the new type of intellectualism in which they were plunged and absorbed was too foreign to that of the Patristic period to make them feel fully at home with the liturgy which came out of that period, or to make them capable of forming the people in that liturgy. Obviously, this kind of intellectualism did not of itself lead to any special form of spirituality, since its aim was only to expose and interpret Christianity along the lines of a scientific cosmology. For this reason, this intellectualism did not precisely develop into, rather it was soon supplemented by a kind of neoplatonic mysticism which was of its nature completely uninterested in the so strongly historic and factual aspect of the liturgical Mystery; it was supplemented by the great and beautiful mysticism of the Rhenish school (Eckhardt, Suso and Tauler) or, in a simpler way, by a popular mysticism, such as that of St. Catherine of Siena, similar to the Franciscan, which ignored, except in a few details, the highbrow intellectualism of the great masters of the Order.

But did there not exist in the Church at this period any men, especially among the clergy, who were still living in the genuine atmosphere of the traditional liturgy, and capable of making the people still live in it? There were indeed. The black Benedictines, especially those of the great Clunisian school, well along into the twelfth and even the thirteenth century, still held to the Patristic and Biblical type of intellectualism, and therefore lived fully in and from the liturgy. And they did so not at all as a mere matter of routine, but with a wealth of personal development which soon was translated into some of the most beautiful products of Christian art. Of this type were men like the Venerable Peter, Abbot of Cluny, Peter of Celle, John of Fecamp, and many others, whose spiritual writings, recently rediscovered, are in the purest line of traditional, and therefore liturgical spirituality. Their contemporaries, the Cistercians of the first generations, accomplished even more. They carried out the first attempt to purify liturgical practice and the spiritual understanding of it from spurious accretions of the "dark ages," by going back to earlier sources, even to the Greek Fathers and to primitive monasticism. By re-interpreting these in a most personal way, they managed often wonderfully to adapt them to the mentality of the times. Such were men like St. Bernard, or better still, perhaps, William of St. Thierry, Aelred of Rievaulx, Guerric of Igny, Isaac a Stella.

Why, then, was their marvellous revival so quickly brought to an end, why did it fail so completely to capture in any lasting way the minds and souls of their contemporaries? The most probable answer is that the great Benedictine and Cistercian monks were too closely bound up with a social structure which was dying, and therefore, they themselves failed to influence permanently the men of their times. The Benedictine monastery, as it was brought to perfection at Cluny, was too much a creation of the feudal civilization which was beginning to crumble just at that time. Monks who were also great landlords could not influence the new urban civilization in which a "bourgeois" craving for freedom from the old system was a decisive motive. And even when the monks were the benefactors of the poor, they were socially so far above them that they could no longer find recruits among them. Even the Cistercians, that is to say the monks who were trying the hardest to be evangelical, could only take the poor into a kind of second-rate monasticism which was, for practical purposes, almost extra-liturgical. This monasticism was that of the lay-brothers, an invention of the Cistercians which would have bewildered St. Benedict himself, since he never intended to have the majority of his monks anything other than lay-brothers, but lay-brothers who were fully living the liturgical life as a matter of course.

Their inadaptability to the social needs of the times was sufficient to prevent Benedictines and Cistercians from doing more than maintaining for some time what proved to be rather an artificial survival than a successful, truly popular revival. Their failure here soon degenerated into an almost complete breakdown, for the monks' immense possessions served only to gain the hatred of the poor, and often to corrupt the monks themselves enough to justify that hatred.

Moreover, in these monasteries, the practice of the liturgy had already begun to deteriorate, and to be invaded by a strange overgrowth which soon developed independently, on its own. At Cluny, the wealth of the monasteries and the practical abandonment of manual work by the monks led to longer prayers. And so supplementary psalms, litanies, and later on offices of devotion (for the dead, of our Lady, etc.) were added to the Office, while two or three community Masses were sometimes sung on the same day. All these practices, of course, obscured the meaning of the liturgy itself; and its original primitive pattern began to be immersed in a formless ocean of inorganic prayer. The Cistercians at first reacted strongly against this tendency, but soon they too succumbed to it, and their Office, as it is today, though characterized by some remarkably primitive features, has actually become, of all the monastic liturgies, the one most overcrowded with secondary prayers.

But even these exaggerated fringes of the liturgy, tending, as they did, to blur its true form, were still permeated, for the monks themselves, by the spirit of the liturgy. This was never true, however, of the new devotions which arose from the developments of the thirteenth century which we have already summarized. The Rosary, like the Offices of Paters and Aves which at Cîteaux were given to the lay-brothers as a substitute for the Divine Office, had the great merit of a primitive simplicity. And it could, therefore, serve to lead toward very pure contemplative prayer, when those who pray it have had at least plain but good instruction in the Christian Mystery, such as that which St. Bernard strove to give the simplest of his brethren in his Chapter discourses. But the popular devotion to the Child Jesus, the Way of the Cross (following the stages of the Passion but with no reminder of the Resurrection), and, later on, the devotion to the Blessed Sacrament thought of as a kind of substitute for Our Lord's sensible presence during the days of His earthly life,—all these were certainly so many developments at least foreign to the spirit of the liturgy, and often unconsciously but all too easily adopted in complete opposition to it.

There is of course no possibility of actualizing the childhood of Jesus here and now: therefore a devotion which was fostered by the imaginative contemplation of the new-born Babe was one which began to go dangerously away from the actuality of the Christian Mystery which is nourished by faith in the risen Christ. Again, a contemplation of the Passion carried on in more or less complete forgetfulness of the resurrection ran the risk of keeping very little of the traditional worship of the Cross, and even led to one or other strange path of mysticism, very far from that of the New Testament and the Fathers. And the new worship in the Blessed Sacrament of a presence which was visualized more and more as an ordinary human kind of presence, increasingly separated from the Mass and even from Communion,—this threatened to wipe out the whole idea of the sacramental order and of the presence of Christ *in mysterio*.

We can see now that these novelties were able to take hold of the minds of the faithful so successfully because the liturgy itself had lost its hold upon them. Moreover, their very success made it more difficult to reestablish a true understanding and practice of the liturgy, since these new devotions involved a mentality not only foreign to that of the liturgy but almost irreconcilable with it. It is when people are no longer in touch with the authentic spirit of the liturgy that such devotions are developed; but once these are in possession, a return to the liturgy is almost impossible. You cannot at the same time hail Christ as if He were still a little Baby in His cradle, and adore Him as the risen Lord, the *Christos-Pneuma*. You cannot weep for His Passion as if you did not know that it has already ended in victory, and also exult in the resurrection. You cannot combine a mysticism centered on Jesus considered as the "Prisoner of the tabernacle," with celebrating the Eucharist as the saving Mystery by which Christ sets us free from all created limitations to bring us into the divine life. The more you are attached to one set of these alternatives, the more you must accept the loss of the other. And thus the way was barred to any possible return to pristine liturgical life.

We must, indeed, say this quite frankly: you cannot eat your cake and treasure it for tomorrow: you must choose. When the development of certain extra-liturgical devotions arises from the fact that the liturgy is dying, and arises from the very causes which are the death of the liturgy, we cannot hope to return to a living liturgy while we concentrate on these devotions and even add to them.

But when we have said this much, we must also repeat in connection with these medieval devotions what we said already, concerning Baroque religion. Taken in their historical setting, these devotions are certainly not to be condemned. If the people of that time had not been given these devotions, they would have had nothing at all, and they would have lost all Christianity. Since the liturgy had become inaccessible to them, something else had to be substituted for it, something which was able to lead them to some Christian religion, if only because it took them as, and from where they were. And this is precisely what these devotions did. But, once more, we must notice the cost of this kind of success. Such forms of piety produce a climate favorable to the growth of Protestantism. This is true not only because the Reformers reacted against the extreme transformations of traditional piety which had been progressively achieved by these novelties, but also for the reason that had Protestantism been such a reaction through and through, in fact as well as in precept, it could have become a true reformation instead. But Protestantism is much more truly the product of medieval piety because it is the fruit of what lay in that piety in seed-form: a naturalistic outlook on religion, a systematic ignoring of the Mystery, a sentimental kind of religious "experience" in place of the sober mysticism, completely grounded on faith, of the great Christian tradition.

But what are we to do now? Now that a rediscovery of the liturgy has been made possible by the progress of historical knowledge, by a renewed understanding of Scripture and the Fathers, should we slash our way through all those modern devotions we have just mentioned, and still more modern ones like that to the Sacred Heart, to find a path back to the liturgy at last? Such a proceeding would certainly be an enormous mistake. We must not forget the fact that some of the historical causes which fostered modern devotions are still operative. Especially must we not lose sight of the fact that our own mentality is still influenced by these factors to an extent which we ourselves cannot fully measure. Let us once more repeat this truth:

we cannot suppress any part of the past, either of the Church or of any individual Christian, just because we are not content with it. Whether they have tended to good or evil, experiences can never be suppressed without creating psychological disasters worse even than the worst of these experiences. Instead, they must be animated, incorporated, and finally swept into the main stream of life, but never left aside. If we fail so to incorporate and dominate such experiences, the rejection of what was spurious will not be effective, nor will be the re-admission of what was wanting. We shall only prepare the soil for various kinds of spiritual neurosis, which will choke what we tried to foster, while the apparently rejected experience will seed itself and take root once more in the most unexpected places.

What we should rather do is apply the very wise and tactful program of *Mediator Dei;* that is, never try artificially to suppress any practice which has in its favor the example of great saints and the unmistakable fruit of spiritual vitality. Instead, we should try, gently and yet firmly, to bring such practices back to the norm of the authentic liturgy, to permeate them with its spirit, and finally to develop into an auxiliary of the liturgy what originated as a substitute for it.

We should not even think, for example, of trying to suppress all that poetry about the divine Infancy which has become so traditional an aspect of the celebration of Christmas. But could we not develop this devotion to the Holy Child in His manger-bed in such a way as to show that behind what can only be a *commemoratio,* of the Infancy of Christ, a memorial of a past forever past, is the actual present fullness of the *Sacramentum,* of the Mystery which began in such a humble and beautiful way, in order to bring us from the life which Christ received from us to that life which He enjoys with the Father? Was not such a development precisely what the great St. Bernard accomplished so wonderfully in his efforts to bring his hearers from what he called a "carnal" love of Christ to a purely "spiritual" love, that is, from a love which is similar to, even though purer than, the love which any human baby naturally awakens in our hearts, to that divine love which springs from faith's acknowledgment of the love of God as manifested through the Mystery?

In the same way, a devotional practice like the Way of the Cross, far from taking us away from the liturgy will in fact bring us back to it, if only we begin to make this Way in the light of the exulting joy to which our Savior's Passion leads, and conclude our devotion with an act of faith in the power of His resurrection. Again, visits to the Blessed Sacrament, adoration of It during Exposition or not, will no longer be misleading forms of devotion if we begin to think of all these practices, not as a substitute for Communion, but rather as an invitation to and preparation for It. The Mystery will no longer be diluted, or obliterated from our minds, if we begin to visit the Blessed Sacrament, not merely to have a talk with Jesus appreciated as a perfect human friend, infinitely purer and higher than our other friends, but also to see in the permanence of the consecrated Bread the unity of all Eucharistic celebration throughout all times and places, and thus acknowledge Jesus in the Blessed Sacrament as both the eternal Priest and the eternal immolation, nourishing our life through His life-giving death.

But the devotional practice which, above all others, can easily be regenerated by being reconsidered in the light of the liturgy, is certainly the Rosary. Its simplicity, its pure and evangelical atmosphere of contemplation, when its "mysteries" are meditated on as being parts of a single whole: the passage of Christ and of ourselves with Him through death to life, make the Rosary an easy way of extending liturgical contemplation throughout the whole of daily life, an easy way of bringing the whole of our life continually back to its heavenly source.

With more modern practices, such as the devotion to the Sacred Heart, such re-thinking along the lines of the liturgy may be much easier in some ways, though perhaps more embarrassing in others. The focussing of Christian contemplation on the Sacred Heart was certainly motivated by an authentic sense of that deep unity of all Christianity in the unity of the Mystery itself as being, finally, the revelation of divine love made to us in the wounded and glorified Humanity of Our Lord. If we wish to find this revelation shining out even through the most untraditional formulas used by the devotion, we need only go back to its origins, to St. John Eudes, and before him to the German Benedictine School of St. Gertrude and St. Mechtilde. On the other hand, at first sight there is hardly anything which seems more foreign to the spirit of the liturgy than the emotional theology which has been developed around the Sacred Heart, and especially those forms of the devotion which are connected with the Eucharistic Presence. The ideas of making reparation for the injuries suffered by Our Lord in the Blessed Sacrament, of bringing Him consolation for the way in which the Blessed Sacrament is neglected and forgotten,—these ideas may often be found expressed in terms which seem to be merely the most crude expressions of a mistaken view of the Eucharistic presence, as though it were the localized and natural presence of a being who can still suffer and die; and of a no less mistaken view of the Cross, as being a human defeat and not the divine victory. But when these ideas are taken as expressing the view that the divine *agape,* until it has won our hearts, willingly takes a humiliated form, the form of the Servant of the Lord, and through that humiliation brings even such sinners as are we to the divine glory —then all the gross misunderstandings of this devotion vanish in the purest light of the Mystery.

Speaking more generally, the value that must be recognized and very definitely retained from amongst the more or less startling accretions of modern piety, is the consciousness of itself that modern humanity has gained, and cannot lose, even when it ceases to be absorbed in itself in order to rediscover the objective Mystery. All the use of systematic reflection, and even of the imagination which is so common a feature of modern piety must not be abandoned, but rather made subservient to a full realization by the changing beings which we are of the unchanging Mystery.

In other words, all the psychological workings of modern piety are to be made more dependent on faith, if only to keep them from the temptation which has been theirs from the first of trying to offer to modern man a substitute for faith.

The application of this principle is of paramount importance in the field of mystical life. Nobody could seriously think of abandoning the mysticism which is the legacy of St. Teresa and St. John of the Cross. But we must never forget that, in their wonderful understanding and description of the psychological and subjective experience of man as he is taken by God here on earth into the divine life, both these saints presupposed as a matter of course what they did not develop in their writings, that is, the sacramental and liturgical life which gave to that subjective experience its necessary objective content. It has been recently shown more especially how St. John of the Cross can only be misunderstood when the Biblical background of his whole teaching is forgotten. With St. Teresa—a woman and not sufficiently learned to use fully and to lay hold of the Latin liturgical tradition—there might have been a greater danger than with St.

John of losing contact with the Mystery, were it not for that hunger and thirst for traditional and sound theological teaching which was made so strong by her sure instinct for the authentic Christian life. The same instinct should preserve her disciples from a mistaken and purely negative fidelity to some of the letter of her teaching. These and all the similar teachings of modern mystics may certainly prove very dangerous to faith if they are taken apart from the Christian and ecclesiastical background in which they were developed. Contemporary experiences give too many and too striking evidences of the fact that an abstract mysticism easily leads to a purely syncretist religion, for us to need to give detailed proofs. The only way to avoid these deadly errors is never to take this modern mystical tradition, which is mainly psychological and subjective, as being a complete whole in itself. Rather are we always to bring back its descriptions of man, and of his self-consciousness as absorbed into God, once more within the framework of a life of faith nourished by the liturgical Mystery. Only then will these modern mystics give all the help they are capable of giving to our modern introverted minds, and not lead them in any way toward a mistaken kind of self-centered mysticism.

These considerations bring us finally to the truth which will give an organic unity to all our observations concerning ways in which devotions may be brought once more into the current of the liturgy rather than simply be cast aside by it. The fundamental approach to the problem of uniting personal, psychological and therefore subjective devotion with the objective discovery of the Mystery in the liturgical tradition must always be that of restoring that Christian culture apart from which liturgy must always fossilize and so become incapable of transmitting the life of which it is so full.

This means that the first and fundamental condition for any liturgical revival which is truly a revival of piety must be a personal knowledge of the whole Bible and meditation on it, both to be achieved along the lines laid out for us by the liturgy; such a revival implies a full acceptance of the Bible as the Word of God, and as the framework and ever-living source of all authentic Christianity. The monks of the Middle Ages remained alive to the liturgy for so long a time only because, in spite of their own defects, they held so persistently to this biblical way of accepting Christianity, of meditating on its truths and of living in them. On the other hand, the common people, contemporary with these monks, were not able, as common people had been previously, to find in the liturgy a true source of life, because various historical causes had deprived them of this direct access to Scripture within the living ecclesiastical tradition of liturgical life. The first necessity, therefore, for a liturgical movement which will lead to an authentic revival of the Church's own piety, is never to try to give back the liturgy to the people without at the same time giving them full and immediate access to the Bible. Only a personal meditation on the Word of God in the school of the liturgy itself will enable the Christian people truly to live in that liturgy, *to live that liturgy again.*

Such a personal meditation on the Bible in the school of the liturgy will mean that the Bible itself will once more be illuminated for us by the reality of the Mystery as it is always present in the sacramental order, and, through it, in the whole liturgy. Thus all the dangers of an approach to the Bible without or against the Church will be avoided. And the Bible in turn, understood in this way and so having become the supernatural world of all our thoughts and meditation and the food of our prayer, will lead us to the full liturgical life, that is, to a life of self-offering in the Eucharistic Sacrifice of Christ and of communion in the fullness, already achieved, of His Mystery. This also means that such a study and meditation of the Bible will lead us again to a life of true asceticism, taking the form suitable to each particular vocation, but always tending to introduce the Cross which we meet in the liturgical celebration into all the affairs of our daily lives. Liturgy will never be lived again so long as it is cultivated as a kind of evasion from actual life, and not as the supernatural leaven by which our whole life must be permeated so as to conform it effectively to the life of Christ which led Him to the Cross.

But this essential asceticism, deriving from the Cross as it is to be apprehended in the liturgical celebration, needs to develop into the mysticism of the risen Christ already living in us, Whom we receive in Communion, or, rather, into Whom we have been fully incorporated by means of Communion. A life wholly lived by faith, this is the ultimate achievement of a participation in the liturgy fully restored to the Christian People. And what is such a life but a life in which the realities hidden with Christ in God have become more real than the realities of common life?

Here we can begin to understand the importance, for any deep and full liturgical revival, of an authentic monastic life truly faithful to its origins. If the great monks of the Middle Ages ultimately failed to influence their contemporaries and to give them the realization of the treasures of piety contained in the traditional worship of the Church, it was because the monastic institutions of those monks no longer possessed and were unable to regain the purity of their origins. This inability was at least partly attributable to the deadly burden of archeologism which has so often been a stumbling block to the best intentioned liturgical reformers and propagandists. Primitive monasticism, following in the steps of the martyrs, not limiting liturgical piety to a special class of society or to a particular type of learning or to anything else, was simply an example of perfect freedom from this world in order to accept fully the Word of the Mystery·in prayer, to dedicate oneself fully in self-offering, and, finally, to live fully in a permanent state of communion with sacred things, with the actuality of the Mystery in the risen Christ. If we can recover, in ways open to all generous souls, such a type of monasticism, the monk would once more become the leader of the whole Body of Christ into the life of its Head.

If all these things for which we hope were to come about, then not only would the liturgy revive in our individual lives, but it would also revive in itself, that is, in its collective and canonical celebration. All those parts of the liturgy which have become more or less affected with sclerosis and so need restoration would, by an easy cooperation between authority and individual efforts, once more surely regain the fullness and suppleness of life. Then all the kinds of devotions which have been developed in an extra-liturgical fashion, would either be taken back in some regenerated form into the traditional liturgy itself, or they would return to the liturgy that life which they helped to keep during the centuries when the apprehension of tradition was low and would disappear themselves in a fuller and purer light.

But let us repeat again and again that in order to reach this goal there are two main ways which must always be taken simultaneously: 1) We must never begin by trying to suppress what is in existence and is giving experimental proofs of its usefulness, especially when we are not sure that we could effectively replace it by better, more traditional and more fruitful practices; but we must always try to reinfuse into devotions—even those which at first sight may seem the furthest away from authentic tradition—the true spirit of that tradition itself. And 2) we must restore that spirit of the liturgy which is the spirit of tradition itself by reviving both the direct full use of the Scripture, always enlightened by the living practice and teaching of the Church, and, on this basis, reviving a life of full participation in and of full correspondence with the liturgy.

Finally, we must always keep in mind that such a revival implies that the Christian must live a life of true asceticism, so that, while not neglecting any of the treasures of Christian experience in this regard, he will keep as his main principle an apprehension, through faith, of the divine Mystery, as disclosed to us in the Word of God and as brought to us in its full and ever actual reality in the sacramental world.

These two principles are those which, as can be easily recognized, underlie the two great divisions of the encyclical *Mediator Dei*. And we believe that the best fruit to be derived from our considerations will be to read that encyclical again in the light of them.

CHAPTER NINETEEN

The Mystery and the World

PERHAPS the greatest, and certainly the most difficult problem for liturgical piety is the one which awaits us when we go out of the church after the liturgical celebration is finished. For, if there is any one point that our study has brought out, it is that the importance of the liturgical celebration itself implies a correlative importance in what we do, after the liturgical celebration, in daily living. The Mystery that is always present and always active in the liturgy can only show its presence and manifest its activity through the whole life of Christians, through that Cross and that resurrection which are their permanent "witness" to the world, their "martyrdom" in the etymological sense of the word.

But this fact raises the whole problem of the way in which we should think about the relation between the world in which we live when we are in church, and the world in which we live outside it. As we have already said, the sacramental world is characteristic of the faith, and of these "last times" of history in which we are to live, in that the sacramental world effects a paradoxical meeting point between this world of everyday life and the world to come, the world of the resurrection into which Christ has led the way. How are we to understand this truth? More precisely, how are we to conceive the relation between the world to come which is brought into contact with us here and now in the liturgy and in the sacramental order, and the world of everyday affairs? We have already clearly stated the witness of Scripture and of tradition to the fact that these two worlds are at enmity. But what does this mean? Just how are we to interpret this enmity?

The actual world in which we live certainly is and cannot cease to be the creation of God. And, through the blessings flowing from the Eucharist, everything in the world which could have been stained by sin is capable of being restored to its original and holy state. How then can St. John say: "Do not love the world, or the things that are in the world. If anyone loves the world, the love of the Father is not in him?"[1] St. John himself gives the explanation when he says a few chapters further on: "the whole world is in the power of the evil one."[2] For the word which we translate by "world," ($\kappa\acute{o}\sigma\mu os$), does not mean simply the beings and things in the world, which are all God's creatures, but rather the reorganization, the order in which they are now arranged; and that order and organization are those of the Prince of the world, the rebel angel who has become the Enemy of God. Therefore, as St. John explains, "all that is in the world is the lust of the flesh, and the lust of the eyes, and the pride of life."[3]

It is to this world that we are to give witness of the divine *Agape,* in order to snatch out of its power the children of God who are there enslaved and bring them to liberty. But this task can only be accomplished by means of our cross and theirs, borne patiently and even joyfully as being Christ's own Cross. And thus we shall come to the resurrection, where everything which we had to lose in order to follow Christ will be found once more in the new *kosmos,* the new order of things and of being, where He is King, having overcome Satan and thrust his power down to hell.

We must frankly acknowledge that this view of reality, which gave no difficulty to the Christians of antiquity, seems very hard for us to face today; it is not at all easy for our mind to accept it. But we need to face it quietly and try to understand it more perfectly, for unquestionably this view of reality underlies the whole Catholic liturgy and is the prerequisite to any true understanding of the central Mystery of the liturgy. We cannot attempt once more to live a full liturgical life and at the same time be able to dismiss this view as one that is too gloomy and fanatical to be taken by any modern, well-educated and sensible Christians. And we must not deceive ourselves with the

[1] 1 John II, 15.
[2] 1 John V, 19.
[3] 1 John II, 16.

hope of finding some easy compromise which would enable us to continue in our comfortable attitude toward this world, while accepting the view of it expressed in the Bible and the liturgy only in such a way as to make it more palatable.

Such delusive attempts at a reconciliation are only too common nowadays. Many people think that, granted that there is antagonism between Christ and the Prince of this world, nevertheless, since the victory has already been won on the Cross, Christians can, as it were, exploit this victory so as to cause Christ to reign, here and now, in this world. Our mission in the world is, it would appear, to redeem it so completely from its captivity to the powers of evil as to make it, here and now, a world that already peacefully enjoys the blessings of heavenly life. The efforts and deeds of Christians would still involve a struggle, but a struggle which could have a successful issue here and now if only Christians were sufficiently filled with faith to bring about a renewed world where God in Christ would effectively be the King.

People who think along these lines usually tend to bring up what was, or is believed to have been, the state of things in the Middle Ages, when Church and state were in perfect agreement and Christian principles were the acknowledged principles of the whole life of human society. Not all these people, of course, hope for a new Middle Age: they realize that the state of things then was bound up with special historical conditions which do not in any way exist today and are not likely once more to become the conditions of the modern world. But, although they do not hope for a new Middle Age, they do hope for something analogous—for a world in which, in one way or another, the law of God should once again be accepted as the general law of society.

Now, to make the bringing about of such a state of things the *final* end of Christian endeavor is to forget two facts. The first is that, whatever qualities might characterize a society which acknowledged God as its Supreme Sovereign, as did the human society of the Middle Ages, neither sin nor death were done away with, or could be done away with, by such a society. It seems, therefore, that to confuse the bringing about of such a society, of such a state of the present world, with the coming of the Kingdom of God is to make a great mistake. The result of such a mistake must be the deterioration of the whole idea of the Kingdom, an impoverishment that takes away from it almost all its evangelical content. Not that all hope in this world is to be rejected. Obviously, a truly liturgical life must be a truly social life, a life which does not ignore man's obligations to his neighbors, but rather fulfills these obligations in the most effective and fruitful fashion. We cannot "witness" to the divine *agape* which is taking possession of us unless we are trying, each of us according to his vocation, to communicate this love of our fellow-men. Or, as St. John puts it, if we do not love our neighbor whom we can see, how can we pretend to love God Whom we do not see. Our Lord Himself said that He would finally judge us on whether or not we have spent our lives in ministering to Him in our neighbors' physical and spiritual needs. But truly ministering to Christ in our neighbor means helping him to find and to become conformed to Christ. Thus we have the paradox that the Christian must try to alleviate the sufferings of his fellow men in order to share with them the Christian secret of fruitful suffering and final victory over suffering and death.

Studied in this light, we can see in their true perspective and value the "Social Encyclicals" and the many utterances of the modern Popes, especially of our present Holy Father, on world conditions and what should be done about them, on the duties of Christians in general and of various social and occupational groups in particular in the world as it is today. As St. Augustine said a long time ago, you cannot preach the Gospel to people with empty stomachs. You must help them to get something to eat before they will be able to listen to Christ speaking through you. So the vast misery of war, of starvation, displacement, unrest that afflict so much of mankind today positively prevents great numbers of human beings from hearing the message of the Gospel. And, also, the materialistic spirit of our age, whether in countries primarily capitalistic or communistic, is in its own way at least as effective as misery itself in preventing people from taking the message of the Gospel seriously. One aspect of the work of Christians in witnessing to the Mystery in the world is, therefore, the task of trying to alleviate the misery on the one hand, of trying to change the organizations, institutions and ways of life on the other hand, which prevent people from even beginning to face the true problems of human and Christian living.

However, in so doing we must recognize the fact that all this work will, so far as we can judge from the hints of divine revelation, never be successful in the sense of establishing any lasting and universal Christian state of things. But our work for the temporal order and our work in the temporal order—from the growing of food to feed the hungry to the passing of laws to benefit the homeless or to distribute the world's resources more equitably—will have eternal results in the human beings, the stones of the New Jerusalem, whom in one way or another we have aided to become members of Christ, or more perfect members of Christ. But the best that we can hope for, in the line of temporal achievement, is a state of society which would positively help man to acknowledge the means of redemption and to use them to the full.

And one may say still more. It is not enough to say that a state of things more or less analogous to the Middle Ages, in which the rights of God over man were commonly and officially recognized by human society, would not be itself the Kingdom of God. Indeed, we may even seriously ask ourselves whether such a state of affairs would necessarily be the most effective preparation for the Kingdom of God. Only a very superficial view of the Middle Ages would give the impression that it was such a preparation. The external success of Christian principles can do as much to rob them of vital force as it can do to facilitate their searching men's hearts. In fact, when we examine closely that period in which Christianity was or seemed to be generally accepted as a matter of course, we can seriously question whether it did not lead to a disintegration of Christianity more than to any effective "christianization" of the world. It is beyond dispute that the Middle Ages have led to a period in which a more pernicious form of unbelief than that of antiquity has appeared. Prior to the Christian civilization of the medieval period, unbelievers were people who did not yet know Christianity, and very often did not believe simply because they did not know. At the end of the same period, the new kind of unbelievers, the general unbelief of the modern world, takes it for granted that it knows Christianity and rejects it because it is so well known that we can at last do away with it. And it appears, as a result of careful study of the Middle Ages, that this new form of unbelief is not a by-product, but rather the final effect of a continuous process which is one with the process of development of medieval society itself.

Taking all these considerations into account, it begins to seem very unsatisfactory to confuse true Christian hope with the hope for any definitive achievement to be expected in this world. Is not Christian hope essentially the hope of the resurrection? How can we, then, seriously pretend to be able to dispense with it? To pretend to bring about the coming of God's Kingdom without the necessity for dying before we enter into it is, certainly, a most untenable position for a Christian. But it is only a more indirect way to the same mistake to hold that we can bring about a state of affairs in this world which will be so perfect a preparation for the Kingdom that the necessity for dying in order to attain to the resurrection would become meaningless. For our task as Christians is not to save the world and ourselves *from* suffering and death; it is to save ourselves and all those in this world who hear the Word of God by means of, *through,* suffering and death. These are two very different ways of understanding salvation, ways which cannot be confused without making Christianity something which it is not and cannot become.

But when we consider some of the tendencies current today, the errors just mentioned may well seem mild and inoffensive in comparison. For the world is now proposing its own ways of salvation, ways in opposition to Christianity, ways which completely disregard Christianity. As a result, we see many Christians attempting to make an alliance between Christianity's ways and those of the world; and we see Christians who are even tempted to believe that the salvation offered by this world is the true one, and that Christianity needs only to encourage it, to bless it with a cheerful acknowledgment of its worth.

Capitalism[4] and communism are equally representative forms of this tendency of the world today not only to ignore Christianity, but to supplant it. To speak more precisely, the civilization of capitalism, as it was developed during the nineteenth century through the application to industry of the discoveries of experimental science, has created the ideal of an increasingly daring scientism trying to achieve by means of purely human efforts that reconquest of Paradise which is part of the eschatological expectation of believing Christians. And now communism, far from diverging from this line of endeavor, has only carried it out to its ultimate consequences, fully and consciously adopting for its creed that veiled and rather timid materialism which was from the very beginning at the core of the civilization of capitalism. Far from being a kind of a way of salvation from the world of capitalism, therefore, communism is in fact nothing but a kind of

[4] By capitalism is not here meant every system of private ownership, but only that form in which money and the profit motives are primary, rather than the just fee and the common good.

would-be salvation to be achieved by means of the complete and total identification of man with that materialistic law of life which was already latent but unacknowledged in capitalism.

The appeal of communism today thus resembles strikingly that which the mystery religions had for the pagan world at the time of the beginnings of Christianity. We have seen in an earlier chapter how these religions, far from attempting to set man free from cosmic fatalism, offered him a way to what was thought of as divinization precisely through identification with the unchanging, fatal law of nature. In the same way today, in a world now called "humanized" —but only in such a way as to "materialize" man himself—communism proposes salvation by means of a voluntary and complete self-surrender of man to that purely materialistic way of life to which capitalism was already tending through its scientific exploitation of the world. The communist vision of man being saved from all kinds of slavery, of man at last fully himself when he has become a mere cog in a world machine which has been scientifically organized to get the maximum of material profit from the world and to provide the maximum of enjoyment for everyone,—this ideal simply makes an absolutist religion of what was a kind of superstition that did not dare to express itself openly in capitalism. For capitalism and communism hold several assumptions in common: the assumption that full material enjoyment of this world is, for practical purposes, identical with human happiness; the assumption that this enjoyment is to be achieved through a scientific organization of the world entirely dependent on human effort, on the capabilities of man's brain and sinews; and, finally, the assumption—made rather shyly and hiding itself under various masks in capitalist societies, but now proudly asserted by communism—that any considerations of the spirit, of morality or even of natural human feelings are to be crushed if necessary in order to progress along this path to universal "happiness."

Now, it was a permanent temptation for all Christians in the bourgeois society of the last century, to agree that the ideas of "progress," "science," "efficiency," were absolutes never to be questioned, and also that these forces were actually tending towards the realization of what had been a mere ideal for historical Christianity. It became the fashion, therefore, among some of the Protestant churches, to discard everything in Christianity which could not be squared with this new creed of man. At the same time Catholics themselves were often far too eager to try to explain the new ideal and the old to one another in order at least to reconcile them for practical purposes, if they could not be made actually to coincide. In order to feel free to bless man's endeavor, Christianity merely asked that Christians be allowed by fellow-citizens to add to the common achievement of mankind a kind of shadowy extension of this achievement into what, in the eyes of these fellow-citizens, was a dreamy, ineffective and therefore inoffensive world of the supernatural.

In the capitalist-Marxist world of today, the temptation keeps on appearing. But it now comes out into the open, for many people, not as a temptation, but rather as a fulfillment of Christianity itself hitherto undreamed of. How many Christians, captivated by the sense of irresistible progress which seems in some countries to cause a capitalist civilization necessarily to develop into a communistic one—captivated also by the perfect self-confidence of communists in their own cause—now seem ready to admit that a communistic society would, after all, actually realize the Christian ideal, though in an unsuspected way? This new human society which, as they see it, stands ready to gather together all human endeavor in a perfectly unified effort to achieve the happiness of all mankind,—this society seems to them a realization of the Kingdom of God needing, in order to be perfect, only the soul which Christians themselves can bring it. They wonder, therefore, whether a society so heavily burdened with a dead past as is the Church can be the true Body of Christ. Would not that Body rather be the community of "militants" which is taking shape everywhere throughout the world in order to make the nostalgic dream of Paradise once again an earthly reality? Are not these "militants," who live only for the achievement of such an idea of general prosperity, realizing, even though they are unaware of it, the creativeness of true charity more perfectly than do nominal Christians, etc., etc.?

Of course, the confusion between the Promethean ideal of modern man and the Christian ideal of God made man is seldom so gross as we have described it, whether this confusion wear a communistic or a capitalistic guise. But it is precisely not the identification of Christianity with its counterfeits but a sub-conscious tending to evade opposing them which is most dangerous. Very few people among those who are truly Christian, are likely to be tempted by any obvious paganization of their faith. But many can easily be led astray by equivocal interpretations of their faith. The worshippers of Satan as such are very few in any generation, and most of these are insane people more likely to disgust than to convert their fellowmen. But there are always swarms of good people who candidly accept Satan when he is disguised as an angel of light, and their number, in spite of all apostolic warnings, grows larger and larger as more and more of them accept, without discussion, his assumed character.

Thus, today we meet many people, and often they are in the ranks of the most zealous apostles, who live only for the conversion of the world to the Gospel, but who do not realize that the methods they are using to accomplish this purpose might much better be called an attempt to convert the Gospel to the world. Under the name of "incarnation," such people attempt in all good faith to incorporate all the ideals held by men today into the ideal of Christianity. But such a Christianity becomes something quite different from the authentic Christianity of the "divinization" of man through the Cross. It becomes instead an unconscious but desperate struggle to avoid the Cross in an effort to "divinize" the world as it is. That is to say, it becomes in fact, under all sorts of Christian phraseology, a purely pagan "apotheosis" of the created things.

A striking example of such a confusion of aims may be seen in the attempt which is being made in some countries to introduce a special feast of "labor" into the Catholic liturgy; and it only makes the confusion worse confounded to call it the feast of "Christ the Worker." Human labor is, of course, something to be blessed by the Church as being, for one thing, a great way by which the Cross of Jesus is to be introduced into our daily lives. The custom of solemnly blessing workers and their work might very well be introduced, therefore, on the day when human society is celebrating "labor" in general. And it would be quite fitting to ask for a special votive Mass, in connection with which such a blessing would be given, just as there are already votive Masses for many other purely human needs. But to make a special feast of Labor is to suppose that human effort as such and of itself is redemptive, that human labor as such and of itself is a constituent part of the Mystery. And this is exactly what no Christian can admit for a single second. For one would cease to believe at all in the Christian Mystery if one held that God in Christ is not the only author of man's salvation, but that man, even if he does not wholly accomplish that salvation himself, still contributes something toward it which has saving value of itself, apart from any root dependence on

God's own work on the Cross. Such an idea supposes that man, in some way or other, is his own savior, that he needs only to present his finished work to God for His divine approval, or, at most, to ask for some external assistance from God in order to perfect his work with God's cooperation. But all this is sheer Pelagianism; it is, as St. Augustine and the Church of his time clearly realized, to bring into the Church itself a kind of pagan idolatry under a Christian disguise.

Yet, when one proposes to people of this turn of mind the perfectly Christian idea of a special blessing for human work, and a solemn supplication for this blessing in a special votive Mass, they indignantly and disdainfully reject such a proposal. For what they wish is not the blessing but rather the formal consecration of human work as being in itself a sacred action; in other words, they do not even want a true consecration, but rather the solemn recognition of a sacred character believed to be already inherent in human work, prior to any action of Christ or of the Church. They want to see men coming into church with their tools and their machines—or, better still, with the finished products of their work as if these had been wrought by purely human effort—to put all these things on the altar as offerings to be united to Christ's offering, and to be considered, if not on a plane of perfect equality with Christ's offering, at least as something which is quite worthy to be compared to His, and even added to it.

Here we can see clearly the capital importance of keeping in mind that distinction which we emphasized above, the distinction between our offering, itself entirely dependent on Christ's Eucharist for its validity and reality, and that Eucharist itself which alone can give value and sacred reality to the acts of man. For as soon as this distinction is blurred, we begin to lose the whole meaning of Christianity and to return from the Christian Mystery to the ideas of the purely pagan mysteries.

What truth, then, are we to oppose to such confusion? Should we try to flee into the traditional liturgy as if it were a refuge in which we could simply forget all about this world and live in a world of our own, carefully secluded from the world where men are living and working? No: nothing could be more misleading than to propose a choice between the practical conversion of Christianity to this world, and an escape of Christians out of this world, as if there were no third possibility.

First of all, let us repeat again: the world of the sacraments, the world into which the liturgy introduces us, is not a world in its own right, standing aloof from the world of ordinary living. It is rather the meeting-point of the world of the resurrection with this very world of ours in which we must live, suffer and die. And this fact implies that liturgical life, far from taking us out of real life, far from making us indifferent to or uninterested in real life, on the contrary positively sends us back into it in order to carry out fully in it the Mystery which has come to us through the sacraments.

But we must not understand this to mean that the Mystery is to comply with the ways of the world, is to adapt itself to the natural evolution of fallen human creatures and their affairs, merely to give these affairs a kind of golden hue, rather like that with which so many painters think it suitable to prettify their purely naturalistic and worldly representations of the Nativity. On the contrary, the Mystery is to take hold of this world, to struggle with it even to death, and only to master it finally in the resurrection.

But here once again, let us not deceive ourselves by the words which we use. For the divine Mystery to dominate the world and so to redeem man who is in it, does not mean simply that some or other clerical politics are successful, or that some bargain is made with a state for a convenient arrangement of the affairs of the Church, nor even that some large segment of the population is persuaded to acknowledge the value of Christianity to some lesser or greater extent. The divine Mystery is to dominate the world and to redeem the men who are in it by taking the world as it is, filled with sin and sufferings and death, by making sin into a starting-point for penitence, and by making of suffering and death the authentic way to the Cross of Jesus Himself.

Moreover, let us notice here how every easy-going method of reconciling the world with Christianity makes light, not only of Christianity, but of the world as well. To think that the world would be redeemed, that salvation would have been achieved for mankind, that the preparation for the Kingdom would be so complete that, for all practical purposes, things would be as though it had already come, all this simply as a result of the fact that the majority of people on earth were practising Christians, or that legislation all over the world had become open to Christian considerations, or that states and civilizations reflected Christian ideals,—to suppose all this is to avoid the major issues of secular life as well as of Christian. Let us imagine that the most Christian civilization possible were established in this world. Would men then cease to sin, to suffer, to die? And since they would continue sinning, suffering and dying, how can we suppose for an instant, or be tempted to suppose, that the greater part of the work of redemption, if not the whole, would have been accomplished in such a "christianized" world? For redemption, properly speaking, only begins when man begins seriously to struggle with sin and with death, because only then does he attack the very roots of human pain and not merely try to alleviate its superficial manifestations.

We do not, therefore, get to the heart either of the problems of the world or of the task of Christianity until we seriously face the problem of sin and accept, not the way of some illusory reconciliation with the world, but the way of conflict which is the way of the Cross, the way of voluntary death in and with Christ.

But does this mean that if we fully accept the Mystery, if we work out the full implications of a liturgical piety in our whole lives, if we try to realize fully the Christian ideal expressed in martyrdom, then our whole lives will become gloomy and our whole outlook will become tinged with pessimism? Not at all. Only the kind of mind which accepts the most superficial view of both the world and the Gospel could possibly think that this would be true. For, as we have already explained, and should now explain once again—death and suffering were in no way brought into the world by Christianity, neither does the revelation of the Mystery in any way render them more gloomy than they were before. Death and suffering are the iron law of this world because it is a sinful world, and sin has these unavoidable consequences whether we acknowledge the fact or not. It is not Christianity which makes human life in this world one that is always liable to pain, since the very growth of this life is necessarily part of its progress towards death.

All those ideals of a possible human civilization, Christian or not, which would make us believe that the riddle of our life in this world would be solved by a more scientific, or by a more in one way or another enlightened management, only avoid, rather than solve, the true problem. These ideal worlds of our planning are only dreams of a wonderland, day-dreams in which man, far from achieving his true self, is only fighting desperately, and illegitimately, to prolong infancy of heart and mind. All the forms of humanism which pretend to compete with Christianity in bringing man back to Paradise, are not real humanisms at all, but should rather be called "infanticisms." The true humanism, the humanism which really opens up for Christianity, the humanism of the *"anima naturaliter Christiana,"* as Tertullian called it, is not like these dreams. It is that humanism whose cry is, *Homo sum et nil humanum a me alienum puto;* and this immortal phrase of Terence is not to be misunderstood, according to the childish translation of the Renaissance, as meaning: "I rejoice that I am human and all that I want is to be more fully what I already am"; but rather, as its author intended: "I am a sinner, weak as are all men, and there is no weakness of mankind that I have any right to pretend to ignore." True humanism, therefore, is one which, at the advent of Christianity, does not find itself embarrassed by the Cross, and is not at once anxious to get rid of the Cross to find out whether, without it, Christianity might not be a suitable golden ornament to perfect man's own natural beauty. Any humanism which is incapable of the fundamental humility of Terence's phrase is a humanism hostile to the Cross only because ignorant of humanity itself. A liturgical life, therefore, is a life of true humanism in the deepest sense of the word, for it is a life concerned with fostering the true interests of human beings as they actually exist in the real order,—the order of grace, sin and redemption.

The work of Christianity for the salvation of men is not, therefore, to confirm them in their illusions, but to bring them first of all to see things as they are, with the certainty that it can also communicate to men the strength of Christ in which they can overcome everything. "This is the victory that overcomes the world, our faith," says St. John. For "who is he that overcomes the world if not he who believes that Jesus is the Son of God?"[5]

But if we are all to accept and understand this truth fully, we must never forget the other truth on which we have meditated already in connection with the fact that the Mystery does not bring the Cross into the world, but finds it here. This second truth is that the Mystery does not transfigure the Cross by making death no longer death, no longer the enemy of God as well as of man, but rather by making death the death of Jesus Christ, that is, a death through which death itself is now to die in the triumph of the resurrection.

Thus, the well-spring of true joy and the assurance of true peace is not to be sought in any opiate that might lull our pain by making

[5] 1 John V, 5.

us dream that it is ended or soon will be ended. This source and this assurance is only to be found in life with Christ, because as soon as this life has been found through the death of Baptism, and as long as it is daily renewed in the death of the Eucharistic sacrifice, we know that through death we are only going to eternal life. Let us remember the testimony of the martyrs, that through the realization of faith, some earnest of the resurrection is already given to us in death, here and now. Men of this world think that they can only enjoy life to the degree that they can forget that their life is leading them toward death. But the Christian is able to rediscover something of the pure joy of Paradise as soon as he consents to face death without fearing it, because he has set himself to follow, now and forever, in the footsteps of Christ. This joy will be possessed fully only when the sacrifice has been fully accomplished; but as soon as we have set forth on the way toward that consummation freely, with every step the undying joy begins to blossom in our hearts. And this is not a kind of disembodied joy, a joy in the abstract, a joy to be found in some pure forgetfulness of creaturehood. It is a joy that we find once more in creatures themselves, as soon as they become for us not a wall which shuts us off from God, but rather a way toward God: as soon as we see God's light shining through them, and do not take them to be lights themselves, only to rest content with their dimness.

In Christian marriage, for example, full human love—that is, love not only of man and woman trying to shut themselves up in romantic isolation, but the love of man and woman which is also the love of father and mother for children and the love of members of the body of Christ who are working together for the fulfillment of a common task in the whole Body—this love can realize a fullness of joy which is not dreamed of by merely romantic lovers, because it has learned to transcend itself, to forget itself when God's call is heard. And in Christian virginity, a renunciation of self even more complete than that of marriage, brings, even in this life, a still higher, because still purer, anticipation of eternal joy.

In everything that he does, in his work, his study, his relaxation, the Christian finds that joy, which is greater because purer than that which the man of this world knows, because his achievements here and now can bring him joy even though he is quite aware of their lack of permanence; for their ultimate and unavoidable passing is for him only a sign of his coming closer to the one achievement which is final. Therefore neither loss itself, nor trial, nor the breakdown of plans and work can deprive him of his joy, for all these things have become the way by which that joy is to be made perfect, to be made secure from all change or decay.

And the Christian knows that he can love forever those whom he loves here on earth, for the reason that he does not love them any longer for himself alone. Therefore, although the Christian is a man of sacrifice, the priest of all creation, he cannot accept—as do so many idealists of this world only—any plan for the salvation even of the whole world which would necessitate innocent death or suffering. Precisely because he has encountered the one absolute end, which is divine love, he can no longer agree that any end would justify the use of perverse means. And this is what brings the Christian finally and unavoidably to the Cross, because when a man refuses to shift the burden of his pain to other men, he cannot avoid taking the burden of their pain upon himself. But this fact also is what causes the Christian to love the world with the love of Him Who "so loved the world that He gave His only-begotten Son, that those who believe in him may not perish, but may have life everlasting."[6]

[6] John III, 16.

On Liturgical Studies

I T MAY BE of interest to readers of this book to have some general
view of the way in which the study of liturgy developed through
the centuries.

The basis of all sound liturgical study must be, of course, correct
knowledge of the development of liturgy, that is, a scientific historical
study of it. The father of this science is Giovanni, Cardinal Bona.
Born at Mondovi in Italy in 1609, he became a member of the Feuil-
lant Order (a branch of the Cistercian family) and died in 1674.
Before his time, scholars such as Gavantus, Goar (famous for his edition of the Greek *Euchologium*) or Morin had published some very
important documents or written valuable dissertations on particular
points. But Cardinal Bona was the first to write a complete and coherent work on the subject, making full use of the materials then
available for historical synthesis. His two principal works, from this
point of view, are the *De divina Psalmodia,* and *Rerum Liturgicarum
libri duo,* the first being on the office and the second on the Mass.
An *editio princeps* of the *De divina Psalmodia* had been published in
Rome in 1653 under the title *Psallentis Ecclesiae harmonia.* But it
was republished ten years later in Paris, by the famous bookseller
Billaine, under the auspices of the Maurist Benedictines, especially
Dom Luc d'Achery, and the work then received the title *De divina
Psalmodia* under which it has been constantly reprinted ever since.
The second book, composed at the request of Cardinal Pallavicini,
was first published in 1671, and is also known under the more explan-

atory title, taken from Bona's own manuscript: *De sacrosancto Missae sacrificio disquisitiones historicae.* All the works of Bona have been collected in a single quarto, printed at Antwerp in 1673 (Opera omnia). But there is also a very important edition of the *Rerum liturgicarum libri duo,* in all three volumes, made by the Cistercian Roberto Sala (Turin), from 1747 to 1753, and enriched with many texts of capital importance that were discovered only a few years after Bona's death. Unfortunately, Sala spoiled this work by interpolating many lengthy digressions and polemics of his own that are of little or no interest.

Immediately after Bona, we must mention another great Italian cardinal, the Blessed Giuseppe-Maria Tommasi, of the Theatines. Born at Alicata in Sicily in 1649, he died in 1713 and was beatified in 1803. His first important work was the publication (Rome, 1680) of a book entitled *Codices sacramentorum nongentis annis vetustiores.* It includes the Gelasian sacramentary, the Gregorian sacramentary, the *Missale Gothicum,* the *Missale Francorum,* the *Missale gallicorum vetus,* all of which had already been consulted by Bona, for they were in Roman libraries, but none had been published in printed form up to that time. Six years later, Cardinal Tommasi published a volume of capital importance for the study of the Roman Antiphonary, *Responsalia et antiphonaria romanae Ecclesiae a Sancto Gregorio magno disposita* (1688). His last great book was his *Antiqui libri missarum romanae ecclesiae* (1691).

But of still greater importance in the field of publishing ancient texts for critical study by scholars, is the work of Dom Jean Mabillon, a French Benedictine of the Congregation of Saint-Maur. Born at Saint-Pierremont, near Rheims, in 1632, he died in 1707 at the Parisian Abbey of St. Germain-des-Prés. A very beautiful life of him was written by his friend and disciple, Dom Ruinart (Paris, 1709). The breadth and depth of Mabillon's scholarship, as well as his solid and mature criticism, made him one of the greatest figures of his time in all kinds of historical research. Two of his greatest works are of fundamental importance in the field which we are now considering. The first is the *De liturgia gallicana libri III* (Paris, 1685) in which he makes full use of the Luxeuil Lectionary (in his *liber II*) which he had just discovered and edited. The second, and still more important, is his *Museum italicum,* in which he makes an inventory of his discoveries in Italian libraries. The first tome (of 1687) gives the

Missal of Bobbio, while the second one includes the first edition of the famous *Ordines romani* (or, more exactly, of the first that he had found). This tome has been reproduced by Migne, (P. L. t. 78, col. 837-1371).

After Mabillon, there is another Maurist, Dom Martene, who should at least be mentioned for his *De Antiquis Ecclesiae Ritibus* (Rouen 1700-1702), which gives many details about the traditional usages, particularly those in French cathedrals and dioceses.

The value of the scientific work done at this time may be inferred from the fact that a book from this period was reprinted only two years ago, and was tremendously successful, so useful is it even today and so modern in all its views. This was a synthetic book on the Mass, first published in 1711 by the French Oratorian Pierre Lebrun, making full use of all the previous publications in the field and entitled: *Explication des prières et des cérémonies de la Messe*.

One priceless discovery remained to be made in the XVIIIth century, that of the book called the Leonine Sacramentary, which was published by Giuseppe Bianchini in 1735.

The eighteenth century also produced two monumental publications, one being the collection of all the texts previously quoted, made by Muratori and published under the title *Liturgia Romana Vetus* (Venice, 1748), and the other a larger (but unfortunately never completed) collection by J. A. Assemani, entitled *Codex liturgicus Ecclesiae universalis* (including the Eastern Rites) in *XV libros distributus*, of which, in fact, only thirteen volumes were to appear in Rome, from 1749 to 1765, and to be reprinted in 1902 (Paris-Leipzig).

After the first publication of this *Codex liturgicus*, there was an eclipse of scientific liturgiology lasting for nearly a century. It almost seemed as if this science had disappeared forever. We have previously noted the weakness (not to say the futility) of Dom Guéranger's work considered from this point of view. But it must be added that those men whose common sense led them to oppose his fantastic theories were no better equipped than he himself to work in the field of scientific liturgiology. The cause of this universal ignorance was the interruption of the traditional teaching of sacred sciences as a result of the secularization or destruction of the Catholic universities and other places of learning that came about in the wake of the French revolution.

But the research accomplished in the seventeenth and eighteenth centuries had been so fruitful that only a few important texts (at least concerning the Western Liturgies) still remained to be discovered. Let us mention only the eleven Masses published by a German scholar, F. J. Mone, in 1850, in a book of little other lasting interest: *Lateinische und griechische Messen aus dem zweiten bis sechsten Jahrhundert* (Frankfurt-am-Mein). These Masses are now recognized as the oldest document we possess concerning the Gallican liturgy, and they were also reproduced by Migne (P. L., t. 72, col. 195-318). In the nineteenth century also two lost *Ordines* were discovered, one by J. B. Rossi and the other by Louis Duchesne. Both were published in an appendix to Duchesne's *Origines du Culte Chrétien* (Paris, 1899).

In the nineteenth century, two great liturgiologists gave their science a new impetus,—the German Probst (1816-1899) and the Englishman Edmund Bishop (1846-1917). A complete bibliography of their work may be found in the *Dictionnaire d' archéologie et de liturgie* (t. 9., col. 1731-32, 1735-36). Edmund Bishop's short essay, *The Genius of the Roman Rite,* which was translated into French in 1921 under the title: *Le génie du rite romain,* is worth being read by everyone, even by people not interested in scholarship, because of its masterful summary, never equalled by any other, of the special spirit of the liturgical tradition in which most of us have been brought up.

We shall conclude this survey by mentioning briefly the three modern schools which have taken the lead in the field of liturgical scholarship.

The first is the English School, consisting mainly of Anglicans, with the important exception of Edmund Bishop, who was a Catholic layman, and also of Adrian Fortescue (who came nowhere near the achievements of Bishop, but whose book on the Mass is the main source for Batiffol's brilliant but superficial treatment of the question). Two men must be mentioned here: Brightman for his most useful edition of *Liturgies Eastern and Western* (though in spite of the title, only one volume has actually been published, on the Eastern liturgies, Oxford, 1896), and W. Howard Frere, whose studies of the Latin liturgy in England all during the medieval period inspired the modern revisers of the Anglican prayer Book. These men have recently had a brilliant successor, Dom Gregory Dix, an author of immense learning with a most arresting style of writing. His book, *The Shape of the*

Liturgy (London, 1945) is already famous. But it is doubtful whether many of his hypothetical reconstructions will survive. Of much more lasting value is the patient critical work of many scholars (not all of them Anglican or English) collected in the volumes of the Henry Bradshaw Society, now numbering more than eighty, which provide us with many priceless texts in editions often nearly perfect.

As to modern scholarship in this field, we have already mentioned Duchesne's great book, *Les origines du culte chrétien*. We should also mention Cardinal Pitra, Dom Cagin, Dom Cabrol, and Dom Henri Leclercq (all of them Benedictines of Solesmes), as well as Msgr. Battifol; but none of these men are of the same rank as Duchesne himself. The bibliography of their work may be found in all the handbooks, so that we do not need to reproduce it here; but let us note the fact that Dom Cabrol and Dom Leclercq, especially the latter, are responsible for that most useful publication, the *Dictionnaire d'archéologie et de liturgie*. In even more recent times, we must mention as scholars of the first rank, Dom Wilmart and his successor, Dom Louis Brou. Dom Wilmart has produced many works concerning not only liturgy in the strict sense of the word, but also the whole movement of devotional prayer in the Middle Ages, the study of which cannot be separated from the study of the liturgy proper. And Dom Brou is still carrying on a most important study of Latin collects of all kinds.

But the only man in France today whose work in liturgiology is of capital importance is Msgr. Andrieu, dean of the Faculty of Theology in Strassburg University, his outstanding achievements being his study of *Les Ordines Romani du haut Moyen-Age* (Louvain, 1931), and his book on *Le Pontifical romain au Moyen-Age* (Vatican City, 1938-41).

To finish our survey with Germany, we need only recall the great names of Dom Odo Casel and Dom I. Herwegen. Let us mention here the famous *Jahrbuch für Liturgiewissenschaft,* and the three series: *Liturgie geschichtliche Quellen, Forschungen, Quellen und Forschungen*. All these studies demonstrate the greatness of Casel's own work, and show also the great influence he exercised on his disciples—many of them not unworthy even of such a master. These studies are not only in the field of purely historical scholarship, but include also that of liturgical theology which we are soon to examine. Before we proceed further, however, we must first mention the very valuable publications (most of them being editions of Eastern texts) issued by Prince Maximilian of Saxony. And we must note also the great creator of the science of comparative liturgy, Anton Baum-starck (like Edmund Bishop, he was a Catholic layman), who, with his immense scholarship, is to be regarded as one of the most creative (perhaps sometimes too creative, and a little among the delusive) geniuses of recent times who have ventured into the field of liturgical studies. For an account of his work, see his own book in French, *Liturgies comparées* (1939), in which he gives a resume of this work, together with a very useful bibliography. Fr. Jungmann, with his great book *Missarum Solemnia* represents the opposite type of scholar-ship in Germany today, that of flawless erudition which refrains from all unguarded speculations, proposing instead an ordered view of all the available material.

In the preceding survey, we have made no attempt to be ex-haustive. Our aim, as we said before, was not to provide a complete bibliography such as can be easily made up from handbooks and en-cyclopedias. We wished, rather, to show how the science of liturgiology was born and developed, when the main discoveries took place, who were the men or schools who played a decisive part therein.

Let us now turn to the theological study of liturgy. Here we must first make a most important distinction. The theology of liturgy is the science which begins with the liturgy itself in order to give a theolog-ical explanation of what the liturgy is, and of what is implied in its rites and words. Those authors are not to be accounted as liturgical theologians, therefore, who go to work the other way round and seek to impose on liturgy a ready-made explanation which pays little or no attention to what the liturgy says about itself. We must emphasize this distinction, since such a mistaken method of theologizing about the liturgy was not born today or even yesterday. It is a tendency which began to appear even in the patristic period, developed in a bewildering manner throughout the Middle Ages, has produced some peculiar fruit of recent growth,—and is not likely to die out soon. But we must notice the characteristic fact that, in spite of such a ven-erable history, these centuries-old mistakes do not add up to a tradi-tion, even a wrong tradition. They are a typical product of individual-ism, and when we happen to find the same explanation given by a series of authors along these same lines, we may be sure that this is only an evidence of that lack of profound personal thought which always goes hand in hand with the superficiality of individualism. The difference between unimaginative compilers who steal from one another's works and creative thinkers who think together is the difference between a dead routine and a truly living tradition.

An early example of this wrong method of theologizing about the liturgy is the work of Theodore of Mopsuestia. His catecheses exhibit the most fantastic kind of explanation, trying, even then, to find in the sacred liturgy a sort of mimicry of all the external actions of Our Lord's earthly life. Most of these explanations are regulated only by the author's own imagination, with no attention given to what ought to be evident from a careful study of the rites themselves. This mode of explanation of the liturgy exercised, unfortunately, some influence over the thought of more than one Eastern Father, including the Pseudo-Dionysius, Narsai, Sophronius of Jerusalem, and Maxim the Confessor. However, in these authors, at least we find, together with the fanciful exegesis borrowed from Theodore, developments along more fruitful lines.

But it was certainly in the late Middle Ages that this kind of fanciful explanation of the liturgy attained what we might call a luxurious as well as a very unhealthy growth. Beginning with Alcuin, Agobard, Amalarius of Metz and Amalarius of Treves, these explanations reached an extreme with Durand de Mende—however expert he may have been on the liturgical tradition of the West. The final product of this school is found in the *Expositiones Missae* of the twelfth century and the thirteenth century, the amazing absurdities of which have been well exposed by Fr. Jungmann. It was against all this that Dom Claude de Vert, the great Cluniac antiquarian of the seventeenth century, reacted so strongly as to deny that any detailed symbolism is to be found in the Mass except by reason of a late and superimposed explanation. The whole discussion of this question, together with very moderate and well-balanced conclusions, is to be found in the Preface to Lebrun's book already mentioned.

Nevertheless, it would be a great mistake to suppose that the Middle Ages produced only such poor explanations of the liturgy. Florus of Lyons, a contemporary of Alcuin's, at once reacted against his artificial constructions, and produced some dissertations of permanent value about the true significance of liturgical rites and prayers and the kind of symbolism to be found in them. The same could be said of Remi of Auxerre, Raban Maurus, and Walafrid Strabo, all of whom, however, in their anxiety to avoid the false type of explanations of the rites, had a tendency to abolish all theological explanations properly so called, to remain on the firm ground of actual history.

But the great models of true liturgical theology are to be found among the Fathers of the Church. The two great men who in the fourth century initiated this study are St. Cyril of Jerusalem, with his *Mystagogic Catecheses,* and St. Gregory Nazianzen, with his great sermons on the Christian festivals, including that of Christian initiation itself. In the West, we have the *De Mysteriis* of St. Ambrose, the *De Sacramentis,* whoever its author may be, the magnificent short addresses to catechumens of Zeno, bishop of Verona, and the great feast-day sermons of St. Leo, which stand out as the permanent type of perfect homilies, arising in the midst of the liturgical celebration from the heart of the liturgy itself.

In the Byzantine Middle Ages, we may also rate highly the great explanations of the Eastern liturgy by Maxim and, perhaps still more highly, those of Nicholas Cabasilas,—in spite of a certain tendency, inherited through the Dionysian corpus, toward fantastic explanations in the vein of Theodore of Mopsuestia.

A sound type of theological interpretation of liturgy is also to be observed in some of the authors we have already mentioned in connection with the beginnings of a modern historical study of the liturgy. An eminent example is Cardinal Bona, who comes very near to the mind of the Fathers. He is at once a scholar, a true theologian and a great spiritual writer; and often we can see in his works at once all these three lines of study, each making its proper contribution, each helping the other with no hindrance or confusion.

But after Cardinal Bona, we must go to the school of Maria Laach to find again the same happy combination of qualities, resulting in the further development of a theological study of liturgy. And this time we come upon even greater genius. What we have said already concerning Dom Herwegen and Dom Casel makes it unnecessary for us to go into further detail here about their school. But let us remark in this connection that a truly liturgical theology is not one which limits itself to the liturgy as its only source—in opposition to a liturgical theology which strives to impose upon liturgy a theology foreign to it. On the contrary, liturgy is so supremely important for the Church, for the whole of Christian faith and life, that a theology can only be properly called liturgical if it begins by putting the liturgy back into both its biblical and its patristic context, and, also, if it never separates the scientific study of the liturgy from its place in the innermost life of the individual Christian and of the whole Church of today.

This consideration brings us to the third way of approaching the study of the liturgy, that is the canonical method. The *historical* study of the liturgy considers it as it has been and as it is now in its historical development; the *theological* study of the liturgy considers its permanent meaning throughout all this development; the *canonical* study of liturgy teaches us what it ought to be, doing so, not by means of any more or less plausible theory of its own, but by stating the mind of the Church. The canonical study of liturgy is thus of primary importance, but here we find ourselves faced with a paradoxical but indisputable fact,—this all-important study is almost non-existent. There are a number of rubrical commentaries on the liturgy, but that is all;[1] and these commentaries, however useful they may be in their own way, bear about the same relation to a canonical study of liturgy that cook-books bear to treatises on the chemistry of food. Indeed, cook-books have a great advantage over handbooks of ceremonies,— when you have some practical experience in cooking and follow their advice quite blindly, you can produce very good dishes even though you do not know why; but blindly following handbooks of ceremonies —because of their purely logical and superficial way of solving questions—will give you only a worship which is apparently correct but may be intrinsically dead.

In the past, the external form of the liturgy was not thus separable from its inner spirit. The great authors of Christian antiquity who were foremost in their theological knowledge of liturgy were also responsible for the development of the classical form of the liturgy in its fullness and freshness of life. The same may be said, though in a lesser degree, of the medieval authors whom we have noted as being the true heirs to the Fathers in this field; and it may be said also of some of the seventeenth century authors whom we have mentioned, like Bona or Lebrun. But if recent years have seen the resumption, after the great break at the end of the eighteenth century, of some first-rate historical study of the liturgy, and, more lately, of its theological study as well, almost nothing has been seen as yet of a renaissance of canonical study in this field. This, of course, is only one particular

[1] Gavantus, in the XVIIth century, was their father. But he is as such also the father of their erroneous method.

aspect of the low state of canonical studies generally today. We may well deplore this situation which can constitute an almost fatal lack in an age such as ours which boasts so easily of its perfect apprehension of the significance of the Church for Christianity.

Such a method, like the general misunderstanding today even of what the science of Canon Law is, may well be the greatest block to any true apprehension of what the Church is. For Canon Law, far from being the dusty and abstract science it is too often supposed to be today, is actually the only means to ascertain what the mind of the Church actually is, what she wants to be, or what she wants to be done.

Index

INDEX OF NAMES